Life of an Exotic Entertainment Photographer

Jack Corbett

Nirvana Publishing Company

Published by Nirvana Publishing Company

1 st Edition

by Jack Corbett Edited by Jeremy

McTeague

For information
http://www.alphapro.com jack.
corbett@gmail.com

ISBN 978-0-9848934-6-1

Other books by Jack Corbett

Death on the Wild Side
Welcome to the Fun House
Dick Fitswell the Man in Quest of the Perfect Fit
Extreme Guns and Babes for an Adult World
Pattaya Pattaya Pattaya Confessions of Sin City

Table of Contents

Foreward

You are probably wondering why you should buy Life of an Adult Entertainment Photographer instead of another book that's been written by other adult photographers. As I've written on its back cover, "Before Facebook and smart phones film was king. In 1996 professional photographers laughed at the cheap digital camera I started bringing into strip clubs, but five years later they weren't laughing anymore. This was the time to create magic." And thanks to so many topless club owner friends of mine, adult magazines I wrote for such as "Xtreme Magazine," top flight feature talent agencies such as Pure Talent, and so many adult entertainer friends of mine, we created a lot of magic. Which we will probably never see the likes of again.

On my alphapro.com website I claim to be the first to bring digital photography into strip clubs. Well, maybe someone else did, but I sure haven't heard about him. While I had a local club provide my own phone line, free drinks on the house, and my own table just five feet from the club's main stage.

I had only a Kodak Dc-40 camera in those days that would do only 375,000 pixels. But club owners, managers and my dancer friends understood we were supplying what no one else did. Which was instant gratification. This was before Facebook. But I had a laptop and we had the Lost Angels chat where we could broadcast our digital images all over the world. No one else was doing it.

Those guys shooting film just didn't get it. While the dancers I knew did. Women like Heaven, Katt, Renee, Skie, Marriah, Alex, Sahara, and Selena to name just a few. While men like Sam Stimmel, Big Daddy, Hawk, Frank Marsala, and Vic Robinson running the clubs were very quick at grasping what this new technology could do for them. Those were incredible times back then. Which in the new world of post Covid

Several years later I would graduate to the Nikon D-1x, a 6 megapixel digital SLR. I put a $2000 Nikon 28-70 2.8 lens on it. Professional photographers shooting next to me were using Nikon F-5 and F100 film cameras. Several of them wanted to switch to the Nikon D1 X, but they were shooting for magazines that insisted in processing their photographer's images in house. This meant film. I could shoot over 1000 pictures a night with the D1 x that could produce 20 by 30 inch print outs. The photographers still using film could not begin to keep up.

19, Facebook and the Smart Phones we are likely to never see again. Which brings up another important reason you will want to read this book. I portray for the most part a very positive look at the movers and shakers of the adult entertainment industry that you probably won't be getting in any other book you might read.

This is because I've been there and done that. And although there were a lot of other adult photographers in those days, they sure weren't writing any books about it. While I was also writing over 80 articles for such adult magazines as "Xtreme Magazine," "Exotic Dancer," "The Wild Times," and "Wood Magazine."

I would wind up covering Feature Showcases for Pure Talent and Continental Agency all over the United States while getting my hotel rooms paid for and constantly being around all the Feature Entertainers doing the Feature Showcases. Driving to Providence, Rhode Island, Philadelphia, PA, Baltimore, MD, Lafayette, Indiana, Des Moines, IA, Springfield, MO, Peoria, Il, and Mobile, Alabama. And shooting the Miss Nude Illinois Pageant at Big Al's, M.S. Texas three times in Abilene, TX, and Wichita Falls, TX, and Sexy Professional Exotic Wrestling (S.P.E.W.) at Big Daddy's Cabaret in Missouri, and Miss Nude World in Des Moines, Iowa. Every year I'd also have my own exhibitor's booth at the Exotic Dancer Expos in Las Vegas, Nevada, where I would showcase my digital photography and website.

I got to know a lot of very prominent people in the adult entertainment world. And although I met a few scumbags, at the level I was operating on, I found most of them to be very talented, reliable and fair minded. And not at all like you might be expecting within these pages. These were the stories I had to write. To give my future readers the real story of the adult entertainment industry from 1995-2005 as I have personally experienced it.

Dedication

To Doctor Doom and all the terrific people I met during my life as an exotic entertainment photographer.

Dollies Playhouse

If you weren't used to hitting most of the Washington Park Strip Clubs in the East St. Louis Metro area you would think the Dollies Playhouse was a dive. But I found it to be a great watering hole. That was a long time ago. So, when Mistress Mary and I indulged in a few playful carnal acts, I didn't think much of it one way or the other. I don't remember what she was doing to me, or what I was doing to her. But I remember us sitting at the bar together, and whatever we were up to, the bouncer had enough of our antics. Whether she was squeezing my balls, and I was kissing her between her legs? Can't remember because that was over twenty years ago.

What I do remember is the bouncer coming up to me and telling me to leave the bar in a loud voice. And hearing a loud female voice from the back of the bar, yelling out, “Jack stays! You can't kick him out.”

And Steve, the owner, standing behind the bar completely unconcerned or unaware of what Miss Mary and I were doing, suddenly looking up.

Watching me, then Marriah who was approaching the bar, telling the bouncer. “Jack stays.” And Mistress Mary telling Steve. “Yeah, we want Jack to stay.”

What it all comes down to is, when Marriah speaks, everyone listens. Even if you are the club manager, or its owner. And doubly so if Mistress Mary agrees with Marriah. Because the credentials of both women are impeccable. Marriah because she's a devout heroin addict who's vocally proud of her addiction and Mistress Mary because she's a total exhibitionist and Dominatrix. Whose most noteworthy exploits are getting a customer up on the stage, tying her victim up and then stripping him to his underwear shorts. Before jamming a high heeled shoe up his anus right up to his prostate. Until her victim cums all over his shorts to the amusement of the crowd. So yes, I was proud of my two friends, who would stick by me through thick and thin.

Marriah

Marriah loved me to death from the very beginning. From the first time I told her how I had beaten the hell out of Larry. My problem was I was still addicted to Nipples. And I was bent on still seeing a lot more of her. Which was not going to be easy considering Art had barred me out of C-Mowes for life, and Nipples was still working at the C-Mowes strip club.

Larry used to drive a limousine that the strip club owned, which amounted to a short time room on wheels. Back in those days it cost $170.00 to take one of Art Mowe's strippers on a 45 minutes joy ride up Highway 157 to Centreville and back. Although Highway 157 was called Bluff Road, due to its skirting the river bluffs that the Mississippi River had formed eons ago. C-Mowes customers hardly had the chance to watch the magnificent scenery flashing by. This was because the customers paying for their joy rides had just 45 minutes to bang their female accomplices.

Although I never took Nipples on a joy ride, I took a few other strippers along with me. Which I made up for by taking Nipples to hotels, my farm, and to other Saint Louis strip clubs where we had sex with each other in hot tubs that several strip clubs had where one could indulge in one's sexual fantasies. Nipples and I had a lot of adventures together that you can read all about in my first novel: Death on the Wild Side. Which details the night I knocked three of Larry's teeth out.

Nipples and I had gone to several strip clubs together before ending up at C-Mowes. Which would have been okay with Larry who had graduated from being Art Mowe's limo driver to being the club's bouncer. Larry's problem was Nipples had worked day shift until 7 p.m. and that is the time the night shift girls came in. So Larry was observing club policy when he asked Nipples and I to leave. The club's rationale being that day shift girls were not supposed to interfere with the night shift girl's money.

But Larry really screwed up when he told Nipples, "you should know better than to come here during the night shift." And then told me, "Jack, I never liked you." Being a take no shit kind of guy, I replied to Larry, "And I don't like you either, Larry." At which point, Larry hit me in the face. Which was an even bigger mistake because six seconds later, I had knocked Larry off of his feet and had started beating his brains out while he was still down. It took three guys to pull me off of Larry. Although it would have taken more than just three guys, but I was still having a little respect for authority.

This led to my having to meet Nipples at other strip clubs and gas stations nearby. The problem was how would I tell Nipples where to meet me after her shift when the strippers at C-Mowes were not allowed to answer their phones during working hours? My answer was to have another girl call the club and ask to speak to Nipples. Making it all out to be a family emergency. My solution was to go to a closeby strip club where I'd have a couple beers and give one of the club's strippers a dollar to call C-Mowes for me. And that's when I started getting acquainted with Marriah. After I had her call Nipples several times for me.

About the third time, Marriah asked me, “why are you having me make all these calls for you?”

To which I replied, “Because I love Nipples.”

“That's obvious, do you want to see mine?”

“Thanks but I've already seen them and a lot more of you while you have been on the stage,” I replied. But the real reason I'm having you call Nipples is I beat the shit out of Larry and now Art's barred me for life from ever coming into C-Mowes again.”

“You beat the crap out of Larry? I used to work at C-Mowes. Larry's a real asshole. You are my hero.”

Luckily for Marriah and me, Nipples had taken the day off which left Marriah and I having a few teqilas together. And as the hours went by I unloaded my situation on Marriah. The essence being that I was living on my farm, and that I had to drive 75 miles back home every night I visited the East Saint Louis area strip clubs.

Being a stripper and a heroin addict with a heart, Marriah asked me to drive her home and to spend the night at her house, which was a shorter drive for me than having to head all the way back to my farm.

Two Heroin Addicts

Marriah, now in her early to mid thirties was hard to refuse. Already having been around the block a few times, she was self confident. Although she was getting to be a little ragged around the edges, she was still full of energy and could pole dance with the best of them.

Because I already had one DUI on my driving record it seemed like a good idea to stay over at Marriah's house. My farm was almost an hour and a half away from Dollies. While Marriah's house in Granite City was just 15 minutes from the bar. But when Marriah offered to do the driving, I was sold.

I didn't expect another man to be staying with her though. Marriah introduced the guy to me as her brother, Doc. And if Marriah looked every ounce of being the hardened stripper, Doc looked far worse.

It didn't help that he introduced himself as “Doctor Doom,” and then told me, “but you may call me Gimp.” I can't remember what the actual injury was, but Doc had a memorable walk that was enough to scare most people who had never met him. Doc also had a face that hardly inspired confidence. One moment it would be smiling, and then it would break into a scowl. And here he was living off a stripper, obviously unemployed.

Pointing at a couch in front of the TV, Marriah told me, “this is where you will sleep, Jack. Let me get a blanket and pillow for you.”

She returned five minutes later while Doc kept watching TV on a second couch that looked like Marriah might have bought at a flea market. Doc didn't say much to me that night other than to ask me where I was from and how I had met Marriah.

I didn't sleep well that night. Although I can't say I was terrified as many others would have been had they been in my shoes, neither Doc nor Marriah gave me any indication of trustworthiness. So, you can imagine my surprise when I opened up my wallet the next morning and found all my money was still there.

*****

Several nights later Marriah took me on my first heroin run. After Dollies closed at 2 a.m. she had me drive her to a street just off Interstate 64 at the last exit before the highway crosses the Mississippi.

It all went quickly with Marriah having me pull up in front of a low rent apartment building. Then she made a quick phone call and went into the building. Several minutes later she came out all smiles.

Once we got back to Marriah's house, I observed Doc preparing a syringe and watched him stick it into his knuckles.

"Leaves no needle marks," Doc told me as I watched the fluid disappear into his knuckle. "Now Jack, you might think that our taking this heroin is bad, but it's much better than Methadone, that awful stuff they use to get you off of heroin. If they made this shit legal, it would be far purer and cheaper, and we wouldn't see all these people dying from overdoses from all that bad shit they use to lace the good heroin."

One night Doc surprised the hell out of me when he asked me to lend him a copy of my book, Death on the Wild Side. Three days later, he gave the book back to me after telling me he had read its entire 464 pages. Above all else, Doc's reading my book, totally transformed my opinion of the man. The truth is I've found that in the U.S. 90 percent of all Americans don't read. Unless they have to. And here's this lazy heroin junkie who's living off a stripper who reads an entire 464 pages in just three days.

As the weeks passed I learned more and more about Doc and Marriah. Marriah later explained to me, "Here I am living in Granite City in a poor white neighborhood. Where I oftentimes am carrying a lot of cash on me that I've earned at Dollies. This is one reason I have Doc staying with me. We never have sex together, which is why I keep calling him my brother. But you have to admit, Jack, that Doc's pretty scary looking. I'd call him pretty damn ugly," she added while breaking into an old ladies cackle.

You are nothing but a goddamn CUNT," Doc replied sardonically. Which means, Marriah, "Cannot Understand Normal Thinking." Then Doc turned to me, adding his last words on the subject: "Jack, all women are cunts. Even my own mother."

Which Marriah laughed off, replying, "Now you see why I call Doc brother. That's because I am not inbred enough to be fucking my family members. Actually Doc's pretty cool. He cleans this whole place for me, and he often does a lot of the cooking."

As the weeks passed I'd be finding Doc to be more and more useful to me. I still was involved with Nipples. Being able to be with her on and off for a week or two. And then she'd suddenly move, and I'd have to find out where her current address was. I once bought a bouquet of roses at a Collinsville flower shop and paid Doc to deliver them to her. And once or twice I had Doc go into C-Mowes for me to give Nipples a note to arrange a place where we could meet. Although Doc's usual personality was of a gruff, take no nonsense kind of man, when it came to having him do such errands for me, I found his attitude to be almost subservient.

By now I was doing a lot of drug runs with Marriah and Doc. Which might sound pretty exciting to many of you, but I will tell you that I found doing drug runs to be incredibly boring and a complete waste of time. But it was Marriah and Doc doing all the drugs. And not me. Yet I found them both to be very intelligent people with some very profound ideas on how the world really worked. So, I began to think of all the drug runs we were doing as a waste of talent. That Doc and Marriah had in spades over most people I had met over my lifetime.

Strange Behavior of Dollies Strip Club Owner at the Exotic Dancer Expo

Meanwhile, I had started shooting digital pictures of topless dancers. No one else was doing it in the strip clubs. I had also just started my own website at alphapro.com. And had just written and published my first novel, Death on the Wild Side. Back in 1996, the Internet was just getting a good start. I had my own chat room on my website, where I could put my digital pictures up. I was naive back then, and I thought I could sell thousands of my new book on the Internet.

"Exotic Dancer Bulletin" (a leading industry trade magazine for adult nightclubs) was having adult entertainment conventions in Las Vegas. So, I sent a thousand dollars to Exotic Dancer for an exhibitors booth at their convention. Since Death on the Wild Side was all about the strip clubs in the Saint Louis Metro East, and Dollies Playhouse was one of the topless clubs in my new book, I felt Steve, the owner of Dollies, would be very interested in my exhibitors booth.

A lot of people have the wrong idea about strip clubs. There must have been over 3000 in the United States at the time of this particular expo. A lot of them are houses of ill repute posing as topless clubs. Which are managed and owned by some real scumbags. But there are hundreds of strip clubs that are owned and managed by some truly excellent people. Exotic Dancer had set out to accomplish two missions: The first was to make a lot of money for its owner Don Waitt. Its second goal was to establish an organization of strip club owners and their top managers, and professional entertainers devoting themselves to the pursuit of excellence.

I don't remember exactly what Don Waitt was doing before he devoted himself to the adult industry. Other than he had previously had a career in music. Not as a concert musician, but as a man organizing various music performances, or whatever. What's important is Don was a musician at heart. But whatever he did he changed careers in 1993 to becoming a champion of the adult entertainment world.

Which culminated in his establishing the first national convention and awards multi-faceted organization devoting itself to the multi-billion dollar adult industry. Exotic Dancer, which would from then on host its annual Las Vegas Gentlemen's club conventions, set out to provide a variety of functions designed to provide a multitude of excellent services to the adult industry. One was the Exotic Dancer Bulletin, which published articles of interest to strip club owners while advertising clubs across the country along with goods and services geared to the needs of the adult entertainment world.

One of the hallmarks of Exotic Dancer's annual expos was its trade show, which offered a huge variety of products and services for the American adult industry. For example, there were booths featuring sound and lighting systems for night clubs. There were booths offering credit card processing systems. And booths for some of the larger strip clubs in the U.S. As well as booths run by talent agencies, which represented some of the finest adult entertainers in the country where the dancers would congregate to network with strip club owners who would later on hire them through their agencies.

To have my own booth at Exotic Dancer's Expo, I had to pay $1000. Whereas, adult professionals had to pay something like $300 just to walk through the front door of the trade show. This included strip club owners, photographers, or anyone else who was interested enough in the American adult entertainment industry to fork over $300. This did not include the costs of one's hotel accommodation which ran from $200 to $300 a night at casinos such as Caesar's Palace and Mandalay Bay, which were large enough to host a large trade show.

For the most part, the scumbags of the American adult entertainment world were not interested enough to pay this kind of money to establish themselves with the upper classes of the adult entertainment industry. As for the respected managers and owners of strip clubs, they started to refer to their clubs, not as strip clubs, but as Gentleman's Clubs. Exotic Dancer might have been the first meaningful entity to start calling such clubs Gentleman's Clubs. Maybe it did, and perhaps it didn't, but I personally believe that it was Exotic Dancer that gave Gentleman's Clubs their true meaning.

Twice each day, Exotic Dancer held seminars geared to making Gentleman's Clubs better, and that meant guiding them to be better at servicing their customers. Who the clubs should regard as gentlemen who wanted to be treated as valuable customers. So, there were seminars devoted to making a club's customers feel more at home. Or how their security guards should behave whenever a customer started making problems for a club. There were marketing seminars, and how to get your club to develop a website. I remember one of the first seminars I attended. Exotic Dancer had a legal panel running that seminar. And I will never forget how one of the lawyers on the panel greeted all the topless club owners in the audience. It went something like this:

> "Gentlemen, you are on the front lines of a tremendous struggle between those who want to silence you and to take away your given rights to freedom of expression. Make no mistake. You are in a war between those who want to shut your clubs down and those who wish to continue providing all the entertainment you are providing.

Later I'd call these Control Freaks, the Mothers for a More Boring Nation.

There were a couple club owners on that panel and several lawyers who had topless clubs as their clients. The panel then gave advice on how club owners could form a much more positive relationship with the citizens of the communities in which their clubs resided. Such as help their communities perform free services for the needy. Or of owners and managers serving on their community's school board. A prime example being Mike Oscello who headed the thirteen clubs in the PT's organization. I would later have many encounters with Mike who I found to be the epitome of gentility.

For years I would continue to have my exhibitor's booth at Exotic Dancer's Annual Expos. As for the first, I think I might have sold three or four books. But in the end having to spend thousands of dollars to take my part in Exotic Dancer's conventions allowed me to do a lot of networking. Which enabled me to meet a lot of serious minded club owners, and of course, a lot of entertainers, who would take me as a very serious player in the American Adult Entertainment World.

But that first year, I was really looking forward to Steve coming over to my exhibitor's booth. But he never came.

He sure was there though, because I encountered him on the elevator. Steve never said a word to me. He had a funny look on his face. And he was dressed in the most God awful attire. I don't know exactly what he was wearing. It might have been a bath robe. But whatever it was Steve might as well have been wearing a sheet that had not been washed for several weeks.
The man was out of it and nothing like the cheerful club owner I had met at Dollies.

The Disappearance of Steve

I was finally able to bring my desktop computer into Dollies. Over a week had gone by and no one had seen or heard from Steve. Marriah had become a great fan of mine and told the Manager a lot of good things about me.

"You must be Jack–I am Hawk," the Manager told me as soon as he saw me bringing my computer into the bar. "I am the Manager of Dollies now. Bring your computer into my office. Marriah keeps telling me some great things about you. I hear you are a great photographer among other things."

I had to bring my 14 inch monitor into Hawk's office along with the desktop computer. After booting the computer up I started showing Hawk a few pictures I had taken with my Kodak DC-40 camera. This camera could shoot pictures at 375,000 pixels tops. When you think of the Nikon D750 camera I'm using today that does 24 million pixels, that Kodak DC-40 was a toy. It really wasn't, but back in 1996 hardly anyone was shooting digital. While every professional photographer I met saw me as a rank amateur who didn't know his place.

I still don't know whether Hawk was a motorcycle gang member or not. But he drove a Harley and he sure looked the part. Marriah said he was, so I suppose I should take her at her word. Because heroin addict or not, Marriah would never lie to me. Or let me down. I don't remember Hawk ever dressing up. Like the managers in the PT's strip clubs do. Playing their parts as authority figures believing that clothing makes the man.

Hell, my dad used to tell me that. Not that I 'm disparaging the PT's managers such as, Mike Oscello, who I had a lot of respect for. But because Hawk and the other Dollies managers were so ordinary. And so much like the typical working man you'd find in your neighborhood bar. Hawk would wear sweatshirts and jeans during the winter months and tee shirts in the summer.

When we think of motorcycle gang members, we tend to think of them as they are portrayed in the movies. As tough guys with loud mouths. Which was not like Hawk at all, who had a soft voice and rarely lost his temper. I hardly ever saw him get overexcited, and whenever I joined him in his office, his face appeared thoughtful. Such as I found him now as he studied the digital pictures I was showing him.

“Those are terrific pictures you are showing me, Jack. How fast can you process them? I've never seen anything like this digital photography before."

It's all done inside the camera, Hawk. This Kodak of mine will produce a picture in less than one second. After that if I want to embellish a picture I have to use my computer. So that I can lighten or darken a picture, for example."

But with that Kodak DC-40 camera I rarely cropped my images. And I don't remember ever having to lighten or darken them either. That camera had a built in flash. And since I almost always took my pictures at close range its flash nearly always did a perfect job. The thing automatically focused on my subject. While the colors it produced were vibrant and spot on. For what it was, it was nearly perfect.

"Let me show you something else, Hawk. I think this will interest you just as much as my camera."

I had started my alphapro.com website a year earlier to sell books. I had my printer print up 2000 of my Death on the Wild Side books for me. Which cost me $6000 for my inventory that I kept in my exercise room. Turned out my website didn't sell many books for me, but I did start up a chat room on Alphapro. My friends and I called our chat group the Lost Angels. Keep in mind that in those days Facebook and other social media groups did not exist. So, we started calling the Lost Angels chat room as the only game in town.

Since Dollies Playhouse didn't have its own Internet connection yet, I was unable to show Hawk how it worked in action. But I had managed to save a couple hundred chat messages of ours as Html files which Hawk reviewed with me.

"This is what we can do, Hawk, with this chat room and my digital camera. I can take a lot of pictures of your dancers and put them up in the Lost Angels. Men can then come in from all over the country, see how good your girls are, and actually chat with them over the Internet. But you will need to get your own phone line into the club and allow us to use it only to access the Internet. That won't cost you very much. But it will certainly draw customers into Dollies who normally would never come here."

"I've never seen anything like this, Jack. This is a great idea. But first I need to talk with Nathan about it."

"Who's Nathan?"

“Why he's the owner of Dollies. He and Steve that is. They are partners. Which reminds me. Can you do something for me?”

“I can try.”

“Well, you know a lot about the Internet, and from what I can see of your Lost Angels you have quite a few members already. This is about Steve. No one's seen him in over a week now. He's not answering his phone. His wife has no idea of where he's at. And they've found his pickup truck somewhere and it's obviously been abandoned. Steve's just disappeared off the face of the earth. So I would like you to ask your friends if they know anything about this. And perhaps you might find some information for me on the Internet on Steve's whereabouts.”

“I will do what I can, Hawk. I saw Steve at the Las Vegas expo for club owners a couple of weeks ago. He really looked strange and he never said one word to me. I've been coming to Dollies several times a week and I've been wondering what's happened to him.”

“All I know is, he came back from Vegas. Came into the club the next night and after that no one's seen him again.”

Nathan, the Other Dollies Club Owner

At first I didn't know what Nathan looked like. Although I had been seeing a slender, dapper looking man come into the bar about every other night. Until Marriah pointed the man out as the other club owner.

"I tell you something about Nathan now," Marriah told me as we sat together drinking tequilas. "Don't tell anyone you heard it from me. But Steve's dead, and Nathan shot him."

"Now Marriah, how in the hell would you know anything about that?"

"I know everyone in this club, Jack. And I've heard from Steve's sister in law that Steve owed Nathan a lot of money. And that when Steve wouldn't pay him, Nathan shot him, or had him killed."

"Nathan seems to be a nice fellow to me, Marriah. He looks dignified. And he never says a word to me whenever I shoot pictures of the girls here."

"That's because he trusts Hawk 100 percent. And Hawk likes you a lot. So Nathan is going to let you do just about anything you want here."

"I want to get an Internet connection here in this club. Dollies will have to pay for an extra phone line, and then I can take pictures of you and the other girls and put them into my Lost Angels chat room on my website."

"Hawk's already talked to Nathan about that and Nathan is going to let you do it. I don't know when, but it's going to happen, Jack. And then we are all going to make lots of money."

"Just think Marriah. If Dollies is going to let us do that, then we will be doing business with a murderer."

"Ha ha ha. But we shouldn't be laughing. Because Steve was a very good man."

"I don't think so, Marriah. Not if he cheated Nathan out of his money."

"Maybe he didn't. All I've been able to find out is Nathan thought so. But it could be the other way around. Nathan might have owed Steve the money and when Steve tried to collect it, Nathan decided it would be cheaper to have Steve murdered."

Grey Ghost

I met Grey Ghost while I was playing volleyball with the guys near my farm. The guys were mostly from Farmersville, Illinois, or from the farms nearby. Most of them were in their twenties and thirties, and many of them had gone to High School together. My closest friends had formed their own team who would play other teams from towns nearby such as Raymond, Morrisonsville, and Virden. When they were not putting their crops in or spending days on end cultivating the weeds out of their fields, they would be practicing four or five days a week. But Grey Ghost was not one of their favorites, and he wasn't on any team either.

Farmersville had a population of 600 and was only five miles from my farm. But the guys often played at an even smaller town, which was just two miles from my farm. Funny thing was, Grey Ghost's real name was Scott Waggoner, and the small town where he lived was Waggoner, Illinois. I had met Scott several years before when he tried to sell my wife and I a computer and a farm accounting system. Then I got a little better acquainted with him when he was playing volleyball with the guys at the old Waggoner grade school. Most of the guys were pretty good playing volleyball on account of their practicing so much. Whereas, Scott certainly wasn't; yet Scott was running all over the court hogging the ball; and more often than not totally screwing things up for everyone else.

Scott was an odd looking guy who didn't look at all like a lot of my other friends. Most of my friends were over six feet tall and weighed well over two hundred pounds. And Scott was under five foot nine and probably weighed 150 on his best day. He was about fifty in those days and wore his long hair in a pig tail which made him look like an over the hill hippy. And a true throwback to Woodstock in the 1960's. His face looked Asian, perhaps Chinese. Which turned out to be not the case since his ancestors had mostly migrated to the U.S. from Germany.

Most of the farmers in my area pride themselves in how neat their houses look, how few weeds they have in their fields, and how often they mow their roadsides bordering their fields. Where most of them do not allow the grass to grow over six inches tall. Now that's a lot of mowing when you consider that each farmer had at least three miles of roadsides to mow. But Scott was no farmer. He didn't even mow the one quarter acre yard around his house very often. While he was oftentimes ridiculed by his neighbors for leaving bicycles, children's toys, and old cars all over the lawn in front of his house.

After meeting up with Scott again while we were all playing volleyball, I ran into him at the Farmersville gas station. I told him all about my book, Death on the Wild Side that I had just published and how I wanted to sell 2000 books that I had stored in my exercise room. And then Scott suddenly started getting real excited and told me, "You need to sell your book on the Internet."

"The Internet? What's that?" I asked.

"It's this huge global network that's all over the world. In which all these computers are hooked in together where people can communicate with each other from their computers. They will eventually be selling all kinds of things from their computers. That's where it's at now."

"I don't know anything about it," I replied.

"Come over to my house tonight, and I will show you."

That night Scott showed me a lot content on the Internet that I hardly even knew existed. We also drank a lot of beer together. It so turned out that Scott's father had been a war hero, being a fighter pilot who had shot down over five German planes. I would have called Scott a liar had it not been for all the pictures he kept showing me. So one never knows. Here I was drinking beer with an overaged hippie who most of the community didn't have a lot of respect for. In this little farm town that had only 200 inhabitants, who were in general looked down on by the residents of wealthier nearby towns such as Farmersville and Raymond.

It didn't help Scott's reputation any that he had also been a drug addict who had left town to live in Austin, Texas, for a few years earning a living as a musician. But after doing far more than his share of Cocaine, LSD, and all the other drugs he was taking, he had come back to his home town to overcome his drug addiction. Ironically, it turned out that he had spent a lot of time fishing in the pond on one of my family's farms that was just one mile from Scott's house.

The pond was right on the Old Highway 66 that now served as a service road for Interstate 55. It was over 40 feet deep in places and it had underground springs feeding into it. Which made the water very clean. I had planted a lot of trees around the pond that ended up making it pretty idyllic and just the sort of place where one could forget about doing drugs.

Over the coming months, Scott and I became great friends. When I wasn't busy farming we would spend practically every night together hatching our plans on how we could make our mark on the Internet. Scott built me a computer. Then we started up my Alphapro website with the help of an Internet provider out of Bloomington, Illinois. It was Scott's idea to insist that the provider create the chat room. And it was Scott who came up with the name of Lost Angels who represented to him all the strippers we would soon be meeting.

Scott turned out to be right on the money in choosing Lost Angels as the name for our chat room. Because it would turn out that a lot of strippers would see themselves as Lost Angels who had lost their way and were now seeking redemption. Which was not to be the case with Thai bar girls I would be meeting years later when I moved to Thailand.

We would soon be attracting our own little group who would be meeting at either my farm or Scott's house. One of them was Luan, an ex girlfriend of Scott's from Farmersville. And then there was Robin, a stripper working at the Platinum Club near East Saint Louis who lived with her husband in Girard ten miles from my farm. Along the way we picked up Dirt, a nineteen year old college student who lived in Springfield. Scott and I hired Dirt to do a weekly cartoon strip on my website, which ran for 120 weeks. Our meetings became a big think tank with all of us sharing our ideas on how we could get more regulars to join the Lost Angels group and how we could get more strippers to become personally involved with us.

In the Lost Angels chat group, Scott took on the moniker, Grey Ghost, after the Confederate guerrilla leader, John Mosby, during the Civil War. Which shows how knowledgeable Scott was of History, music, and all sorts of other subjects. I can only say that Scott was a wonderful guy, who had a great off the wall sense of humor, and was a brilliant artist, who could draw outstanding cartoons. He knew computers inside and out while being a very talented website designer.

Chatting in the Lost Angels at Marriah's House

Marriah became addicted to our Lost Angels chats in short order. I doubt it she even finished High School. But some people have got it and others don't regardless of education. I'd say she was about 35 when I met her. Which for strippers is well past their prime. I can't count the many nights I slept with her. But like Doc, I never banged her because it would have been like sleeping with a sister.

Her face showed the hard life she had been living, but most of her customers never saw that side of her in the darkness of Dollies. She was a powerful dancer and still had a good figure. But her customers also never got to see her taking her false teeth out when she went to bed at night. And as for her being on heroin, you never could tell when she was on it, or not, except when she was going through withdrawals.

Many times we'd go out after Dollies closed when she'd make phone calls from one phone booth after another. When she's often being told by her dealers that they were out of the good stuff. Then we'd go back to her house where she'd tell me she was feeling sick, and she'd crawl into bed knowing that she would score the next day

Marriah would never complain about anything. She'd just start feeling sick, and then she would just wait it out.

And she loved driving my car, which started out as a 1993 Mazda Miata sports car that had a 1600 c.c. engine with 116 horsepower. I took after my dad, however, who once owned a 1953 Chrysler New Yorker that he got up to 120 miles an hour. After that he bought two Buick's, a 1955 Road Master, which never could make 120 miles an hour. So he traded it in for a 1956 model, which never equaled the Chrysler's top speed either.

So, I fitted my Miata out with oversized wheels and tires to handle a lot of extra horsepower. Equipped it with a Sebring supercharger that made it feel like it had a V-8. And an after market free flowing muffler and header, and an air intake to get cooler air into the engine. And then, the final touch, a roll bar that made my Miata look like a race car. I never put my Miata on a Dyno, but I'd say she had over 180 horsepower. I got it up to 140 miles an hour numerous times. But it could do far better had it not been for the rev limiter that stopped the engine once it hit the red line at 7000 rpm's. The problem with Marriah is she didn't have a driver's license. So, here I was using her as my driver due to my having a DUI, and she would have wound up in jail just as surely as I would have been.

By this time Marriah was renting a new house, having moved from Granite City to Collinsville, which was 8 miles from Dollies. Doc moved out of their house in Granite City, but only stayed with Marriah in Collinsville for a short while. As I said before, Doc was awfully smart. So, he moved out of the Collinsville house because he felt Marriah was getting to be too careless with her heroin addiction. Marriah's new roommate was, Taylor, a new dancer at Dollies, who was one of the most beautiful women in the bar. By the time Taylor arrived on my radar, Dirt had started to spend a few weekends with me. Which I couldn't blame him for since he was nineteen years old and still living with his parents while attending college.

In Illinois it's against the law for anyone to drink at a bar who's under twenty-one, so you can imagine how thrilled Dirt must have been to be considered an honored guest at a strip club like Dollies, which normally carded anyone who looked under age. But by this time Dirt was doing my website due to Grey Ghost having other commitments. He was still doing the Death on the Wild Side cartoon strip. The Dollies dancers were well acquainted with the cartoon strip thanks to Marriah, so Dirt found himself in the cats bird seat when it came to getting a lot of attention from the girls.

One Friday night after Dollies closed, Dirt and I followed Marriah and Taylor back to Marriah's house in Collinsville. I don't remember exactly who drove with who; or that possibly all four of us might have managed to sandwich ourselves into my little sports car; but we all wound up drinking beer together at Marriah's where I booted up my laptop computer and got everyone in the Lost Angels chat room.

PlONe (pronounced: P-L-ONE) from San Francisco was in the chat room that night and so were several of the other guys. By this time Marriah was getting to know PlONe pretty well in our chats while Taylor who had never chatted with anyone online before thought the whole thing was pure magic. Here we could all chat in real time and PlONe was in California over 2000 miles away. Taylor of course was stunning, and I was taking great pictures of her with my Kodak, which I could put into our chat messages while all these guys were telling her how beautiful she was.

When it comes to all that partying and beer drinking for so many others there has to be some bathroom breaks. But Taylor's and Marriah's toilet sessions were heroin breaks. Which left Dirt and me drinking our Budweisers as we waited for the girls to come out of the bathroom after shooting up. Dirt was like me, having no use for drugs. While we both thought heroin was a useless waste of time and money that could better be spent on tequila, we gave the girls a pass. As far as we were concerned they weren't doing anything immoral. And the girls still behaved perfectly normal to us while they were still under its influence .

****

It was a good night. We all had a lot of fun chatting with our friends in the Lost Angels while Dirt and I got to cut it up with two fun loving strippers. So, we all decided to get together the following weekend at Marriah's after Dollies closed.

Dirt and I made it to Dollies just as we had promised the girls. But my Dad was dying in Arizona from a stroke. I had managed to visit him twice, each time thinking that I'd never have the chance to see him again. Each time it seemed he would start to recover a bit and then he'd go through another serious relapse.

I had an answering machine on my telephone back at the farm; so I called it from Dollies to see what condition my father was in; while half expecting to hear a message from a family member telling me that he had died. So, when I called it I learned from my nephew that my father had just died. That meant that all of our plans for the rest of the evening were off. Because I would need to go back to my farm to call my nephew back and my sisters about my father's death. This meant a hundred mile drive for me all the way to Springfield to take Dirt back to his parents house and for me to drive another thirty miles back to my farm.

Marriah and Taylor were disappointed just as much as Dirt and I were, but I did what I had to do, and finally went to bed early the next morning in my own bed at the farm.

Death of a Customer

The next morning Marriah, then Taylor called me. Both women scared to death. Counting on getting a ride from me in my sports car, Marriah had to have one of her customers take her home. While Taylor no doubt went back to Marriah's house in the same car; but that's over twenty-five years ago; as I sit here in my Thailand condo, I can't remember the exact details; because so much has happened since then; but I can almost hear Marriah's voice again, terrified of what would happen next.

"Jack, Taylor and I woke up this morning and found my customer dead on the couch, his face blue from the heroin we had given him."

Whoever the man was, I had never met him. But he was from a Saint Louis suburb with a Middle Class background. He might have been a drug addict. Or possibly a voyeur who only wanted to try something he had never experienced before. Wherever the girls had gotten their heroin, the two dancers had obviously not been affected that much by it other than to get their usual high. So, I suspected the customer wasn't an addict whose system could not take whatever dose the girls had given him.

Both girls insisted on coming to my farm before the police would arrive. Marriah especially had every reason to be terrified of the police. Because this was the second man who had died of a heroin overdose while she was close by. The first man being an ex-husband of hers.

Taylor had a regular customer who drove them to my farm that afternoon. I can't remember exactly what we all did then, but I think I put a couple pizzas in the oven. And of course all four of us downed a few beers. But as the sun started to set Taylor told Marriah: "We had better be getting back to Collinsville. Jack's father has just died and he' s got enough problems without having to put up with us tonight."

But I will never forget Marriah telling me, "I want to stay here with Jack."

I remember Marriah staying with me; not for just a few days, but for several weeks. We watched a lot of satellite TV together, and drank a lot of alcohol. That first night she told me: "I want to shoot your 30-06 rifle. I want to feel its kick against my arm.

It had already gotten dark. I had over 30 guns in my farm house that night, but out of all of them my 30-06 was my pride and joy. I had bought it from a Staunton, Illinois, cop when I was only twelve years old for fifty dollars, which I had to work all summer for. Its shells were 3 inches long and it could shoot through 2 foot diameter trees. And for a twelve year old boy, its kick was very noticeable. Which I'm sure it had to be for Marriah. So, we set up several milk cartons filled with water and put them out in the yard a few feet from my back door. I watched Marriah blast away, hitting most of them, her eyes squinting, her face showing no fear of the rifle's recoil.

Marriah Escapes to the Farm

Marriah never went back inside her house. But her two sons did, one of them 17 while the other was in his early twenties. She never was apprehended by the police because if she had I would soon be visiting her in jail.

We went to a Collinsville car rental business where she had me rent a self drive U-Haul for her, and then we left it for her sons to pick up. A day or two later, the older son drove it to my farm filled up with Marriah's furniture and personal belongings that included a lot of clothing. Then the three of us put it all in my barn.

Meanwhile, Doc shows up. Can't remember exactly when, but I must keep in mind that Marriah was a heroin addict. And for three or four days I watched both of them going through heroin withdrawals together. What I saw was nothing like you see in the movies. There was no kicking and screaming. There was no drama. I only saw two good friends getting sick together, and staying sick as if both of them were experiencing multi-day hangovers.

Doc had been laying low trying to keep a low profile. Because he knew all too well that Marriah was prone to being a loose cannon who was dangerously outspoken about all the drugs she was taking. If I were to compare the two of them, I would say that Marriah was often impulsive whereas Doc was nearly always deliberate.

Being a farmer, I couldn't have both of them staying with me forever. Although I was doing everything I could to keep them comfortably occupied while being fully aware that if I didn't, both of them would start doing heroin again. I had two desktop computers then and two separate phone lines into my house. So, I had both of them going online a lot, and watching a lot of television off my satellite I had in my back yard.

Luckily, I had the perfect solution for both of them. Grey Ghost and I had been renting an apartment on Toronto Road, which was at the southern end of Springfield, the state capital. In those days you had to use a telephone line to access the Internet. But when it came to telephones most farmers in my area were getting the shaft. I had to pay $35.00 a month to Illinois Consolidated just for local phone service. But on top of that I had to pay long distance charges for my phone calls to nearby farm towns that were only ten miles from my house. When I first started my website I was paying a minimum of 8 cents a minute to

Microsoft Network to get online. Which went as high as 14 cents a minute depending on what time of the day I went online.

After a few months I found cheaper ways to access the Internet such as Wam Computers in Litchfield, Illinois. And finally from an Internet provider in Springfield, Illinois, which still meant long distance telephone charges for me. Unless, I could go online in Springfield. The hitch was I would have to rent an office in Springfield. Grey Ghost, of course, had the same problem as I did in having to pay prohibitive long distance charges from his house in Waggoner, Illinois.

The solution to our problem was our finding a two bedroom apartment on Toronto Road where we set up two desktop computers to access the Internet at local phone rates. One can easily understand that it was far less expensive for me to pay half the monthly rental for an apartment compared to my having to pay up to $1000 a month in long distance phone charges from my farm.

At first it was a wonderful adventure having a second home within the Springfield city limits. But after awhile it all got pretty old for me, even though the apartment was just 26 miles from my farm house. I loved that farm house. And I loved the yard surrounding it where I had planted over one-hundred trees. Grey Ghost wound up spending many nights in our apartment while I usually went back to my farm where I was keeping all my guns while having all the comforts one could think of including a wide variety of content I could get from my satellite television service.

Later on Grey Ghost's visits to our apartment became increasingly infrequent. I suppose, like myself, Grey Ghost felt much more at home in his spacious house in Waggoner. Both of us were still bound by what remained of our one year lease. But neither one of us were using the apartment anymore.

Grey Ghost might have been looked down on by much of the farm community, but one thing he had in spades was a heart of gold. So it didn't take much to talk him into giving up our apartment to Doc and Marriah to help two heroin addicts overcome their addiction to drugs. So, we agreed to keep on paying the rent on the apartment provided that both Marriah and Doc would keep a low profile and stay away from doing drugs. Marriah wanted to go into rehab in Springfield while Doc didn't think much of rehab, electing instead to swapping his addiction to heroin to a new addiction to computers and the Internet.

I bought a television for the apartment, which Doc and Marriah moved into early in the morning while their neighbors were still asleep. The idea being that no one would notice that the place had two new residents who were not on our lease.

Satin, the Beautiful Dancer from Deja Vu

There's a strip club in Springfield, Illinois, called Deja Vu Showgirls and is just one of over fifty Deja Vu clubs nationwide. And like most of its sister clubs, the Springfield club is a juice bar that serves no alcohol. Which is exactly what the movers and shakers of the Deja Vu organization intended. Due to many state laws prohibiting full nudity where alcohol is sold, Deju Vu went the full nudity route for most of its franchised clubs. As for myself, I like to drink and I've been used to drinking in the Saint Louis Metro East for years. So Deja Vu is not my kind of place.

But Deja Vu's only thirty miles from my farm, so once in awhile I would check the place out. Which is what I set out to do now that I was trying to get new clubs online with me in our Lost Angels chats.

Near the front entrance at Deja Vu there was a semi-private booth where a dancer could get some degree of physical contact with a customer. I found a pretty black dancer standing just outside the front entrance close to the booth. Who was obviously serving as hawker trying to get potential customers to come into the club and pay their hefty cover charges. The dancer was very attractive with an outgoing personality. So, I flirted with her for a few minutes before going into the night club.

At Deja Vu you pay a cover charge that entitles you to two non alcohol drinks. Which I paid that night to enable me to talk to the club's managers. Once I got inside the night club I encountered one of the Managers - a big guy who introduced himself to me as Ted. I don't know what state Ted came out of. I would have guessed Texas because he had a southern drawl that reminded me of many Texans I had met.

I found Ted to be a pretty coarse kind of guy. He was friendly enough, but he kept joking around about how many dancers I was fucking. There was another Manager standing close to Ted, who was far more reticent, and knew a lot more about the Internet and websites than Ted. This was Mike Parker. I would run into both Managers numerous times a year later when Deja Vu moved both men to Collinsville, IL, where I would soon be renting an apartment. On Highway 111 close to the Highway 64 exit there was an upper scale strip club called Hollywood. The owner of the Springfield Deja Vu franchise wound up buying it. Then he transformed it into another Deja Vu franchise. About a year after that, he changed the name to Hustler Club after buying into the Hustler brand.

The good looking black dancer turned out to have a drug problem. By this time Marriah was going through rehab in Springfield and that's where she met Satin.

Meanwhile, things weren't going too well for Doc and Marriah who had started living in the Toronto Road apartment Grey Ghost and I had been renting. Once again my brain is getting foggy as I try to remember exactly what happened. But either one of their neighbors complained to the owner of the apartment Grey Ghost and I were renting from, or the owner saw one, or both of them entering the apartment. Marriah had a lot of tattoos while Doc looked like a rough character you wouldn't want to meet in a dark alley. So, the owner became alarmed and called me about my subletting her apartment out to a couple who didn't meet her standards for Middle Class up-righteousness.

I really can't blame the owner of our apartment for evicting Doc and Marriah. Because quite honestly neither one of them inspired a lot of faith in Middle Class American values. And during this same time period, the house Marriah had been renting in Collinsville burned down. Which I found to be very suspicious since the fire occurred within a couple of weeks after Marriah and Doc had relocated to my farm. Although I can't prove it, and Marriah never admitted it to me, I think she wanted to make a very thorough house cleaning to destroy any evidence that might help the police find her. She had a lot of stuff in that house and although most of her clothes and furniture wound up in my barn, the U-Haul we had rented couldn't begin to hold everything she had been keeping in that house. So, who knows what might eventually have been found in that house. Perhaps some old pictures or addresses that might incriminate her, or give her friends or relatives away that the police could question later?

I will say that both of her sons were very devoted to her. And that either one of them was capable of torching that house. Although Marriah had been living on the fringes of society, down deep she was a completely honest woman. Who paid me back for renting the U-Haul. And contrary to what one might expect out of a stripper working at a club next door to East Saint Louis, she was as reliable as a clock.

Doc was able to rent out another apartment close-by. But a few weeks later, Marriah decided that she had better resume her career as a stripper.

I don't know if she went back to drugs again. But she went back to Collinsville to continue her misadventures at Dollies. Only this time she took Satin with her.

Fun Times at the Collinsville Hotel

This left Doc homeless, without a job, and no desire to play maid for another stripper. By this time Doc was getting along very well with Grey Ghost and some of my friends from the farm area. And here I had three bedrooms leaving me two to spare. So when Doc swore to me he'd never do heroin again, I let him move in with me.

Doc was an excellent mechanic. Whereas, I wasn't. It still amazes me that I was able to be a successful farmer for twenty-three years because I sure wasn't very handy with my hands. Except when it came to boxing, which I was very good at. In general farmers are some of the best mechanics in the world. They have to be because they are always having to deal with tractors, electric motors, farm implements, grain augers, and pickup trucks, which most of them could repair themselves. I just didn't have it in me to be more than a novice when it came to dealing with machinery. So, Doc with his natural mechanical ability represented a solid choice as my live in hired hand.

I used a small room in my farmhouse for an office. While my ex wife had been using an alcove at the other end of the house as her office. A desk was already there with a bathroom adjoining the alcove. Doc made this alcove his favorite place in the house. Where he soon started getting a thorough knowledge about computers and the Internet.

I think Doc missed his natural calling because he could have easily gotten a job with the CIA. Using the desktop computer I had given him, he could find just about anyone anywhere, and he often looked up prisoner friends of his doing their time in the penitentiary.

Unlike Doc, Marriah found herself completely homeless after the mysterious cremation of her Collinsville home. So, she found a hotel in Collinsville right off the Interstate that was just seven miles from Dollies. Satin took a room in the same hotel and immediately resumed her stripping career at Dollies. Their rooms at the hotel cost each of them forty dollars a night, which they were able to negotiate down from an even higher rate due to them staying there for months on end.

The hotel was very attractive inside, with a large swimming pool and an indoor garden surrounding it. I had stayed there several times before on those nights where I didn't want to drive all the way back to my farm. So, I wound up making a deal with Marriah and Satin. And that was whoever I slept with on a night that I didn't drive back to my farm, I'd split the cost of the room with, which was a great deal for all three of us.

By this time I was going out at night almost as often with Satin as I was with Marriah. So, twenty dollars a night represented a considerable savings for both of the girls.

Dollies Playhouse Gives Me My Own Phone Line

By this time, Nathan had authorized Hawk to allow me to put my own phone line in the club. They would have allowed me to do it earlier had it not been for one problem, and that was who was going to do all the work putting in the phone line? I suppose they could have had the phone company do all the work, but for some reason they didn't. The solution turned out to be Satin, who not only was sharing her room with me at the hotel, but who also had me drive her to her mother's house in Springfield two to four times a month. It was no big deal for me to drive her to her mother's, due to it being only thirty miles from my farm. Which was hardly out of my way because of my doing most of my grocery shopping in Springfield, due to the greater selection than the much smaller supermarkets had in nearby Raymond or Litchfield, which were twenty miles from my farm.

It took Satin and me two or three days to do the wiring at Dollies. The club had a large upstairs which it gave Satin and me free reign to. So, we bought a couple hundred feet of phone wire which Dollies reimbursed us for and then we got down to work. When we finished we had put in two outlets. One was just five feet behind the club's long stage in the bar's main room. Behind it was another large room where the club had two additional stages. At the time Dollies had become very popular and was able to have a lot of customers in both rooms where it was even able to employ two bartenders, one servicing the main room where the club had its front entrance, the other in the backroom.

Satin and I put a T between the phone line going to the front room and the second phone line we put in to a small recessed area near the back bar.

This setup allowed me to have my own table just five feet behind the long narrow main stage in the main room while having a second line in the back where we placed a television behind the bar, which we turned into a Web TV with its own software and Internet connection.

Good to their word, I always got my first two beers free from Nathan and Hawk. While I was able to politely ask any customers who sat at my private table in the main room to sit elsewhere, due to my having to hook my laptop to the phone jack behind my table.

You can just imagine how many people wanted to join me at my table. A lot of the strippers did, as well as some of the club's regular customers. We were, after all, the only game in town.

There was no other club in the United States that was doing what we were doing. I could take pictures of the club's strippers all night long. And within minutes of taking them put their pictures into our Lost Angels chats. The girls loved all the attention they were getting from men all over the United States. And so did several of the Dollies Managers.

Big Howard

I didn't like Howard very much when I first met him. Serving as the club's main manager after Hawk, Howard oftentimes worked the club's front door. Howard was also the club's main bouncer, so when a customer started to get a little rough, Howard would set the customer straight about who was the toughest man in the bar.

Howard had been a starting lineman on the Collinsville High School football team. So, although I found his manner to be gruff and a little intimidating when I was first getting to know him, I later found a different side to him. This was the side that had endeared him to many citizens of Collinsville who had known him since his football days. Although he was capable of becoming very angry at times and had a voice that could shake the needles off a cactus, most of the time Howard was a gentle giant with a sweet mouth who could charm the socks off practically anyone.

Howard usually worked day shift which gave him the whole night off from five or six p.m. on. But being Howard, he was able to put those hours to good use drinking beer and tequila with me at my table where I kept my laptop computer and digital camera.

When he was not at Dollies, Howard could often be found at Killians, his favorite watering hole on Bluff Road just one mile from the motel Marriah, Satin and I often stayed at. There's a beauty about that section of Bluff Road near Killians that has to be experienced - a beauty that really comes into its own after dark. I would oftentimes join Howard at Killians. And so did Doug, who was another Dollies Manager working under Hawk.

Jade

About the time Satin and I put in the phone line at Dollies, another one of the strippers started to hang around me. Her name was Jade, or at least that's the name she danced under. In many ways Jade was a lot like Marriah. Because like Marriah she was a real kick ass woman who wouldn't back down from anyone, be it man, woman, or beast. But Jade became completely fascinated by computers, digital cameras and the Internet.

Now a lot of you have probably gotten the false impression that most strippers are rather stupid, or that they are all about money. This is certainly true about most bar girls in Thailand where I reside now, but it's totally false when it comes to most of the strippers who became good friends of mine.

The more time I got to spend around Jade, the more I started to appreciate her for her intelligence and strong desire to learn all she could about the Internet, digital photography and computers. Most people would start calling Jade - Jack's digital disciple.

It didn't take long for Jade to start renting a room at the same hotel Marriah and Satin were staying. And when she did, I started sleeping over in Jade's room just as often as I stayed in the rooms of the other two women.

Whenever I'd stay at Dollies until the club closed, Marriah and Jade would almost be fighting each other over who'd leave the bar with me. Sometimes we'd all go back to the hotel and crash. While other times we'd go to another strip club that closed two hours after Dollies; or one of the Collinsville bars on Bluff Road; or Pops, which shared the same huge parking area with the two PT's Sauget clubs: PT's Sports and Diamond Cabaret.

To those who don't know any better, the night life of Saint Louis isn't all that terrific. The bars on the Missouri side of the river all close by 1 a.m. But over on the East side of the river, which most of us call the Saint Louis Metro East; a strip club such as Dollies will close at 12:30 a.m. on Sunday evenings, but stay open until 2 a.m. on Mondays through Thursdays. And on Fridays and Saturdays Dollies Playhouse will stay open until 4 a.m. That's for what I will refer to as the roadhouse style clubs such as Dollies, C-Mowes, and Miss Kittys. But the more upscale clubs such as PT's Sports, Diamond Cabaret, or Platinum and Roxys would stay open until 6 a.m. on weekends and 4 a.m on Mondays through Thursdays.

But if that's not enough late night action, there's always Pops, which is a large bar with a huge second floor balcony that's right next to the two PT's Sauget clubs. Sauget is right across the river from Saint Louis, so one can get there within five minutes after crossing the Mississippi from the Missouri side. A lot of St. Louisans go to Pops after the Missouri clubs close at 1 a.m. even if they are not interested in strip clubs. But Pops will stay open until at least 8 a.m. So, a lot of men and women who work in the strip clubs will often go to Pops.

There are many other clubs and bars that I could mention and Jade knew them all, which meant that my friends and I would often be led astray by Jade who seemed to know all the gay and swinger's bars, along with all the places I already knew about.

Both Jade and Marriah shared a common trait: This being a complete loyalty to me as their good friend who they would fight to the death for should anyone threaten me.

Crazy Czech

“You are not going to believe this guy who's coming to Dollies tonight,” said Marriah.

“Who?”

“C.C.”

“Now who in the hell is C.C., Marriah?”

“Crazy Czech, Jack. And he's one crazy motherfucker."

“As crazy as you, Marriah? As crazy as me?”

“Crazy Czech is crazier than all of us."

An hour later, a tall bearded man came in. Marriah rushed up to the big man and put her arms around his waist.

“Come here Jack. I want you to meet C.C.”

“Name's Bill, Jack. Marriah has been telling me a lot about you.”

“Such as?”

“She's been telling me you are even crazier than me."

”Where are you from Bill?”

“From Indiana originally. I have a house there. But right now I'm working in St. Louis doing some special computer software projects.”

“You are a computer programmer then?”

“I'm more like an engineer. I'm into systems design.”

“Well Bill. I'm into a lot of drinking. So let's start on some Tequilla.”

“Sounds good, but before we get too wasted, I want to talk to the Manager.”

“You want to talk with Hawk?" Marriah asked. “What do you want to talk to him about?”

“I've got this great idea. Jack. I've looked over what you and Marriah and a lot of others are doing in the Lost Angels chats. Your digital pictures are astonishing. I've never seen that done before. But we need to talk with Hawk because I've got this idea that will bring lots of customers into Dollies.”

“What's that, Bill?”

“Dollies Trendy Toilet Sex.”

“We can't do that here,” Marriah replied.

“Sure we can. Get Hawk over here. I want to talk to him about it.”

A few minutes later, Marriah came out of the office with Hawk who joined Bill and me at the back room's bar.

“Hi. I'm Hawk the General Manager here. Marriah tells me you want to have a lot of sex in my bar.”

“I'm Bill, Hawk. But Marriah's giving you the wrong idea. I'm not interested in having sex in your bar. I want everyone to enjoy sex at Dollies.”

“What do you have in mind, Bill?” Hawk asked.

“By now you've gotten used to all Jack's digital photography. And how he puts all his pictures into his Lost Angels chat messages. I hear it gets a lot of guys coming to Dollies who normally wouldn't come here. Especially from across the river in St. Louis.”

“Well yes. We've had some success getting some new interest in the bar.” Hawk replied.

“If we start doing Dollies Trendy Toilet Sex you are going to get a lot of new faces coming in here.”

“What do you mean, Bill?”

“Every Saturday night we can have your dancers and some of your customers playing around in your toilet. And once Jack takes pictures of what's going on in your toilet he can post them in the Lost Angels chat. I think you will have a lot of guys from the St. Louis side coming here to get in on all that action. And from other areas of the country besides St.

Louis."

"I'm interested Bill. You and Jack need to get together on a plan on what goes on in that toilet, and then the two of you can get back to me about it. I'll run it by Nathan then to get his approval."

By this time I was getting well acquainted with a 21 year old blonde who was going by the stage name, Alabama. I informed Crazy Czech about the night I had gotten much better acquainted with Alabama after we wound up leaving the club together and I brought her to this little motel I was staying at. And how we talked all night as I watched her eyes, which kept widening until I thought they were glowing in the dark. Now I know the reason why she wanted to talk all night: She's a crystal meth addict.

When I told Crazy Czech what happened that night, he replied "That's perfect! We already have Marriah who's a devout heroin addict and now we can add Alabama, who's a crystal meth addict to our team that's going to spearhead our Dollies Trendy Toilet Sex extravaganzas."

"I'm glad you recognize her qualifications for helping us propel Dollies to new horizons in the strip club stratosphere, Bill. Alabama is perfect and I'm going to tell you why."

"Reassure me please, Jack."

"Last week was Halloween. Alabama came to the Dollies Halloween party wearing a nun's outfit. And she looked terrific in that. I think many men fantasize about having sex with a young, sexy nun, and let me assure you, Alabama's damn sexy wearing that nun outfit."

It didn't take a lot to convince C.C. that I had the perfect plan for introducing the first episode of Dollies Trendy Toilet Sex. When we outlined it all to Hawk he gave us approval for implementing it. But by then I had gotten Hawk's measure, so I knew he could not refuse us. Because Hawk would play the male lead with Alabama playing the heroine of Dollies Trendy Toilet Sex. By the time we finished doing Episode 1 of Dollies Trendy Toilet Sex practically everyone the bar the bar loved it. I provided the script out of my own demented imagination.

> Sister Margarita a young nun at a nearby convent suddeny decides to get a taste of freedom that the convent has denied her. She borrows a car and bottle of whiskey, proceeds to drive around town drinking

straight from the bottle. But suddenly she has to take a shit, so she starts looking for a place where she can relieve herself. Now a completely inebriated Sister Margarita wanders into Dollies completely oblivious to its being a strip club. She finds a toilet in the bar, and spreads her nice bottom all over the toilet seat while she continues to drink out of her bottle of whiskey.

Then Hawk comes into the restroom and starts urinating into the urinal. At first he's completely unaware of the attractive nun who's watching him urinate as she continues to drink from her bottle. And then Hawk catches the attractive nun from the corner of his eye. After he finishes urinating, he goes over to Sister Margarita and starts drinking with her. Then a customer comes into the men's room. The man hasn't shaved for several days and he's brought a razor and shaving cream into the restroom bent on making himself presentable to all the strippers. Hawk is now almost on top of Sister Margarita while the customer goes over to Hawk and Sister Margarita to get his share of Sister Margarita's whiskey. Sister Margarita then proceeds to shave the customer as several customers and strippers join them in the toilet. I go into the toilet with everyone else and proceed to kiss one of the strippers on her ass.

Sam Stimmel

I took Grey Ghost with me to the next Exotic Dancer Expo in Las Vegas. On Grey Ghost's recommendation we took two desktop computers with us, two computer monitors and several boxes of promotional materials. Taking everything we needed to set up our exhibitor's booth we drove 1800 miles in my pickup truck.

Our exhibitor's booth gave us a lot of well deserved credibility. With both club owners who felt we were a force to be reckoned with and the entertainers at the convention.

One of them was Jules, who would often visit our booth. Jules was a very talkative outgoing House Dancer working for Stimmelators in northern Indiana. I'd say that roughly half the entertainers at the convention were Feature Entertainers trying to gain a lot of publicity. While the other half were House Dancers. Jules was a House Dancer working at only one club, Stimmelators, which was owned by Sam Stimmel.

The Feature Entertainers were a different kettle of fish from House Dancers such as Jules because most of them were not affiliated with a single club. Instead, they did a lot of traveling from club to club across the United States to do special shows for club owners

At this point it is essential to establish what a Feature Entertainer is. There are House Dancers and there are Feature Entertainers. The House Dancer works for "the house" which is a single night club. Whereas, a Feature Entertainer works for herself and typically travels throughout the United States from club to club. The club hiring the Feature Entertainer will pay her a rate of $100.00 to $1500 a show. The Feature will typically perform three to four special shows per night for several nights in succession.

There are two basic types of Feature entertainers: There are the Porn Stars and there are the Burlesque Style Feature Entertainers. The Porn Stars have typically established notorious reputations as Porn Stars while the Burlesque Style Feature Entertainers are in most cases not nearly as well known as the Porn Stars. Due to their notoriety the Porn Stars can command a much higher price per show than the Burlesque Style Feature Entertainer. The Burlesque Style Feature Entertainers are able to perform high quality shows where they can show off their superior dancing skills, the originality of their shows, & costumes. Their shows can oftentimes be very comedic.

willing to pay them anywhere from a couple thousand dollars for three or four nights to fifteen thousand dollars or more.

There were several Feature Entertainers at the expo who could easily afford their own booths, due to their being very highly regarded by the upper echelons of the Adult Entertainment world. A prime example being, Adara Michaels, who did special shows with her "twin sister." Who was not really her twin. But similar enough to Adara that they could pull off their twin sister acts to their audience. Adara used the moniker, "Scandalous" to identify their twin sister shows. At this particular convention Adara not only had her own booth, she also had a stage close to her booth where she and her "twin sister" could dazzle the crowd of topless club owners. Who would later book her for her feature acts at high dollar prices, which would more than justify Adara's investment in her booth and stage.

Other feature entertainers at the Exotic Dancer Expo could be found representing the booths of the best known talent agencies such as the Pure Talent Agency, Continental Agency and Universal Talent. The talent agencies would deal directly with club across the country for a 15 percent commission off what the clubs paid the Feature entertainers they would book from the agencies.

But practically all of us were out to network with the other adult industry professionals on one level or another. Jules, although she was a House Dancer, still dreamed about becoming a feature entertainer. So she would go from booth to booth meeting everyone she could such as the owners of the Pure Talent Agency and club owners who might eventually hire her should she ever become a feature entertainer.

Other than booking Feature Entertainers I have found such talent agencies do a great talent job protecting their "Feature Entertainers" from unscrupulous night clubs that do not live up to their contractual agreements with the Features they book. Examples of not fulfilling the terms of such contracts might include no payment, or underpayment to the Feature Entertainers, non payment of essential travel expenses, failure to provide adequate dressing room facilities to the Feature and sexual harassment.

The highest number of Feature Entertainers I've ever photographed at a single Feature Showcase was 19 at the 2002 Big Al's Feature Showcase in Peoria, Illinois. The showcase ran for three consecutive nights during which I averaged over 1000 pictures a night.

Grey Ghost and I soon met Sam Stimmel through Jules. And when Sam showed an interest in the Alphapro website and the Lost Angels chat, which Grey Ghost and I showcased on the computer at our exhibitor's booth, it didn't take long for Grey Ghost to convince Sam to visit us in our hotel room.

Now that Grey Ghost was one helluva salesman. By the time he finished showing off what he could do as a website designer, he had gotten a check from Sam for $250 to get Stimmelators listed in the Jack Corbett Guide, which didn't even exist. And wouldn't exist until a month later after Grey Ghost and I drove up to northern Indiana to visit Sam and his club.

Grey Ghost's next victims were the owners of Pure Talent Agency, Jim and Anne Marie Hyatt. Who Grey Ghost also invited up to our hotel room. I had already taken a few pictures of several Feature Entertainers at the Pure Talent booth. Which Grey Ghost put on his desktop computer in our hotel room. As Anne Marie and Jim watched Grey Ghost pulled the pictures into photoshop and went to work.

“Jim and Anne Marie, I am going to show you what I can do with all the Feature Entertainers you represent. As an example we will use this single picture of one of your Feature Entertainers. Now, when you look at it closely you will see the woman has a few small wrinkles in her face. Now watch what we can do with her face.”

Grey Ghost pulled out the lasso selection brush from his Photoshop tool box and selected parts of the entertainers face. He then selected from the Photoshop menu a blurring effect.

“I'm not going to go too wild with this because this entertainers wrinkles are not too bad. They are noticeable though. So, I will apply the blurring effect at the 5 % level. Take a look now. Notice that she looks a lot younger now that the wrinkles have all been blurred out. This is what magazines like Penthouse and Playboy do. It's called airbrushing. But I'm going to take this one step further. Notice that this woman's eyes are dull and listless. So, I am now using one of Photoshop's paint brushes to create a small rectangle. I am going to make it very small and color it white.”

Using the magnifying glass tool Grey Ghost zoomed the image so that only one of the Feature Entertainer's eyes filled the work space. Then he dabbed a small rectangle into the center of the entertainers eye.

“I'm setting this paintbrush tool at a 5 pixel size. Notice that I've colored the rectangle white. You see it as a rectangle though. Now watch what happens when I zoom the picture out so that the entertainer's entire face is now filling the work space. You can't even see now that I painted in a small white rectangle. But notice how her eyes are much more lively now."

"Amazing, Grey Ghost. That's just unbelievable."

"I tell you what, Jim. I can create a website for your Pure Talent Agency in one hour, and you can watch me do it."

And true to his word, one hour later Grey Ghost created Pure Talent's first website and put it live on the Internet.

The site was very rudimentary of course, but from that point on for the next two years Grey Ghost had landed himself a job as the website designer for Pure Talent Agency. Which paid off hugely for me as well, because it wouldn't be long that I'd be traveling all over the United States shooting Feature Showcases for Pure Talent. While getting my hotel rooms paid for while becoming very well acquainted with dozens of entertainers who I'd later feature in my articles for "Xtreme Magazine."

Before the convention ended Grey Ghost and I were having a few beers with Jules and Sam in his hotel room. Although Grey Ghost and I would stay for two more nights at the Exotic Dancer Expo, Sam and Jules had to catch the plane back to Indianapolis the next morning.

"Grey Ghost and Jack. I have no more use for the beer I have in my car because I can't take it on the plane with us tomorrow. So I'm going to give it to you. I'm sure you will make good use of it."

On that note Sam and I took the elevator down to the hotel lobby and then we went to Sam's car and took several six packs out of his trunk. Then he said to me, "I'll see you in several weeks. You and Grey Ghost can stay at my house when you come visit us."

Stimmelators

Over 400 miles from my farm, Stimmelators turned out to be totally different from Dollies and any other St. Louis Metro East strip club I had ever visited.

Although a first class gentleman's club, Platinum Club was in Brooklyn, Illinois, within one mile of East St. Louis. While Roxy's, a PT's strip club was across the street from Platinum. Both clubs were close to where the old East St. Louis stock yards used to be. I had found Brooklyn to be the epitome of seediness.

To get to Brooklyn one drives up Interstate 55 towards St. Louis. But when the Mississippi River that separates Illinois from Missouri is only several minutes away, and the St. Louis Arch looms large, you turn right off the last exit before you cross the river. Which is Route 3. Until then everything's well lit up. And then within the first half mile of Route 3, you are entering a poverty stricken area that can be very frightening to the uninitiated. Both Platinum and Roxys are two miles off the Interstate. But on the short drive to both you are likely to see crack whores looking for tricks. So you will want to park in one of the club's parking lots or within one city block of them.

There is a club called Pink Slip just two blocks from Platinum and Roxys. This is an all black club, which I went to once. Where I was warned not to visit from several black employees at Platinum who told me they wouldn't even go there.

PT's Sports and Diamond Cabaret were in Sauget right across the Mississippi from St. Louis in an industrial area very few people would want to live. While Dollies, Chameleon, C-Mowes and Hollywood were in Washington Park which was just as impoverished as Brooklyn.

My point is to differentiate Stimmelators from most of the St. Louis Metro East clubs that were located in areas where very few people would want to live and were allowed to exist because there weren't any wealthy citizens there to complain. So, Grey Ghost and I were surprised to find Stimmelators on Main Street in North Webster, Indiana, which was in the middle of an idyllic tourist area in northern Indiana.

Beer was cheap here. With the club serving more as a watering hole for the locals than a strip club encouraging all kinds of sexual activity. The dancers all wore pasties and they danced in turn on a long stage in the main room downstairs. Grey Ghost and I were stunned when we found out how milk toast the whole thing was, due to each girl dancing one at a time on the long stage for several minutes after which she'd walk around the room getting dollar tips from the customers. Each customer giving her only one dollar, and then she'd shake her pastie tipped breasts a foot in front of the man's face.

Grey Ghost and I were greeted like royalty from the moment we entered the club. The doorman was about sixty and appeared more like a fatherly neighbor than the sort of man who could be called in as an impromptu bouncer should any trouble makers get out of line. We also met a couple DJ's; neither of them showing the slightest semblance of arrogance.

Most of the customers were good old boys who were out for a few beers who enjoyed being around a lot of beautiful women. Which Stimmelators had in spades.

Grey Ghost and I soon found ourselves sitting at a table with a sensational looking dancer and her boyfriend who introduced themselves as Katt and Rocci. Katt was prettier by far than any of the Dollies girls with a sensational body, full breasts and a face that was so striking that she could have been a model practically anywhere.

But Katt was much more than a pretty face. Although she went on and on about how she had worked for some of the best clubs in Las Vegas, she was just as interested in my laptop computer and my website as she was talking about herself.

Stimmelators had a large upstairs where there were several stages, a bar, and Sam's office. Where Sam soon took us to show off my Alphapro website and our Lost Angels chat room. But once Grey Ghost and I got Katt posting messages in the Lost Angels chats, Sam could hardly get her back downstairs to do her turn on the stage.

With Katt now being occupied with collecting her dollar tips from over twenty customers, Sam introduced us to a very attractive blonde, who I liked on first sight. Who would be perfect for me to use as a model for showing off what we could do with my digital camera and the Lost Angels chat. I wouldn't be the photographer, however. So I had Grey Ghost shoot a few pictures of Renee and me lying on a couch. Where Renee and I hammed it up pretending to be drunk and very much in love. Shooting a sequence of pictures of Renee and I sitting close together on the couch Grey Ghost's final shot was of me lying on top of Renee with my head on her lap as if I had passed out from drinking too much.

Once again, Sam took us into his office where Grey Ghost and I put the new pictures into the Lost Angels chat. By this time Marriah and Jade were posting messages in the chat to PlONe and a couple of the other guys.

Renee watched Marriah post, “Look at Jack. See how drunk on his ass he's gotten.”

As Renee looked at Grey Ghost and me, and asked, “You can do that?”

“Yes. Marriah and Jade are dancers just like you, Renee. But they are down in East St. Louis messaging us. They know me all too well.”

“As a drunk?” Renee asked me with a laugh.

“Jade, Marriah and me. We get drunk together all the time.”

Once again, Sam took us downstairs where he introduced Grey Ghost and me to a third dancer. Who if it were at all possible was even more stunning than Katt and Renee.

A tall slender blonde, Heaven, had just the right name to describe herself. Which turned out to be her real name and not just a stage name. She had high cheek bones and the look of a real movie star you might find in a James Bond movie. And an aristocratic look that belied the fact that she was only a stripper. Unlike Katt and Renee who had obviously been quite taken with Grey Ghost and me and even more impressed with the new technology we had shown them, Heaven showed hardly any interest in the digital pictures we had started to show her on my laptop. Obviously, she had much better things to do such as chatting with her friends and getting customers to buy her drinks.

Suddenly Jules shows up. But when Sam tells Jules that Grey Ghost and I are staying with him, Jules tells her club owner. “I want them to stay with me, Sam. You are awfully busy. So, if they stay with me I can show them around.” With our bags still in my car, we still haven't seen Sam's house, and we wind up following Jules to her house after the club closes.

Grey Ghost and I drove back to my farm the next afternoon. But before we did we went back to Stimmelators around eleven in the morning. Where Sam showed me a note he had gotten from Renee. It read, "I want Jack to tell me where I can find his website. I won't be in the club for the next few days, so please have him tell me so I can look it up from home."

PlONe

Within the first few weeks of our putting the Lost Angels chat on my website, two men found it and became regular members, the Baron and PlONe. As a reminder PlONe is pronounced like this: P-L-ONE.

Baron was a writer whose real name was not Baron, who wrote a lot like Ernest Hemingway. Who like Hemingway lived in some far away places far away from Middle Class American mediocrity. For years Baron had been a fisherman in Alaska, and later moved to the Olympic Mountains in Washington.

About the same time Baron became a Lost Angels chat regular, PlONe started entering our Lost Angels chats. But unlike Baron, who preferred living in the wilderness with very few creature comforts, PlONe was a high powered computer programmer living in the San Francisco area.

Then Grey Ghost and I found Scarlet the Harlot who also lived in San Francisco. A stripper turned whore Scarlet was a civil rights activist for strippers who were being abused by the club owners they were working for. So, it didn't take long for Grey Ghost and I to convince Scarlet to join us in the Lost Angels.

With Grey Ghost's blessings I decided to meet Baron, PlONe, and Scarlet up close and personal. So I booked three flights, one to San Francisco, another to Seattle, and the third my trip back home to St. Louis from Seattle.

On my first night in San Francisco I arranged to have dinner with Scarlet who met me at Sinbads, which was a terrific seafood restaurant that had a spectacular view of the Bay Bridge. I had been to Sinbads a few years before where I drank a few bottles of Anchor Steam beer, which was being produced by a small San Francisco brewery and had a very distinct taste.

Scarlet and I spent a few hours together at Sinbads enjoying the view while discussing what she was doing for San Francisco's whores and strippers. Just as I had found in the Saint Louis Metro East strip clubs, in San Francisco most club owners were requiring their dancers to pay a tip out for the privilege of working in their clubs. Scarlet was trying to unionize the San Francisco strippers, so that they could strike for real wages and outlaw the tip outs the clubs were charging their dancers. Which amounted to Scarlet becoming a very vocal advocate of strippers' rights to a decent wage, health insurance, and being eligible for collecting Social Security that would be based on the income they'd be reporting to the IRS.

I found Scarlot to be a very intelligent woman with a heart of gold, who really wanted to make a difference for a better world.

The next night I met PlONe for the first time at Mitchell Brothers, which was the most glamorous of San Francisco strip clubs. Unlike the Saint Louis Metro East Clubs customers were not allowed to drink or smoke in the SF strip clubs. I did not find any meaningful degree of socialization there among the customers, managers, or between a stripper and her customers. What the clubs did have was a lot of sex between the dancers and their customers. But the sex came at a high price tag. While many of the strippers, especially the ones I encountered at Mitchell Brothers were off the scale gorgeous.

For example at Mitchell Brothers I remember the cover charge being $45.00 just to get into the bar. Fortunately, I found PlONe to be extremely knowledgeable about the admission prices at nearly all the San Francisco bars. An example being one could get into Mitchell Brothers for around $25.00 if one arrived early in the afternoon.

Once I got inside Mitchell Brothers I was able to view some really sensational girls lying stark naked on small stages which customers could gather around with large bulges in their trousers. I can't remember what the best looking girls were charging their customers for sex, but I think it was in the $200.00 range and up.

Out of all the San Francisco clubs, Mitchell Brothers, was by far the most widely known, due to its being featured in "Behind the Green Door" starring, Marilyn Chambers, who would take the world of Porn to an entirely new level. Besides being a very beautiful woman, Marilyn could have become one of Hollywood's superstars due to her excellent acting ability. Unfortunately, Marilyn sacrificed a career in Hollywood. Porn was for Marilyn and many other Porn Stars after her, the Rubicon that once crossed would ban them from main stream cinema forever.

The Market Street Cinema was a strip club that had been converted from an old movie theater. I found the cover charge to be reasonably priced at $20.00. Which entitled a man to be able to sit in a section of old cinema seats from where he could watch the club's dancers perform shows at a distance. I found most of these dancers to be mediocre compared to the Stimmelators girls. The better looking girls could be found in a backroom of secluded small areas where a man could get a blow job in a standing up position, or in small short time rooms that offered a full menu. To gain admission to this backroom area I had to pay another $15.00 or $20.00.

I was eventually able to talk PlONe into taking me to a normal bar where we could drink beer together. It was at this bar that I learned for the first time that PlONe had his own airplane and a pilot's license.

Although the San Francisco Metropolitan area has over 4 million residents and covers a large area on both sides of the bay, San Francisco itself is quite small. Which I could easily cover on foot. So my having to walk back to my hotel was no problem. While PlONe had to drive over the Bay Bridge to get to his home in Oakland. We were walking together past a lot of homeless people sleeping on the sidewalks when a woman came up to me and asked for a cigarette. PlONe had parked his car close by. So, we said goodbye to each other after agreeing to meet at Chez Paree the next evening.

Watching so many beautiful strippers at Mitchell Brothers had made me pretty horny, so one thing led to another with the woman who asked me for a cigarette. She followed me back to my hotel while this little voice in my head told me to restrain myself. But the little head rearing its prominent head inside my pants prevailed.

The woman was beyond wildness, almost neutering me with her nearly tearing my dick off while we were having sex. At the same time I found it all to be incredibly exciting, so we did it again. But I didn't get any sleep at all that night, due to the woman turning the radio's volume up.

Thankfully, she left the next morning, which enabled me to finally get several hours of sleep. Until I heard someone knocking on my door. Terrified, I went over to the door and looked out through the small peep hole to see who was there. Only to find out that my worse dreams had just come back to haunt me, but after a few minutes when I didn't answer the door the girl disappeared. Only to come back a few minutes later. For once prudence ruled. This time I opened the door to tell the girl, “Go away. I have another woman in here with me now.”

I met PlONe later on at the Chez Paree, where once again we were not allowed to have alcohol. Inside the club we found several men chatting on a desktop computer that the strip club had provided for them. Chez Paree had two phone lines, one for its desktop computer, the other one for customers who wanted to bring their laptops into the club. A lot of the Chez Paree dancers and customers would be chatting with other dancers and customers who were posting messages to them out of their homes.

The Chez Paree group was using an ancient IRC based chat in which they could post their messages only in text. Whereas, we could send pictures to each other in the Lost Angels, due to its being based on HTML Code. Later, as PlONe and I became much better friends I would give him my password and username that would allow him to improve the Lost Angels chat. With PlONe's improvements we could post private messages to each other, or post messages to any subgroup we wanted to without giving the other members a chance to read our messages.

But no one from Chez Paree was interested in the Lost Angels, or in our ability to post digital pictures into our chat messages. We were state of the art, leaving the rest of the world far behind. But back in those days hardly anyone was interested in digital photography.

The Chez Paree group looked at us and would continue to view us as a bunch of upstarts who didn't know their place. And at me, in particular, as a hick farmer living in Central Illinois who couldn't ever hope to live up to San Francisco standards of sophistication and urbanity.

And as for PlONe, the letters in his name spoke for itself. Although he had been a member of the Chez Paree chat group, he and a couple of his friends were not very highly regarded by some of the strip club's strippers who started calling them losers. As did some of the more uppity customers in the group. So not to be outdone, PlONe and his friends, who all regarded themselves as men of superior intellect compared to the rabble trying to make fun of them started calling each other PlONe and PlTWo, and so on. Which they told everyone who would listen stood for Pathetic Loser One, Pathetic Loser Two—. But their subtle sense of humor was entirely lost on the rabble who had no clue that Pl was the name for a computer programming code.

So, what was unsaid and certainly would have been misunderstood by the rabble was that this small group considered themselves as a superior elite of superior intelligence who were making far more money than those who were calling them losers.

Baron

As soon as I got off the plane in Seattle I spotted the Baron looking directly at me. I was wearing my hat, so even though Baron had never met me before he certainly recognized me because of that hat.

My first impression of Baron was of a sixty year old farmer who had faced the elements all his life, which had left their indelible mark on him. Although he looked older than he seemed in the pictures he had shown us, he still looked every inch of the mountain man. Which was the very the image he wanted to project due to his turning out to be exactly what he proclaimed himself to be.

Baron had this old two wheel drive Japanese pickup that looked like it had been around for eons, and this is what got us to his trailer up in the Olympic mountains after three or four hours during which we had to take a ferry across Puget Sound. As we approached his trailer, Baron pointed out a far smaller trailer, which wasn't much more than a U-Haul, that I couldn't imagine anyone living in for much more than a night or two.

But if Baron 's former home where somehow managed to maintain an Internet connection and desktop computer left a huge amount to be desired short of being a doghouse, Baron's new trailer didn't amount to much either.

It was a single wide trailer that supplied only about half the living space of a double wide. And although it often got cold up in the Olympic Mountains Baron only had a worn out 1500 watt heater that had lost half it's original 1500 watts of electricity leaving him with just 750 watts, which was barely enough to keep his water pipes from freezing. But Baron was still able to keep himself comfortable with the wood burning stove he had in his living room. And while he was keeping an ample supply of firewood just outside his trailer, the wood was a very soft quick burning wood that would die down to ashes within several hours.

At my farm I had two stoves. One I could fill with either coal or wood. And this could supply heat for up to 24 hours before the last flames would go out. The other was a small but very beautiful Scandinavian stove that could only burn wood and only up to 15 inch logs at that. Yet it was sufficient to heat a large room from wood that was far superior to Baron's because it could keep a flame going for a good ten hours.

Baron would sleep in a small bedroom at the far end of the trailer, while

I got to sleep on a couch next to his wood burning stove. I suppose Baron had long ago gotten used to sleeping in the cold. Either that, or he was sleeping in a very well insulated sleeping bag. While I had to keep feeding his wood burning stove with fresh wood to keep myself from freezing my ass off.

Mike, which was Baron's real name, had several guns mounted on the wall of his small living room behind his wood burning stove. One was a .22 rifle that he used to target practice with and shoot birds. He also had a shotgun that no true mountain man can afford to do without. While the last was a 1996 Swedish Mauser that fired a 6.5 millimeter bullet that Baron swore could shoot as flat as a 300 Magnum.

Which it could almost match. Baron swore up and down that he could take Elk or even Moose with it, which it so turns out many hunters in Sweden regularly did with their 6.5 Swedish Mausers. But I had gotten used to my 30-06's, which I felt was a lot more like it for shooting such large animals as Moose and Elk.

Baron might not have had much in that small trailer of his, but he kept his priorities straight by maintaining a desktop computer, a passable Internet connection, and a good supply of alcohol. +So, I was able to look at the ballistics of the Swedish Mauser round thanks to his internet connection. And although it was pretty much of an ancient round that on paper could be easily outperformed by what most of America's hunters were now using such as 30-06's, 270's, and 7 mm Remington Magnums, it had developed a great reputation for having excellent killing power and deep penetration on big game animals at much lower recoil than the others I have just mentioned.

“Watch me take this bolt out of the action,” said Baron. This old Swedish Mauser is much better built than the 98 Mausers the Germans used in the World Wars. Notice its attention to detail. It has great accuracy and it won't punish your arm at all. So, you will never flinch while shooting one.”

“Baron, you have convinced me. I have to get one. Where can I buy one?”

“I can take you to a gun store tomorrow. With any kind of luck they will have one that you can buy for only a hundred dollars.”

The next day, Baron took me to a favorite gun shop twenty miles from his trailer. Where I was elated to find a pristine 1996 Swedish Mauser for $100.00. I bought 40 rounds of modern 6.5 mm shells to go with it, which were lighter than the ones the Swedish military was using at the turn of the century. Not only were they higher velocity and flatter shooting; they were also hollow points; which I felt confident could take down anything Baron and I would ever find in his Olympic Mountains. While leaving the gun shop, its owner warned me, “you can take the rifle back to St. Louis on the plane, but you won't be able to take the ammunition with you. So, be sure to shoot all of it while you are here.”

I couldn't wait to shoot my new rifle. So, the next day Baron and I set out for a small lake he knew about where we could put both rifles through their paces. On the way, Baron started to get very excited and pulled his pickup to the side of the road. A small tree had fallen on the road, which would have stopped us from continuing, but then Baron gleefully shouted, “Road Kill! Jack, this is a lucky break for us.”

From the back of his pickup truck Baron produced a chain saw which he fired up. And then he started severing all the branches off the tree. Each time Baron cut a limb off, I'd put it inside the bed of his pickup until we had gotten it half full and most of the tree had disappeared from the road.

It is hard to believe, but we never found anyone on that snowy road. Other than my backpacking with Outward Bound when I was sixteen and later with the National Outdoor Leadership school in Wyoming, I had never in my life been on a mountain road that was so completely devoid of cars. And as far as my traveling through the mountains at Outward Bound, or the National Outdoor leadership school, the terrain we covered was far too rough for motorized vehicles of any kind.

We finally found Baron's lake. Where no one would ever find us. Here we could shoot our rifles with no one to question what we were doing there. Where we could shoot out to 200 yards at willows and large twigs in the lake, or on the shoreline across from us. While Baron shot in sitting down position I got in a much steadier prone position. With my chest in the snow I started firing away while being pleasantly surprised by my rifle's low recoil.

A half hour later Baron and I had enough shooting. It had already started to snow with both of us knowing all too well that Baron's truck was two wheel drive. By the time its wheels were spinning in the snow I knew we had gotten ourselves into some very serious trouble.

“Baron, do you have a shovel in your truck,”I asked.

“No, I don't.”

“A lot of good that chain saw is going to do us now,” I replied as I looked in the back of his truck for something we could use to dig his rear tires out of the snow.

But all I could find was a claw hammer and a large screw driver. Which would have to do. But spinning his rear tires in the snow had dug a deep rut behind both tires. Had we been anywhere else, I think we both would have given up trying to dig the truck out of the snow. But we had seen no one on the two lane road we had taken to the lake, so it was unlikely that anyone would come and bail us out. And that left us scraping furiously with the two hand tools, which were still far superior to having to dig the tires out with our fingernails. Then I remembered the branches in the pickup truck's bed that Baron had shortened with his chain saw.

We cut gaps in the snow behind the back tires in which we could place the tree branches. Which gave us a firm foundation that the tires could grip. As Baron started the truck's engine he was able get the truck to move a few inches forward, and then back against the tree branches which stopped the tires from spinning. Putting his gear shift into drive, Baron was finally able to get his truck to move forward out of the ruts as I kept pushing on the tailgate. Finally we were home free although we wouldn't be out of the woods yet.

By the time we managed to get out on the road, the snow had picked up. But after we had driven a few miles, I noticed that the snow was starting to fall even harder. So far, I had trusted Baron. After all these were his mountains so he had to know them well. But when I saw the sun peering every now and then through the clouds I knew something was wrong.

“Where are we eating, Baron? And do they have beer there?”

“Los Angeles City, Baron replied. “I know a great restaurant there where they have great food and enough beer to keep both of us happy, Jack.”

“And is Los Angeles City North or South of us, Baron?”

“Why it's South. Is something wrong Jack?”

“Can you see the sun?”

“Sure I can although it keeps hiding from us.”

“And is the sun on our left, or our right?”

“It's on our left.”

“Baron, the sun sets in the West. It's now 4 p.m. So this means we are heading North, not South. And we are gaining altitude all the time as we keep going higher up in the mountains. The snow is going to become a blizzard and then we are going to get stuck in the snow and there will be no one coming to get us.”

“Shit Jack. You are right. I'd better turn this thing around and start heading South right now.”

Luckily, Baron was able to get the pickup turned around on the narrow two lane road without getting us stuck in the snow. Twenty miles later the snow had slackened and we arrived at a nice warm tavern where they had hamburgers and beer.

By the time we got back to Baron's trailer both of us were in the mood for doing some serious drinking. We drank vodka until the bottle ran out and then we started drinking whiskey as we got my laptop online, so that we could chat with PlONe and some of the girls in the Lost Angels.

To this day I'll never forget, nor will I stop laughing at what Baron posted into the Lost Angels chat.

> “Here we are back at my home thankful to be alive. We got stuck in the snow today while shooting our rifles. Then we were lucky to dig ourselves out. But we got lost in those mountains, and we would have died in those mountains had it not been for Jack. Jack, is the greatest mountain man whoever lived. Greater than Daniel Boone and even greater than Abraham Lincoln."

The next morning I woke up to the sound of shooting. And found Baron outside the trailer shooting at ducks flying overhead with his .22 rifle. He didn't hit any, which is quite understandable, and I really didn't think he was very serious about the whole thing. Had he been using his 12 gauge we would be eating roast duck that night. I had never shot a bird on the wing with a rifle before, although I had shot several fast moving rabbits with .22 rifles and my .22 Magnum Revolver. But I couldn't do it very often, and had always figured that shooting flying birds with a rifle was only done in the movies. With the exception of a few great marksmen who would always be far better than I'd ever be.

That afternoon Baron took me to the Big Quilcene River and showed me a dam that had created a beautiful mountain reservoir. We looked at the dam and then we started skirting the reservoir where Baron took a picture of me smoking a cigarette that I still have on my website. We must have hiked around that lake for a good two hours while Baron kept talking about all the things we could soon be doing on my website.

“We can do movies, Jack. But because the Internet's so slow because we are using phone lines people will have to download these movies. We already have Heaven and Katt chatting in the Lost Angels every day. They are both brilliant actresses. And Katt's so pretty. She's much prettier than most movie starlets today. As for Heaven: What a kick ass bitch, she's sensational! Just think what we can all do together, Jack. And we can start making some real money.”

“That's an idea, Baron, and I think Heaven and Katt would do it in a heart beat. Then there's Renee. She'd be excellent in the movie also.”

“She hardly comes into the chats , Jack and I don 't think she compares to Katt and Heaven."

“Well, I must admit that I'm a little disappointed in Renee not coming into the Lost Angels very often, but I still like her a lot. There' something about her, and you have to admit--she's gorgeous."

“Tell you what we need to do, Jack. I need to get over to Stimmelators with you soon. I can help you set the whole thing up there."

Brandy, the New Girl at Dollies

The new girl at Dollies was slender and very beautiful. As I watched her from my little table close to the long stage where several girls were dancing, I decided that I had to meet her right away. I had several girls with me already who were watching me post messages into the Lost Angels chat room. So, it didn't take much for me to approach the new girl and ask her to join us.

Only nineteen, the girl's name was Brandy. I soon detected that she had little in common with the other Dollies dancers. For Brandy had the sweet innocent look of the girl next door. While I soon found out that she hated customers touching her. Which was the normal modus operandi most of the Dollies girls followed. Because at Dollies the name of the game was for the girls to put out the bait, by luring their customers to believe that sooner or later they'd be having sex with them. The hook would come soon after, with many of the girls actually having sex with their customers outside the bar. Or at least leading their customers on by making them believe sex would come later.

But Brandy wouldn't even put out the bait, due to her planning on stripping only for a couple of months after which she would get a much more normal job. But she needed the money over the short term, due to a friend staying with her running her phone bill up to over $1000.

Although Brandy never finished High School, I soon found out that she would have been a far better than average student. But after committing a few minor disciplinary infractions she smarted off to the school's superintendent, who suspended her from school. Ironically the superintendant had been my best friend when I was in Junior High School.

From the very beginning Brandy became addicted to computers and the Lost Angels chat. At first I'd bring my laptop computer to her house where she'd spend hours with me learning just about everything I could teach her. I soon became acquainted with her twenty year old boyfriend, who never was able to hold onto a job more than a few weeks.

While Brandy was as sharp as a tack when it came to computers, Joey just didn't have it in him to even come close. But that being said about Joey, to this day I have no complaints about him. He was a great guy who was up for about anything. Brandy and Joey would oftentimes visit me at my farm.

After Marriah stored her furniture in my barn,I warned her to come get her furniture, or suffer the consequences. I found Joey to be a worthy accomplice. I told Marriah that if she didn't come get her furniture I'd burn all of it. So,several weeks after I warned her, I had Joey and Brandy come to my farm for Halloween. And we had one helluva weenie roast at the bonfire Joey and I made out of Marriah's furniture.

Sometimes Joey would stay in Granite City while Brandy would visit me at my farm for weekends. I don't know if it was because Joey didn't have a jealous bone in his body; or that he regarded me as no threat whatsoever to his relationship with Brandy; who never made it a secret that she felt I was far too old for her.

So Brandy was becoming like Jade, another digital disciple. While becoming just as fiercely loyal to me. I found both women to be terrifically smart, and both to be excellent fighters. Which I hardly expected out of Brandy who only weighed about 110 pounds. But I soon found out that she had another side to her that belied her innocent little girl next door look and demeanor.

Brandy had a violent temper, which she had so far managed to hide from me. But Brandy and Joey both had soft hearts which made them willing to take in every stray hard luck case who were having problems paying their rent. All of whom were women. Unfortunately which is so often the case, most of these women were either unwilling, or too lazy to do their share of the household chores. As I kept getting to know Brandy better, I would often hear her yelling and screaming at her roommates to do their share, or "get the fuck out!"

So, I started believing Brandy when she kept talking about beating women up who had crossed her. Meanwhile Brandy was becoming so adept with computers and the Internet that she would brag to me how she could give people viruses who were giving her a hard time.

That's when I decided to buy her a desktop computer. Although it cost me over a thousand dollars I bought it expecting her not to pay me back–figuring anyone who spent so much time learning all she could about computers, deserved one.

But when Joey 's mother died and left him forty -thousand dollars , Brandy paid me back even though I insisted that it was my gift to her, and that I didn't want her to pay me back a single cent.

Jules Visits me at my Farm

It only took a couple weeks after Grey Ghost and I stayed all night with Jules after visiting Stimmelators that Jules decided to visit me at my farm.

But that was so long ago that I can't remember all the exact details. While I sit here in my Thailand condo at my keyboard trying to digest it all. I am at a total loss over why she decided to leave so early when we had both been planning on her staying longer.

Do keep in mind that a lot of these women had boyfriends and that I certainly wasn't one of them. So, it is likely that Jules had a boyfriend who wanted her to come back for whatever reason. Perhaps they had split up, and that's why Jules wanted to venture far from her home. But here I'm just clutching at straws. My dealings from then on would be with her club owner, Sam Stimmel, and the club itself. Along with whichever girls I could get involved with us.

And here's another thing that I'd like to instill in all wannabe professional adult photographers. You don't fuck the girls, guys. Because if you do the word will get around that you are just another clown who's only out to get his dick wet. And the real professionals in the adult entertainment world won't want to have anything to do with you. Now, I'm not about to say for one minute that I didn't ever fuck one of the entertainers I was dealing with, but when I did, it was always the entertainers idea and never mine.

So like most of them, I never had sex with Jules. And when she visited me at my farm I had her stay in her own bedroom, so that I'd never be tempted to have sex with the nice warm body lying next to me. Which I think suited Jules perfectly who no doubt wanted to get away from it all while getting to experience a new part of the country with its own unique identity. Which the farm area I was living in certainly had.

I honestly can't remember what Jules and I did to entertain ourselves. Perhaps I had taken her to a Farmersville bar or two to enjoy some fun times with my country boy friends. Or perhaps I had taken her to a strip club or two in the St. Louis Metro East. But whatever we did together Jules must have thought that it was time for her to get back to her daily routine in North Webster, Indiana. Because one afternoon after we had only spent several days together I suddenly found that Jules was gone, with not a word of warning from her about how, or why she had changed her plans.

The Next Trip To Stimmelators

By now several more dancers from Stimmelators had become regulars in our Lost Angels chat. While at Dollies: Brandy, Alex, Jade, Marriah, and Satin were chatting in the Lost Angels everyday. I was finally able to get a televison installed at the Dollies back bar and got Nathan and Hawk to agree to paying a fee that transformed it into a Web TV, which we plugged into the phone line Satin and I had installed in the back room.

The girls from the two topless clubs loved chatting with each other. Surprisingly, Heaven took center stage among the Indiana dancers. Along with Katt, the two of them competing against each other for attention. But it soon became apparent that there was no love between them.

Heaven could easily become a top earning model anywhere had it not been for the large tattoo on her back. And Katt knew it. While Katt had great looks in spades, was intelligent and had great leadership qualities, Heaven was off the charts. She was the kick ass queen of the club and everyone knew it.

Jealously is a sin that I cannot overemphasize. Because I would soon be kicked out of half the clubs in the St. Louis Metro East. And now that I've been living here in Thailand for the past fifteen years doing a cracker jack job as chairman of the committee running my condo building, I've learned a lot more about jealousy.

And so it was with Heaven. I'd start to hear rumors of Heaven stealing from the other Stimmelators dancers while committing other crimes as well. But I would soon be getting to know the real Heaven, who would be writing poetry that I'd put on my website along with three other Saint Louis Metro East dancers I would be meeting later. But of the four, Heaven was a real poet who made most of her verse rhyme.

You can still read a lot of Heaven's poetry on my website, and there's a lot of it there. No. Heaven never stole from anyone as far as I am concerned. And as far as any other wrong doings she might have done, most of them were created out of thin air, coming out of the mouths of much lesser women.

By now Doc had been living at my farm for months trading his heroin addiction for his new addiction to the Internet. If he went back to Collinsville it might have been only once. And when he got there, he was scared to death of running into his heroin junkie friends.

He soon met a girl online from the East Coast. And fell in love with her. I remember Doc once telling me, "the real monkey on my back is alcohol. Not Heroin."Which he proved during those month he spent on my farm.

There was a gas station in Farmersville that had a Subway adjoining it. But I didn't go into Subway nearly as often as I went into the main room where they sold hot dogs, chili, donuts, and sweet rolls. One must keep in mind that while farming, most farmers are really under the gun, so there's not a lot of time for eating at a sit down restaurant. Which made me a great customer of the Farmersville gas station, because I could down a couple hot dogs, or a bowl of chili in a few minutes.

It soon became a joke among the attendants at the Farmersville gas station that I'd eat my breakfast there while Doc drank his. This was because Doc would drive my pickup truck once or twice a day to buy half pint bottles of whiskey. The bed of my pickup truck soon became littered with empty whiskey bottles proving Doc's point that whiskey was his strongest addiction.

I was too busy farming to remember what errand I sent Doc on. But by the time he brought my supercharged Miata sports car back, the engine was overheating. I could see the smoke coming out from under the hood. And then I looked at Doc's uncomprehending face. Somehow he had blown the engine. For that matter I had already blown two engines while trying to get my sports car to exceed 140 miles an hour. Which really pissed me off. After all, I was the one paying two thousand dollars for each blown engine, and now I'd be paying for a third engine. And not that Doc was trying to set any speed records. He was drunk off his ass and probably wasn't paying any attention to how much he was exceeding the red line on the car's tachometer.

After he sobered up, Doc must have felt very badly about blowing up my Miata's engine because he soon bought himself a used car for one hundred dollars, which would be as I suspected very unreliable. And Doc proved that one winter's day when the temperature went below zero. His car suddenly stopped running several miles from my farm house as Doc found himself in the middle of a blizzard fueled by the strong prairie wind. Luckily, Doc managed to walk back to the house.

Later Doc would tell me, "That blizzard saved my life. No one came while I was walking back to your house. I thought I would freeze to death. So, I started promising God that I would never do heroin again as long as I lived. I probably would have eventually gone back to doing heroin, but God was with me, and I survived. And never as much as thought about doing heroin ever again. Jack, you saved my life, and I will never forget that."

Doc even cut down on his drinking, although we'd often drink beer or whiskey together. Oftentimes, Jade would visit us at the farm. While Robin and her husband, a couple of neighbors living only ten miles from us, would visit us several times a week. We'd have small parties at my farm, or over at Grey Ghost's House on his porch.

But Jade, Satin, and Brandy were itching to meet their new friends up in Indiana. So I asked Sam, can I bring several of my Dollies dancer friends to Stimmelators for a weekend? To which Sam replied, "I guess they can stay at my house. "Although Heaven and Katt were coming into the chat several times a day every once in awhile Sam would also, which gave him the chance to get the measure of the Dollies dancers.

But the Dollies girls still wanted to make money. Which would mean their dancing for tips at Stimmelators. Although Sam didn't like the idea of temporarily hiring the Dollies girls he reluctantly agreed to allowing them to compete against his own dancers for tips.

*****

It was Doc's idea to rent a large van to take our group from Dollies to Stimmelators. I picked Dirt up in Springfield, and then we went back to my farm for Baron and Doc. Baron had flown into Saint Louis a few days earlier. So there were four of us taking my pickup to the Collinsville car rental to get the van. Which we took to Dollies where Jade, Satin, and Brandy were waiting for us in the parking lot. Then we drove over four hundred miles to Stimmelators to meet up with the rest of the gang.

This would include Heaven, Katt and the rest of the Stimmelators girls. But also Crazy Czech and PlONe who had made their own travel arrangements to Stimmelators.

By this time I had designed a special black jacket that I would use to advertise my alphapro website and our Lost Angels chat group. Which I'd give to the most prominent members of our group who wanted to wear them. The members getting jackets from me would include: Dirt, Crazy Czech, Katt, Heaven, Jade and Satin. The Alphapro jacket had a large alpha wolf logo on the left front side in bold white lettering. While the right side of the jacket displayed the members name and the alphapro.com URL in yellow lettering. The jackets were stunning. And believe me, whenever I'd go into a club with a couple other members of the Lost Angels wearing their jackets, everyone around us were wondering: 'Who are these people?' I had also designed several t-shirts. One was the Pink Giraffe t-shirt advertising a bar that never existed other than it being a fictional night club I wrote about in Death on the Wild Side. I also designed a Dollies Trendy Toilet Sex t-shirt that featured Alabama's sitting on the toilet in her nun's outfit.

Back in those days, we were the only game in town. With even the most beautiful strippers such as Heaven, Satin, and Katt, and much later on, Renee, being proud of being seen in the Alphapro jacket.

But, poor Sam. He had promised to let us all stay at his house. But Baron and I managed to get a hotel room close to the club while Crazy Czech and PlONe made separate arrangements. This left Satin, Brandy, Jade, Dirt and Doc staying at Sam's home.

Although Sam's house was large, it didn't have enough bedrooms for all of Sam's new guests. I can't tell you who slept where due to Baron and I staying in our own hotel room, but at least several of my friends had to sleep in Sam's living room on couches, or on the floor.

There were others joining our group at Stimmelators such as Keith Miller who lived a few miles from the club and a couple of other guys who I don't even remember. There was also another dancer who I had met in a Fort Wayne strip club who joined all of us for our big party.

A lot of the dancers at Stimmelators resented the Dollies girls who they viewed as competitors competing against them for tips. Sam knew this would happen and I'm sure he heard a lot of complaints from them about the Dollies dancers. While the most beautiful Stimmelators girls rapidly grew quite fond of the Illinois girls. This would include Katt and Heaven, a tall blonde who called herself Nipples, and a very pretty twenty year old who was using Marriah as her stage name.

Looking back on the whole thing, I think Sam liked Satin best of all out of the three Dollies girls. But the real hit with Sam would turn out to be Doc. One reason being that although the Dollies dancers loved swimming in Sam's pool, it would be Doc who would clean it afterwards. In his garage Sam had two very pricey sports cars: a Ferrari and a Porsche 928. Neither one of them running correctly, but somehow Doc fixed both cars, which convinced Sam into calling Doc and me into his office on our last night.

“Doc. I want to thank you for everything you have done for me this weekend, Sam told us in a soft voice. I don't know how you were able to fix my two cars, but I have to hand it to you. I can't say when, but I would like to offer you a job working for me.”

“Are you sure you want to Sam?” Doc replied.

“Sure. Why shouldn't I?”

“Because I am a heroin addict. I even went to jail because of my drug addiction. But now I am a recovering drug addict.”

“Doc. I believe that everyone deserves a second chance. So I am giving you one. But it is going to be a few months from now.”

“Sam, I sure appreciate the offer. And I will take you up on it, and I promise you that I will never do heroin for the rest of my life.”

The weekend turned out to be one helluva party. With our group becoming so large that Sam had to open up his whole upstairs to us that included our very own bartender. The only thing that was missing was Renee, who for some unfathomable reason or another, was my favorite of all the girls.

Dealing with Nipples

Out of all the guys in the Lost Angels, Crazy Czech was probably the most colorful one of them all. And out of all the Stimmelators dancers his favorite girl was Nipples. I think the main reason C.C. liked Nipples so much is that she had a certain sadomasochistic streak in her that reminded him of his Goddess, Mistress Mary. Nipples was every inch of being five foot eight or so, and had these oversized nipples that she would stretch into a long oblong appendage. Which she thoroughly enjoyed using in all kinds of strange ways. That knowing Crazy Czech most likely included whacking him across his lips with her tits.

But I was still having my own problems with my own Nipples. Who unlike Indiana's Nipples had breasts that were quite small although they were crested with much larger than average nipples.

By this time most of the girls in the Washington Park clubs knew that Nipples was the main female character in my book, Death on the Wild Side. And so did Nipple's young boyfriend who both Grey Ghost and Dirt used to make fun of in our Alphapro cartoons, who they kept referring to as "Boner" because of his Neanderthalish lack of intelligence.

And although a Saint Louis police officer had warned me to stay away from Boner because the police officer thought he'd kill me, I had often mocked him such as the time I had gone to the house he and Nipples were staying at while posing as a new candidate running for school board. But, I won't give you any further details about how badly I humiliated Boner and his pals. You will just have to read about it in Death on the Wild Side.

One night while Jade, Marriah, and I went out to Pops after Dollies closed, we found Boner and some of his friends drinking in the bar together. And Marriah being the loose cannon that she was went over to talk with Boner and his pals. This must have been about 5 a.m. when Marriah came back to rejoin Jade and me with a gleeful look on her face.

“Jack, I just told Boner and his friends that you are over here and that you can hardly wait to kick all of their asses.”

“Thanks, Marriah. For wanting me to fight four guys at the same time.”

Which is one of the reasons that we didn't take Marriah with us when we all had that party at Stimmelators. Sam had made it very clear to all of us that he didn't want Marriah anywhere near his club because there was no controlling her.

"Don't worry Jack. You and I will kick all their asses together," said Jade. Who meant every word of what she was saying.

And that is one of the reasons that Sam had warned me to be careful about bringing Jade to his club.

About 6 a.m. Boner and his buddies disappeared from Pops, and Jade, Marriah, and I went back to our hotel.

******

But I was going out with a lot of girls back then. And not only with the Dollies dancers. I don't remember what club the girl was working out of, other than she was a real whore. Marriah wasn't, and neither was Jade nor Brandy. But the woman wanted to go to Pops, and I had that beautiful Miata sports car–and so we went.

As the girl and I got out of my car, after I parked it fifty yards from Pops, Boner and two of his friends suddenly appeared.

"Nice car you got here," said Boner, who was obviously spoiling for a fight. "Too bad that we are going to really fuck it up."

Expecting Boner to start keying my sports car's finish, I was going to have to stand my ground when the girl took me by the arm, and told me, "Let's go into Pops, Jack. These little boys aren't going to do shit to your car."

As the girl and I started walking toward the nightclub, I turned my head to look at Boner, and told him, "Go ahead Boner. I will know for sure who's done it, and then you will have to explain everything to the police."

The girl and I took our time having a few drinks at Pops while Boner sat with his friends in the next room. Although I still thought I'd have to fight Boner and his pals the girl and I eventually left Pops and called it a night.

******

But I sure didn't want to be worrying about Boner anymore. Because there would come a time when he might catch me off guard. Thinking that surely Nipples had told her boyfriend that I had knocked all of Larry's teeth out at C-Mowes, and to this day I don't know if I did, or if I didn't. Nipples would have thoroughly enjoyed embellishing her story of what actually happened that night. So, it was likely that Boner was a lot more scared of me than I was of him.

I had a beautiful exercise room at the farm that had once been a one car garage. Having two cousins who were carpenters, I had them insulate the walls, which they covered with drywall. Then they plastered and painted it a bright yellow. To give the illusion of making the room appear much larger than it actually was, I bought some very large expensive mirrors and had my cousins put them up to cover an entire wall. Then I had them lay concrete over what had been a dirt floor, and had a large carpet shop in Raymond lay carpet over the concrete. Then we put a propane stove in to heat the place during the winter. The final touch was my buying a wallpaper mural online of the mountains rising majestically above the Snake River. And then I hired the best wall paperer in the area to create an entire wall that would be so realistic that I actually would feel that I was in the mountains, such as I actually had been while going through Outward Bound's mountaineering course in the Colorado Rockies, and National Outdoor Leadership's one month expedition in Wyoming's Wind River Mountains.

Then I bought a two stack Universal gym, which set me back another $3500, a Schwinn Aerodyne, and a Nordic Trak Cross Country skiing machine. I finally bought a heavy bag that I hung from the ceiling and had my cousins install the wooden speed bag platform my step grandfather had made for me when I was ten.

I was originally from Staunton, Illinois, my dad's hometown. Where I grew up living on the edge of a golf course with large trees surrounding the other three sides of our house. My dad kept two horses in a barn. And had a wire fence constructed from the barn out into the woods. It was a great place to grow up where I learned to shoot guns and bows and arrows and to ride horses at the age of seven.

I learned very early on all I would ever need to learn about jealousy. Because from the first grade on I was viewed as the little spoiled rich kid. That's what a lot of parents told their children about me and my family. And Staunton was a very tough town, that had numbered over 7000 inhabitants in the 1930's. When the town reached its peak as a coal mining town with the majority of its immigrants coming in from: Germany, Poland, Hungary, Russia, Italy and Ireland.

So, little spoiled rich kid got into a lot of fights from the first grade on. But my Dad's father who owned a furniture store and a funeral home died when I was still a baby. This was before we moved out next to the golf course when I was five. So, I got to see a lot of dead people because I was living in the funeral home, and I got to watch my Dad operate on a lot of dead people, due to his being a Mortician.

One of the first boys I had to fight was Henry Porter Lloyd. Who would end up being both my good friend and my nemesis from the first grade up until I graduated from Junior High and moved with the rest of my family to Saint Louis. Henry's idol was: John Wayne, who he used to watch in a lot of movies. Later Henry would become a Green Beret and do four tours of duty in Vietnam. Over a period of eight years we had a lot of fights with a pattern of one year Henry would keep getting the best of me in our fist fights, while I'd get the best of Henry the following year.

Another good friend of mine, was Sanford Bloemaker. Who was two years older than me and by far the toughest boy in the school. Sanford would wind up weighing only 140 pounds or so as an adult, but he was faster than greased lightning and afraid of absolutely nothing. He would later become a tunnel rat in Vietnam.

Sanford would generally leave me alone. Unless I teased him, so I was really asking for it whenever he would beat the snot out of me. But other than Sanford I could kick just about anyone's ass in the school, and often had to if only to prove that I was not the spoiled little rich kid practically everyone thought I was.

When I was ten, my Grandmother decided to get married again to George Timmerman, who was superintendent of one of Staunton's coal mines. George had been an amateur boxer who oftentimes served as a referee for both amateur and professional matches. In his younger days George and a couple of his pals would spar a few rounds and then they would run eighteen miles from Staunton to Litchfield.

One of the rumors circulating around town about my Dad was that he had been caught screwing a man's wife and when the enraged husband came home to find my Dad in bed with his wife he cut my Dad's balls off. Which never happened of course. Although my Dad had developed an enviable reputation as a ladies man and a womanizer.

But had a man come home and found my Dad in bed with his wife, my Dad would undoubtedly kicked the husband's ass if it ever came to a fight, because my Dad was afraid of nobody.

But my Dad never stood a chance against my new Grandpa Timmerman, and one afternoon George brought to our house a platform bag setup, and a heavy bag which he installed in our basement. I don't remember who challenged who for that boxing match but I saw George knock my father down three times even though Dad was 45 and George was seventy.

So, I learned a lot from my new grandfather about boxing when I was ten. And had a speed bag and a heavy bag to practice on after George showed me how to keep the speed bag moving with just his elbows.

My family spent the entire summer in our house on the golf course when I was nineteen even though they had moved to Saint Louis in a second house, so my sisters and I could go to school in St Louis suburbia. Since I was soon going to go through a one month course with the National Outdoor Leadership school on what would become a continuous expedition in the Wind River Mountains, I thought it would be a good idea to get my body in the best shape possible.

I developed a routine of running between three and five miles everyday and spent an hour each day hitting speed and heavy bags in my Grandpa Timmerman's basement. But, I wasn't the only young man using Grandpa Timmerman's gym. So, I would often spar with some of the other guys - and always won.

Not that I was the toughest guy in Staunton who had frequented my step grandfather's gym. Grandpa kept telling me about Myron Spenser who was so good that he might even win the Chicago Golden Gloves. But, I would never meet Myron until the summer before I moved to Thailand.

One story I heard about Myron is that he and Larry Degear got into a fight with three guys from another town. And that Myron knocked all three of them down before they started to slink off into the sunset.

When Larry who hadn't lifted a hand to help Myron finally told Myron. “Let's go get them Myron.”

I'm now going to cut this short before I keep rambling on about all the boxing I would do later, but I sure knew how to fight. And I had a big score to settle with Boner, so it was time to turn nineteen again.

One night when Nipples met me when we went from strip club to strip club together, she showed me how her face had been sliced up by Boner who had beaten her up. We got very drunk together that night, and

Nipples started to get very jealous over how some of the other strippers were paying too much attention to me. So, Nipples punched me in the face a few times while I was driving, and after I had enough I dumped her out of my pickup truck at the intersection of Highways 111 and Interstate 64. Then when I came to my senses and couldn't stand the sight of Nipples having to walk down Route 64 and have to hitchhike a ride; I got out of my truck so that I could convince her to go back to my truck. We started arguing and then the police arrived. They put me in jail for the night, but they let me out the next morning. The police then informed me that I would have to go to court. And when I asked them what the charges were, expecting to be charged with a DUI, they informed me that Nipples had sworn out a complaint against me for beating her up.

I didn't beat Nipples up. I never laid a finger on her. But Boner certainly had, and he should have been the one to be put in jail. The asshole was a woman beater and now I was going to punish him in a way that he'd never forget.

For the next three weeks I worked out furiously on both the speed and heavy bag, until I had satisfied myself that I could take a man down with either hand.

The plan that I concocted was not just to knock Boner down, but to put him in the hospital as well. I would go after him at Pops where I figured I only had a few seconds before the bouncers could get to me. I had it all planned out in my head as I continued to pummel the heavy bag. I would knock Boner down and then I'd keep kicking him in the head until the bouncers got to me. And should any of his friends try to help him I'd knock them down also.

When PlONe came to visit me from California I decided to put my plan into action. Because if I took PlONe with me he would certainly bail me out of jail.

When we first entered the nightclub, we saw no signs of Boner, or Nipples, but I knew Pops had a pool room, which is exactly where I found my Nipples playing pool. I knew Boner had to be somewhere close, so I decided to use Nipples for bait.

I was smoking a cigarette when I approached her and started to engage her in conversation. When suddenly Boner arrives and starts getting into my face, playing the bully. So, I casually took off my jacket, tossed it to PlONe and put my cigarette into an ashtray. Then I turned on Boner.

"Hey asshole. I owe you one for beating up Nipples. You think you are a tough guy don't you? You are, but only when you are beating up women." I was right in his face as I moved in on him waiting for him to throw the first punch.

Fully expecting me to back down, Boner took a step backward as I continued to move in on him. While I screamed into his face. "Hey pussy! Come on, so I can kick your ass. And then I am going to kick the asses of all your brothers. Come on pussy. Throw a punch. You woman beater. You are a piece of shit!"

But Boner kept moving back; he must have thought I was crazy; and I was. Finally, he turned his head and walked away.

So, it all came down to nothing. As I would later continue to find out that women who are abused and beaten up by their boyfriends nearly always go back to them, which is why policemen are so reluctant to get into domestic disputes. Years later while living in Thailand, I would find out the same thing was true about most Thai bar girls who are constantly being beaten up by their cowardly Thai boyfriends. They nearly always go back to them. Because they understand the Thai man and his ways and are used to all the abuse. Whereas, they can't understand an European or American man being nice to them. Such women are all the same.

The Night They Pepper Sprayed Stimmelators

I was soon traveling up to Stimmelators every two months in spite of having to drive over 400 miles to visit my new friends. But from now on I'd be staying with Sam. Who would become my mentor, teaching me all the ins and outs about how to run a strip club and the trials and tribulations serious minded strip club owners go through.

And if I had ever dreamed of owning a strip club after this experience; any thought of being a club owner or manager was forever banished from my mind.

I remember one night at midnight, Sam's asking me if I wanted to go with him to take a new girl home. The girl was from South Bend, Indiana, sixty miles from Stimmelators. It was her first and last night working for Sam. But when she arrived at the club, she soon learned that she was completely out of her league. She hardly made any money that night having to compete with the likes of Heaven or Katt.

Sam felt sorry for the girl and decided to take her back to South Bend once he found out she didn't have a ride home and hadn't made nearly enough money to get a taxi. We didn't get back to Sam's until past three that morning.

Although Sam's club was milk toast when it came to any form of sexual activity, there was a huge amount of activity from what I'd later call the “Mothers For A More Boring Nation” to shut him down along with every single adult night club in the entire state of Indiana. All of which resulted in the do-gooders convincing the politicians into erecting a couple hundred billboards across the state announcing all the evils the clubs were committing against all the morally upright Christian folk of Indiana. The billboards proclaimed that strip clubs would turn all their children into drug addicts and low life scum bags who would later on fill up all of Indiana's prisons. And that merely having a strip club in the community would cause epidemics of Syphilis and Leprosy.

Which led to not only Sam and a lot of Indiana strip club owners to fight back, but also a large number of strippers. In order to learn more about what the clubs were doing to hold off these Mothers For A More Boring Nation, who were so determined to shut them down I drove down to Fort Wayne, Indiana, to find out for myself what all these night club folk were doing to counter all this negative publicity. In Fort Wayne I found a group of several bars that had joined together to form a united front promoting the virtues of the clubs while disproving through a legal format all the false allegations against adult clubs and all the dancers, DJ's, managers, bartenders and doormen working for them.

Here I found a number of the Stimmelators girls working at booths where they handed out fact sheets disproving the propaganda that was being circulated by their Mothers For A More Boring Nation opponents. While those women who were not presently working at the booths were busy circulating handouts throughout a large night club proving that there was absolutely no link between crime and drugs and the strip clubs of Indiana. Here I found Heaven and Jules and Ruby, a friend of Heaven's who was working in a Fort Wayne strip club along with Jazzy and several other Stimmelators dancers.

I eventually found myself with several of the Stimmelators girls at a large table all of us finally relaxing over a few beers. That was the first night I met Tornado who was one of our newest Lost Angels members. Although Tornado lived in South Bend, Indiana, he was oftentimes visiting Stimmelators where he had become good friends with Jules and several other of the Stimmelators dancers. Tornado wound up paying for most of my beer, and from that moment on we became fast friends.

Later Tornado would join me at two of the Exotic Dancers Expos in Las Vegas; two of the Pure Talent Feature showcases I would be doing at Big Al's in Peoria, Illinois; and another Pure Talent Feature Showcase in Mobile, Alabama; along with several other Pure Talent Feature Showcases that I have long ago forgotten about. Eventually, he would turn up twice in Thailand after I moved there, and fell in love with a Thai woman who he would marry in Si Saket. And later take with him to Indiana where he would help her raise her eight year old daughter.

*****

But the most ignoble night in the Indiana clubs occurred while I was visiting Sam. I had brought Alex and her husband with me, which was a good thing for me because Alex's husband did a lot of the driving.
I can't remember everyone sitting with me that night at Stimmelators when the unthinkable occurred. But suddenly the entire room filled up with smoke. At first I thought a fire had been the cause of so much smoke. Then I saw two customers beating a hasty retreat out of the club having an argument with the Doormen. I watched a dancer falling off the pole onto the stage. While nearly everyone around me started coughing who then started pouring out of the club. One of the club's DJ's soon joined the Doormen who were obviously trying to help restrain the two customers. That was when I decided to help provide a little physical assistance. But as soon as I got up close to the four men I

suddenly started sneezing. And hated myself for having a physical weakness that might stop me from effectively dealing with the two customers.

By this time practically everyone inside the club were rushing towards the exit, panic stricken. I heard loud coughing and sneezing all around me, while I wasn't affected so much. Being able to move through the crowd quickly I was able to follow the two customers as they rushed outside to their car. And watched the driver start the car's engine while his accomplice proceeded to yell out obscenities at the Doormen and DJ they had been arguing with. The man yelling out obscenities soon got into the car with the driver.

As the car proceeded down main street to the stop light at Highway route 13 I started to run after the car, got a good look at its license plate, and somehow memorized it. I kept chasing after the car until it turned right at the intersection and sped off North towards Syracuse.

By the time I walked back to the club, I found a small crowd gathering about a man who had collapsed just outside the club's front door. The man was covered with wet chemical that had soaked his clothes and gotten all over his face and glasses. I then asked the men who were all around me if anyone had a cell phone. And when one of them volunteered that he had one, I gave the man the license plate number that I had just memorized. After the man called the police, I watched several men helping to take the club’s Promotion Manager, Ford's, clothing off which had gotten covered and wet from pepper spray.

By this time Sam was just outside his club talking to the customers who had gathered at the door. One of them volunteered to drive Sam in his car to Syracuse. Sam immediately took the man up on his offer. Then I turned to watch the man lying prostate on the concrete in front of the club's entrance. The man kept sputtering and coughing as I watched Sam and his driver disappearing toward Syracuse. Ford who had been lying on the pavement in front of the club had been trying to play the part of Manager even though Sam didn't even have a Manager. So, he had obviously been involved in some manner or another with the two customers who had pepper sprayed the club.

Sam came back to his club an hour or two later, his face livid. By the time he and his customer got to Syracuse, a small resort town just ten miles north of his club, he found that the police had already been able to stop the two customers who had pepper sprayed his club. For the first and last time I was to ever hear Sam swearing, I listened to him tell us how he had gotten out of his customer's car and started walking toward the police who were questioning the two men who had pepper sprayed his bar. But when Sam yelled at the police officers to arrest the two men, one of them shot back at him. “Get back in your car, or we will have to put you in jail.”

“So, what happened to the two men who sprayed your club?” I asked Sam.

“Nothing. My dancer who fell off the pole had to go to the hospital due to her injuries, but the police just let those two criminals go.”

I will never forget that night. The two men doing the pepper spraying had assaulted virtually everyone in the club that night. But the way the police had looked at it: we all were getting our just desserts for hanging out in a strip club while they viewed the two villains as two heroes who were doing their best to rid their precious state of Indiana of an evil strip club, and all the criminals who were there that night.

Return to Visions

Visions, an upper scale Gentlemen's Club in Centreville, Illinois, was almost the polar opposite of Dollies, which I have previously described as a roadhouse type of strip club. Drinks were much more expensive at Visions with a bottle of beer costing $5.50 versus $4.00 that was typical of Dollies and other bars such as C-Mowes and Chameleon on or close to Highway 111 in Washington Park, which borders East Saint Louis. To get there from Interstate Highway 55 one drives down Highway 157, which is also called Bluff Road. Immediately to the left are the bluffs left behind after the Mississippi River receded to its present location. The bluffs rise more than a hundred feet above the road to Visions. On the way, one can take a right onto Collinsville Road, drive a mile, and arrive at the Cahokia Mounds. This is where a powerful Indian civilization built a city that numbered over 20,000 inhabitants by 1050 AD. To those who are ignorant of its History, their population exceeded that of London. Here its citizens created over 100 mounds from baskets of earth. The highest of which would later be called Monks Mound, rising 100 feet above the prairie. On its summit, lived the Great Sun, ruling a great civilization of Native Americans who inhabited hundreds of much smaller city states hundreds of miles from Cahokia.

Driving down Highway 157 is an incredible experience. It's beautiful. And it's haunting, With the ambience of this ancient civilization permeating the valley beneath the bluffs.

Before Highway 157 makes a 90 degree turn, is Visions Gentlemen’s Club, which is lit up at night in sharp contrast to the two lanes one is traveling on. While to the left of Visions is PT's West, which is one of four PT’s chain of clubs in the Saint Louis Metro East.

But all that was long ago. As I reflect sitting here at my keyboard in my condo now that I am living in Thailand, I think it's best that I quote from the article I wrote in the "Wild Times," which was THE local strip club guide in the area:

Return to Visions

> On a quest for a great night and with all of Friday night before me, I headed out to the Visions Gentlemen's Club only 12 miles from my Collinsville apartment straight up 157 in Centreville. Charles was managing tonight and another manager, Charli, was tending bar. Couldn't miss with old friends already there and new ones to meet, I would not go

anywhere else. This was the place, an upscale night club I would never forget. It had never failed me, being one of two clubs I frequented that had never barred me.

Seemingly overshadowed by Crystal Palace and PT's next door, Visions lies back nearly a quarter mile down a little lane. One might easily miss it, but shouldn't since it's the crown jewel of the three, or at least I think so. There's an ambience there that begins with the drive down 157 either leaving the club or approaching it, a drive that takes one around the bluffs on high ground with a flood plain just below you to the West and lit up on a clear night you see the St Louis skyline. I call it memory lane. Driving the Miata top down with a good friend next to me or a girl from one of the clubs. Or a small group of us in a car or pickup hitting Visions and some of the other bars in the area. Always----our focus was Visions and with good reason.

Visions had undergone two major restorations, first as the Paradise Club right after Platinum Club bought it and renamed it Platinum Paradise Show Club, the second restoration last summer, after a restaurant consortium bought it, put another quarter of a million dollars into it, and reopened it as Visions. I had just done my laundry and had found two free passes to Visions that a girl named Selena had signed on the back (I owe you one Selena).

The new entrance to Visions is impressive----the reception just inside the door even more impressive. Mike was handling the door and I had only met him once----a week ago when Kasey Karrington was featuring and I had come in just to see Kasey and her boyfriend, Vic. But he remembered me, accepting my free pass with a grin.

Guess where my first move's to? If you know me by now----the bar and with it beer number one. I see a friendly cute face over there and she's sitting at the optimal location for securing beer after beer with the minimum amount of distraction. Beer's important to me and watered down stuff like Bud Lite just won't do. It's Poison, a little brunette, who used to dance with Brandy and sit with us but that was over a year ago.

Got my priorities straight now. Have a beer in front of me. Pretty girl next to me. Now--food. And that's where part of that $250000 renovation comes in. A small kitchen.

Charli places a small menu in front of me. I order a steak sandwich for around $5.50 which comes with my choice of potato chips and either potato salad or slaw. Was going to grab food on the run from McDonalds and eat it on the way to the club but this is going it in style. Smart business move on the part of Visions and here's why. Any club that cannot offer its customers food, if only a micro waved pizza, had better be looking at changing its management. Customers get hungry and if they can't eat in the club they are going to go elsewhere, often not returning to the club. Here I have a number of choices from the menu. Touch of class here.

While waiting for my food I flip myself around so that I'm sitting on my bar stool looking at the stages and the rest of the room. Getting analytical now, I'm studying the place--asking myself, "Why do I like this club so much?"

There's four stages, three of them in use, a dancer performing at each one, with two stages equipped with poles. Here, if a girl can really dance, she can strut her stuff, and show what she's made of.

The bar has four sides, the back side being a wall. Theoretically girls and patrons can sit on three sides of the bar although the club is presently using only two sides for its customers and dancers. Unlike last week when I came in to watch Kasey Karrington feature, the club is more dimly lit tonight which gives it the old atmosphere I liked so much----pure glamour. The DJ has total control of the club's lights from his stand being able to dim or brighten the lights. Someone tells me they have turned off the lights above the bar so it's not the DJ who has adjusted the lighting. It's the four foot long aquarium in the center of the bar that furnishes the only lighting in this area. Perfect.

There are mirrors on three sides of the room and on part of the fourth, the rest being taken up by a lengthy VIP room bathed in red neon where the girls can sit with their customers and do private dances. Inside the VIP lounge are several small couches and a few small tables and chairs. Small lights that look like candles rest on each table. The VIP room is glassed in. You can look inside from a distance and get an idea of who's in there if you have good eyes which most of us don't and if you really want to you can walk up to it and peer into the large glass windows although you are going to look like a fool and might even trip over the three couches just outside the VIP lounge or the small table and chairs which rest just below the large glass windows. Here men can sit alone or with a favored girl while watching the dancers perform on the stages.

In the center of the room hanging from the ceiling are two large globe lights slowly spinning out multi-colored light in a mild strobe like effect which gives the stage and the dancer performing on it just a touch of surrealism, but here the key words are "just a touch". The whole effect with the kaleidoscope of lights ever changing throughout the room is what strip clubs were meant to be--------a fantasy land carefully planned and created by its owners to take the clubs patrons into a different realm where everyday problems are forgotten for a few brief hours.

Suddenly reality hits me in the back of my head. My hat is stolen from behind. I turn around to see Charli putting it on her head adjusting it to a jaunty angle as she smiles at me. Have to say one thing, it probably looks better on her than on me.

"That'll cost you, Charli," I tell her.

"You can't threaten me, Jack," she answers with a smile. "I"m your bartender and I'm the one who's getting you your beer."

"Still a manager here, Charli?"

"Yes, but normally only one night a week. Most of the time I"m just bar tendering."

"For wearing my hat I want you to promise me to let me dance on your stage and do the pole. I'm a lot better at it now than that time you let Nipples and I do it together."

"Not tonight," she replied.

"Which means possibly some other night?" I ask her to which there's no reply. I'm thinking now of both the past and the future and if I handle it right someday she's going to let me do it. There was that first time a few years ago when Nipples who inspired the Lori Mellon character in my novel

Death on the Wild Side was working here.

Charli was just as she is today, a hard working assistant manager who was very competent. She could joke around with the best of them, was very fair the way she treated both the customers and the girls, but at the same time she'd stick to the clubs rules and one of them I'm sure was not to let customers get on the stage and do the pole.

One night Nipples was drunk and I was even drunker and somehow I managed to convince Charli to let us do the pole together. Went up on the stage with Nipples. Both of us grabbed the pole, nodded at each other as the signal to have at it, then the two of us started rotating around the pole in tandem. Here I was with the best dancer in the house making a public spectacle of myself. I still don't know what happened but after doing only one turn I fell right on my back--then just lay there trying to comprehend how I had fallen.

Had a lot of practice since, taking girls to the back stage at Dollies where I'd spin around the pole by myself or do it in tandem with them. Done it in Indiana too, showing off to a club owner friend of mine and others in the room. For me, it's easy and fun. Especially that night a Dollies bartender and I did it for over half an hour as a manager took pictures of us. Got a stress fracture in my right foot because I was wearing sandals. Didn't sue the club since that's not like me so if Charli has any hesitation, next time I ask her I'll just remind her of that or bring 12 dozen releases and sign everyone of them.

Then I catch a glimpse of Charles who manages five nights a week, hop off my bar stool and going up to him ask "Want to talk with you in your office, Charles. Whenever it's convenient for you, just let me know."

He's got lots of things going on, he tells me but will let me know when it's a good time, which is fine with me since I have a lot of beer I'm planning to drink.

Back at the bar a pretty blonde has just sat on the stool next to me. Immediately I catch her eye and ask--------"Wasn't that you who went to Dollies last weekend with a date, then returned here where I saw you again after I came in to see

Kasey feature?"

"That was me. I sometimes go there to have a few. I saw you at Dollies and was wondering what you were doing."

"I was online with my laptop. A group of us meets over at my table where we go online and chat with the group on my web site. I also do a lot of digital pictures of the girls."

"They let you do pictures there?"

"All the time as long as I use common sense such as not doing them in the back room when a private dance is going on or taking them in the front room where most of the customers are (here I was lying to her since I usually don't use common sense although I follow these guidelines).

"What do you pay them?" she asks.

"Nothing. Done well over 100 girls and over 3000 pictures. I don't even know how many. Most of them like having their pictures taken and put on the web site in our chats." Probably more than half of them I've taken there but I've taken lots of pictures of dancers in Indiana, Las Vegas, and around here in the St Louis area at other clubs. Even here in this club."

"Not me. I don't want my pictures on the Internet." "No big deal. Some feel like you do. Most want them taken and you'd be surprised at how often they come up to me first to see if I'll do pictures."

Wanting to meet the club's new DJ I see him walking around close to the bar and jump off my bar stool. The man is close to my height, wears his dark hair long and has glasses.

"Hi, I'm Jack Corbett," I introduce myself while holding out my hand.

He grabs my extended hand and shakes it profusely, grinning at me. "And I'm Jesse."

"Been wanting to meet you Jesse. Knew your predecessor pretty well. Steve. Always liked him."

The conversation then turns to Steve, where he was working, and Steve's having his picture in my novel sitting in my Miata with its top down. That afternoon, Steve had taken a few minutes off to drive my Miata, the two of us sitting side by side, on a warm afternoon with the little car's top down. Then later on I took the pictures. Steve and I had become fast friends and my initial impression of Jesse is that I'm going to like him. Seems eager to meet new people, has a ready smile and a firm hand shake.

Food arrives just as I'm returning to my bar stool. As I sit down to my beer, a good sandwich, potato salad, and the chips, I'm thinking-----"This is a lot better than McDonalds. Good company all around. Pretty women and I've got a Budweiser to wash it all down." This time facing the bar since I have my food to contend with while sucking beer from the bottle, a hand reaches up behind me giving my arm a gentle squeeze.

Turning around, I see it's Sahara, who was handling the bar last week while Kasey was featuring. I had been hoping to find her here.

"Hi Jack. How are you?" Sahara's eyes smiled at me as she spoke.

Always liked Sahara. When you meet her you forget you are in a strip club. Laid back, with a nice smile, she's easy to talk with and she never seems to care if you are buying her a drink or not. Kind of woman you could take anywhere, she's a lady through and through and I don't want anyone to tell me you can't find ladies in strip clubs because you can. Besides...she's damn attractive. Pretty in the face, with medium length hair, nice eyes that look right into yours, she's just hard to beat. Best part of it is, she's a real kidder. I like sharp witted women who aren't abrasive or cruel who are pleasant in a bantering kind of way. And see----------I said all these good things about her because I meant them and didn't even mention her figure. But now I will. Dynamite. Okay...you got it. She's slender and beautifully proportioned. Now I"ll just have to talk about her later on since I've got a meal to finish and another beer to drink.

The food's good and the beer----that's always good. Just don't ever serve me Bud Lite. Too watered down. But now

I'm starting to feel sorry for myself.

Charli's still wearing my hat. For two hours she wears that hat. Dancing behind the bar, or handling drink orders, or hustling about, always on the go, that hat's going wherever she's going being firmly attached to her head. I feel denuded. I'm bald. I feel complete loss sweeping over me.

But suddenly I feel better. Another blonde sits next to me. Earlier I had seen her walking around the room with a single flower in her hand, then later I observed her on the stage, dancing a little unsure of herself as if she was wondering what to do. "She's obviously new at this game," I had told myelf. "Still...cute. Appealing with that lost angel look about her. After several minutes of conversation at the bar she has to get up on stage again. I watch her walk away thinking how she reminds me of another blonde I know from another club who I had once felt close to.

A few beers later, I catch Charles's eye from the other end of the bar. He gives me a pleasant nod which means-------"Let's catch up with each other in the office."

It's a small office. Nothing ostentatious about it. There's a large camera monitor which he can watch while sitting at his desk as he checks up on what's going on throughout the club. I know from previous experience what kinds of things they can check up on and have been in that office a number of times. There are cameras all over the club. This time Charles is checking to see what's going on in the VIP room. "Look like the judge is back there again and ready to do another private dance," Charles remarks to me as he watches the screen.

I've gone online in that office with a laptop and shown him my web site but that was a year ago. Done it several times. Once, with PlOne with us visiting from San Francisco and Philip21 from Indiana, the three of us talking with Charles while we put the laptop through its paces.

Back then, Brandy was dancing. Worked at Visions since it was easy for her to catch rides back and forth to work with Charles since they both lived on the same street. I remember how he had taken me out to show off his car stereo in the club's parking lot back then. 1500 watts of amplifier power in his trunk with speakers all over the inside of the car. That car seat would resonate with sound when he'd turn it up a bit. And if you'd sit in it when he gave it a little base it would about lift you off your duff, the bass coming right up out of that seat.

"Still got the car with the great stereo, Charles? "

"Got rid of it. Now working on another one and this one's really going to kick some ass."

Tell you one thing, it's easy to relate to a manager who's got a lot of kid in him. But just ask around about Charles and you will very seldom find a dancer who doesn't respect him or like him. And you will never hear anyone question his integrity.

It was a year ago when the new restaurant group bought the majority interest in this club and renamed it Visions. Platinum Club in Brooklyn and the Centreville club were owned by the same people and Charles had been General Manager of this club. Brandy was working here then, and Brandy's one of the finest girls I've ever met from the dancing profession. A new man took over as General Manager. And Charles went back to being an assistant manager at the Brooklyn Club. Just one of those things that often happens when a change of ownership occurs.
I remember how Brandy almost cried when she found out she would no longer be dancing with Charles as her manager or that she would be catching rides with him. She worked a few days at the Brooklyn club--then quit dancing. And has not danced since.

Visions still has Bob as General Manager. And Charles is back. It's like old times as I tell him my latest plans that can affect the club and the two of us swap stories. There is a knock on the door. Every so often there's a knock on the door and it's almost always a pretty dancer. This time it's a brunette and she sticks around. I offer her my chair telling her I can stand. After a few minutes Charles pulls out this large glass jar that is full of chocolates. Some of them enclosed in their individual wrappers, others bare, ready to be eaten. He offers me the jar and I take one or two when the door opens and Jesse, the DJ comes in.

"I came in for some candy, Charles," Jesse says grinning at us all.

"Have all you want," Charles answers as he extends the jar to Jesse.

Now it's four of us in the office talking with Jesse and Charles kidding each other about an embarrassing incident that Jesse blames Charles for as the two men laugh it up. Don't remember how it came up but somewhere along the line Jesse starts kidding the girl.

"I will not and do not go out with you dancers," he tells her.

"Why not?" the girl asks.

"Because you are all crazy. That's why."

And wouldn't you know it and I know you aren't going to believe this but within five minutes of Jesse's saying that the girl somehow sends Charles' jar of chocolates crashing onto the floor. Glass all over the floor now, we start picking up chocolates and shards of broken glass. "That's exactly what I meant," Jesse announces good naturedly. "You girls are all crazy."

We are all throwing the chocolates whether wrapped in paper or not into the waste can along with the glass. "It's a liability thing," Charles explains to us. "One little bit of glass on a chocolate or wrapper and a customer or the wrong employee gets into contact with that glass and this club can be sued." But he takes it in stride, never showing a moment's anger to any of us. But what a waste. That stuff was good and now I can't have another piece.

I turn to Jesse and ask: "Where are you from, Jesse?"

"Missoula, Montana, he replies, which sends back memories of a woman I had met on a frigid morning in Sun Valley, Idaho where I had rented a condo to ski for a month.

It was thirty three below zero that morning and deciding that skiing in such cold conditions was total insanity I had started walking and running to the local library where I could warm my feet by the fire while reading ski magazines (I was really into skiing in those days). I ran around a corner and almost knocked a blonde off her feet. Later on, meeting her in the Ketchum drug store I asked her to have lunch with me.

That night I was moving her stuff into my condo after first telling her she'd have to move out before the next weekend since I'd be having friends coming in from Illinois. She had hitched a ride from Missoula, Montana to Sun Valley with two guys she had just met and started working at Adkins Market, the local grocery store.

That started Jesse and I swapping stories about skiing-----how we had both skied Big Mountain in Montana, Grand Targhee and Jackson Hole in Wyoming. I then told him how the blonde just wouldn't leave when her time was up and my friends were about to arrive. And how I dealt with it.

"What's her name?" Jesse asked. "I might know her."

"Don't remember," I replied. "That was awhile back."

Finally I excused myself and returned to the bar. Plunged in thought I thought about writing. Time for another beer, then another. Taking in the music now, I watched the room. This club's got good music and after awhile it just becomes a part of you. The music's non stop and with the lights with their strobe like effect it creates just the right mood.

Seductively it all sneaks up on a man----or a woman. I say a woman because right now a pretty blonde has come in out of nowhere and is sitting at someone's stage. At first I hardly notice since I'm consumed in my thoughts and letting the club's sounds wash over me as I become part of the scene. Thinking too that in any club in this area at any time I never know what the night will bring-----who's going to be in the club or who's going to walk in the door. Always..there's that adventure lurking around the next corner. I never know when it's going to happen or who's going to share it with me.

A few minutes later I notice that the blonde is sitting a few stools down from me at the bar looking at me with a puzzled expression on her face. I remember her. She's a nurse-----an RN living over a hundred miles from the club. We've not seen each other in years. A mother and a nurse she was well respected in that town but she had always dreamed about what it would be like to be a stripper. Until she finally took the plunge and would come in on weekends, living out of a close by motel. There had been an intellectual side of her that was painfully obvious at times but she was a pretty woman and I had met her here when Visions was Platinums Paradise Showclub.

Back in those days I used to go to dancers' stages. The nurse often wanted me at her stage but refused me when I offered to tip her.

Back at the bar she had once told me: "You are very intelligent and I love talking with you. You don't ever have to give me money." She often told me about how she had two lives and had decided that October 2nd would be her last night dancing. That was months before the final day of her dancer's clock. I have often regretted that last night she danced. Blew it. No one's fault but my own and I'm not going to tell anyone here what I did. But it was one of the cruelest things I've ever done to a woman. Months later I called the hospital she was working at. Her voice was cold. But I still got her home address and sent her one of my novels. Never heard from her or called her since.

No time to waste-- I walk right up to her.

"What are you doing here?"

"In town so I thought I'd stop in to see if anyone was still here I knew."

"Sorry I was such an ass that last night you worked."

"You are an ass, Jack. Admit it."

"That night was the worse ever. Just sorry it had to be you. Wish I could make up for it."

"You can start by buying me a drink."

"I have a better idea. At least I hope you think it is," I suggest to her.

"Oh no. Something tells me I don't want to hear this."

"I wish it were summer. I'd have the top down on the Miata. Let's just go out and drive around. We have a lot of catching up to do and it's a nice drive."

"What? Me drive around with you. You are crazy, Jack. Absolutely nuts."

"What do you mean you driving around with me. I have two DUI's," I tell her as I hand her my car keys. “You are driving me around, and by the way, I just happen to have both tequila and beer in the car."

"Okay," she replies doubtfully, but if you try to pull one of your old tricks on me, I'm bailing."

"I don't think you'll mind. Let's go."

Outside the Miata's looking low slung and fast. I had a lot of work done to it having had it lowered and racing springs put on all four corners. Oversized wheels with low profile tires and stabilizer struts put in both the front and rear of the chassis to make her corner even flatter. A little work under the hood too--such as a header, an air intake, some porting of the cylinder heads, and a couple other modifications to give it more horsepower. Used to run a supercharger on it for an additional fifty horses which made the car really fly but after blowing three engines I took it off.

Heather got in behind the wheel as I opened the door for her. Then I got in the passenger seat from the other side. Reaching back behind the seat I pulled the six pack out.

"Beer for the road?"

"Why in the hell not?" she laughed. "Just don't tell anyone back in my home town I was drinking and driving if you ever meet anyone there. Remember back there, I'm not Heather. Heather was my stage name. I'm Lillian, a nice and proper nurse who works in the cardiac ward of the local hospital. I have children. I go to PTA meetings and do all the nice things that good parents are expected to do."

Handing her the beer, I pop open my can and take a deep swallow. "Just take 157 straight out north around 10 miles or so. Go straight through Collinsville. I'll tell you where to turn. Trust me."

"Trust you, Jack! Not on your life."

Within five miles she's grinning as she revs the car up through the gears. I tell her to shift at close to 6000 rpms where the Miata's got good power. Didn't think she'd be taking the corners this fast. I had the matronly nurse in mind and had forgotten that she had been a stripper.

"I love this car Jack. You are forgiven if you give it to me."

"Sorry, but I don't tip."

A few minutes later I tell her to turn left on Collinsville Road. Then have her park the car in a lot several miles later.

She looks at me as if I'm crazy and asks---------"Are you out of your mind? If you've got sex in your mind you sure picked the wrong car to do it in." Which she was right on since Miata's are not much bigger than go karts.

"Trust me," I reply.

"Oh God. Do I have to?"

Luckily I have two dark blue quilted jackets in the sports car's little trunk, coats I had been using down at the farm, dusty from wearing them while working on tractors and other machinery. I also have a wine skin full of straight tequila.

"I'm not wearing that dirty jacket, Jack!"

"You will if you don't want to get cold."

Don't know how I did it but I somehow convince her to walk with me a mile to Monks Mound, site of possibly the most advanced and definitely the most populous Indian civilization ever seen on the North American continent--and easily within four miles of the Washington Park clubs.

"Cops will pick us up if we park next to the mound," I tell her, "and we are going to need these coats since it's too cold tonight and their dark color will help hide us as we climb the mound. They constantly patrol around here and the museum does not want people climbing this thing at night."

There was another night more than a year ago when a pretty girl who worked at Dollies drove me to the mound after the club closed. I had started walking toward the Mound with the girl following me. But the night's chill was too much for her and she told me she didn't want to do it after we had walked only fifty yards.

Heather and I didn't take the large concrete steps but climbed the side of the mound thinking once again of the cops. Minutes later we were at the top looking at the St Louis skyline lit up majestically to the West. The view–incredible.

Thinking about how most motorists driving by the mound on I-55 either didn't notice it, or thought someone had just planted it there from the sky, I start to tell Heather about its history. How the Mound Builders or Mississippians as they were often called worked for six hundred years to build the huge earthen edifice which rose over a hundred feet in the air and had a larger base than the Great Pyramid in Egypt.

"There were over 20000 residents here who had this mound as its center. In 1250 AD there were more people here than the City of London had at the same time. They called this Cahokia.", I explained as she asked me countless questions.

Sometimes we wandered around the top of the mound trying to peer off into the distance but it was a cloudy night and we couldn't see much. Most of the time we sat huddled close together with our arms around each other talking quietly--not that it mattered since there was no one out there but us. At last the sun started to come up and we began to see the trees slowly appear. A heavily wooded area began to take shape off to the South and then the other mounds started to appear. The last thing to take shape out of the darkness was the museum just across Collinsville Road, a striking building in which one could learn about this advanced civilization that disappeared more than six hundred years ago-----the cause for its decline and disappearance unknown.

"Can you imagine what it would be like sitting up here on the Fourth of July at night while watching the fireworks display on the St Louis Riverfront?" I asked.

"Incredible," she replied.

"And we can sit up here with some of our friends imagining all those thousands of people on the other side of the river like rats in a trap fighting traffic to get home."

Sitting up high like the Great Sun himself, who was the absolute ruler living in a house on top of the Great Mound we then started talking about the club and clubs in general. We watched the sun climb higher into the sky imagining ourselves living 800 years ago and joked about how we would have lived where we were presently sitting, not down below with the common men and women who toiled for the Great Ruler.

"There were no stars last night." she said to me and I replied,

"Yes there were and they were us. We had fun. I picked this place. Time for breakfast. Your turn. I'll take you anywhere you want."

The Creation of Dick Fitswell

I wanted to publish “Return to Visions,” badly because it encompassed so much about the Collinsville Centreville area while capturing the essence of a great night club and the people I was meeting there. And above all, what it's like visiting the Cahokia Mounds, which I would end up doing on countless occasions. I would celebrate Fourth of July there watching the fireworks ten miles away near the Saint Louis Arch. And of surrounding communities on the East side in Collinsville, Belleville, and Granite City. I would later rent an apartment just four miles from the great mounds, which would be one of the foundations for my entire exercise program. And would include running up and down the steps of Monks Mound six to ten times. Which I would follow up with a two to three mile run on trails that meandered around the mounds where I would encounter a lot of deer.

I found the mounds to be just as haunting during daytime as I found them at night when I wrote "Return to Visions." There were big trees everywhere. All around me there was a commingling of huge white oaks with brush and smaller trees that created a nearly impenetrable forest. Even in broad daylight it would get pretty dark where the trees and shrubs started to crowd each other out.

Looking for a publisher I called Jim Lilly up, who met me the next day. By this time my Dad had died, which provided me with enough income that I could quit farming. Since I loved Dollies and the other Saint Louis Metro East clubs so much, I decided to move close by.

I picked Woodhenge Apartments in Collinsville, which was just one mile from the hotel I was staying at with Jade, Marriah, and Satin.

Woodhenge is located high up on the bluffs just off Highway 157. And now that Jim Lilly would be meeting me to discuss my article "Return to Visions," I found it to be ironical that Cahokia Mounds is only four miles from my new apartment.

I had always found Jim Lilly to be a hustling energetic extremely affable young guy who seemed to be everywhere. Which he had to be since he was the owner-editor of his "Wild Times" magazine rag that focused on strip clubs in the Saint Louis area

.

The “Wild Times” only amounted to forty or fifty pages, but it was the only publication in the St. Louis Metro East area in which strip clubs such as Dollies could advertise. And not just strip clubs, but massage parlors, tattoo shops, and other businesses related to the strippers and night clubs in the area. But "Wild Times" was a free magazine that relied entirely on advertising for its revenue. So by necessity Jim had to be a fireball of energy because he was all things in one. As owner, salesman, photographer, and the man who wrote most of the magazine's articles, photographer and graphics artist.

I didn't really think much of Jim all those times I encountered him in the Metro East strip clubs. But later on as I got to know him much better I learned to appreciate him as a jack of all trades who did many things so well.

Jim met me at my new Collinsville apartment. But right off I found that he had an agenda that was radically different from mine. My article "Return to Visions" oozed with romance and nostalgia. Which would hopefully provide the cornerstone for the kinds of things I wanted to write about. And which I believe I became very successful at doing while writing for "Xtreme Magazine," "Exotic Dancer," and other adult publications. I already knew that many strippers were very intelligent, talented women who were underappreciated by Americans who didn't know any better. Who I already understood wanted to be recognized as much more than the outward perception of being just tits and ass.

So, I was nearly horrified with what Jim was proposing to me.

"Jack, I want you to create a character for me who I can put into my "Wild Times" magazine. To give you an idea of what I'm talking about, here's a printout from the Nashville Times about this character it's created called Dick Biggs."

"Never heard of it, Jim. What is the Nashville Times?"

"Just this little Internet rag about Dick Biggs who has a big dick."

"Sounds really out there to me. Don't you find this to be a bit boring?"

"No. Not if you can outdo the Nashville Times. Jack, I want you to write about a new character who we will call Dick Fitswell. This character will have an oversized dick. Can you do that for me?"

"I don't know. I can try. But if I do, I want you to publish my article "Return to Visions" in the "Wild Times."

"You have a deal. If you can give me a Dick Fitswell I can publish, I will print "Return to Visions" for you.

Alex

Thinking that I was selling my soul to the Devil I decided to ask Alex what she thought of my writing pornography stories for the "Wild Times."

I had first met Alex when she was stripping at C-Mowes at the same time I was falling for Nipples who was working the same shift. But I found Alex to have two very distinct separate lives.

Although Alex worked as a stripper in some of the seediest clubs in the U.S. close to East St. Louis, she lived about as far away as she could from the sordidness she had to put up with to make a decent living. Later, I would visit her at her home out past the city of Washington, Missouri, which was far west of the suburbs of St. Louis some sixty miles away from Dollies. She had a nice house that was typical of Middle Class America. She had two daughters and a husband who I would later come to like. And she already had a computer in her house with an Internet connection.

In our Lost Angels chat, PlONe had refined it, so that we could private message each other and the other members would not be able to read our private messages. I used the chat's private messaging feature, so that no one other than Alex could read my messages.

I started off by typing to Alex, "Alex, I can't write porn. Jim Lilly won't publish anything for me unless I create this character called Dick Fitswell who has a huge penis."

Alex replied: "Jack, I am the first to read your novel, Death on the Wild Side. All five hundred pages of it. Believe me, you wrote some pretty sexual stuff in it. I know you can write about Dick Fitswell. Go for it. You won't regret doing it."

Alex turned out to be right. By the time I had completed my first paragraph of what would become Dick Fitswell the Man in Quest of the Perfect Fit, I got completely hooked on my own creation. Before writing the book, I got five or six of my Fitswell stories published in "Xtreme Magazine," three or four in the "Wild Times," and three or four in "Wood Magazine." Jim Lilly would have published far more Fitswell chapters because the whole idea of Fitswell was Jim's. But something happened to Jim. He simply finished publishing the "Wild Times," and disappeared off the face of the earth.

But my addiction to my own Dick Fitswell character never waned. So, even when I stopped writing for adult magazines such as "Xtreme" and "Wild Times," I kept writing more and more Dick Fitswell misadventures, putting them in my own Looking Glass Magazine section on my Alphapro website. And finally putting over twenty-four Fitswell stories into a book that is sold all over the world in paperback, and e-book editions. And to think I only had to write this much to addict myself to Dick Fitswell:

> I'm the real man...the man on the prowl...looking, always searching for the perfect woman-not for brains or heart, but for the perfect fit. So, listen up all you men who really want to score and see why I'm called Dick Fitswell. I've been the man with the plan--- the man who makes it happen. Now, let me tell you about last night.
>
> I hate country bars. The music's terrible, and the conversation's piss poor. But they got women in this place and that's the bottom line. I need it bad tonight because last night was such a bummer. The girl was too damn short for me and it just didn't feel right with her clinging onto me...as she kept crying out, “I love you Dick!” I spy a tall blonde with great breasts. I can feel myself inside her already. She's mine. "She's not looking at me yet," I tell myself as I pull my shirt up a bit which exposes my magnificent chest. I tighten up my arms and watch the veins pop out in my forearms. I'm the shit. "How would you like to fall in love tonight?" I ask her.
>
> Good line. I used to use--"Got a light?" but a lot of women don't like the smell of cigarettes on a man. Now I'll often get myself into a little sweat by exerting myself outside a bar before I walk in such as running around its parking lot a few times to give myself just the right amount of B.O. A lot of women love that smell. Makes them think they're with a real man”

Chameleon

I was driving back to Dollies after doing a photoshoot at Miss Kittys of one of the girls when I saw the blinking lights behind me. But I didn't think much of it because I had only a beer or two. When the police officer asked me for my driver's license, I asked him why he pulled me over.

“You weren't wearing your seat belt", the police officer replied. I want to see your insurance card.”

“It's in my apartment. But I can guarantee you, officer, that I have good insurance.”

“I need to see it though. If you don't have it with you, you are breaking Illinois state law.”

For once I was almost as sober as a judge, but that didn't matter to the police officer who was obviously out to write up as many tickets as he could. Giving me two tickets, one for not wearing a seat belt and the other for not showing proof of insurance, the officer confiscated my driver's license. I'd beat the ticket for not being able to produce proof of insurance later on in court, but not wearing a seat belt would stick on my driving record. Which would show two moving violations, due to a speeding ticket I had gotten two weeks earlier.

I would have gone straight to Dollies until this little voice told me to go straight to Chameleon, a small club only several hundred yards past the turn off to Dollies. There I would be sure to find Tommy Davis, the bar owner, who also owned a tow yard.

I found Tommy sitting in his usual chair on the very front of the bar, grinning like the Cheshire Cat as soon as he saw me walk though the club's small front entrance. But behind that Cheshire Cat grin, lurked an aura of menace. For Tommy was the nearly perfect incarnation of evil. And I loved him for it.

A short, heavy set man, one might think that Tommy couldn't fight his way out of a wet paper bag, but I knew better. I had seen him hard at work many times operating his tow trucks. Often times freezing his ass off in the snow chaining cars to one of his trucks, or having to change heavy tires, and in general having to manipulate, or move some very heavy objects. I also knew that Tommy had a sawed off Louisville slugger baseball bat close to his right hand and a .357 Magnum Revolver that he wouldn't hesitate to use. Tommy was a tough man who had no scruples whatsoever.

From his favorite chair Tommy could scrutinize anyone coming through his front door. He had an eye for undercover cops and troublemakers who he'd immediately ask to leave by telling them that his place was open only to club members.

“Well, if it isn't Jack Corbett,” Tommy greeted me with a grin. Have you fucked any new girls?”

“No Tommy, but take a look at these two tickets I just got from the police. One for not wearing a seat belt, the other for not carrying proof of insurance.”

As I handed Tommy the tickets he asked: “Washington Park Police or State?”

“Unfortunately it was an Illinois State trooper. So, I doubt if you have any pull with him.”

“Give me the tickets, then. We will just have to see about that,” Tommy replied as I handed him the tickets.

Dialing up a number, Tommy ambled out of the bar into the parking lot already talking with whoever was on the other end. Five minutes later he came back into the bar and handed me my driver's license.

“You can tear up these two tickets now. But if anyone asks, you never saw a thing.”

“Got it Tommy. I never knew you were that well connected. You are something else.”

“Don't mention it.”

Chameleon was breaking nearly every law in the book, which it could get away with due to Tommy giving the Washington Park Police a cut off every vehicle he could tow into his tow yard. This partnership between thieves encouraged the Washington Park Police to pull vehicles over for the slightest infractions. But charging drivers for DUI's was the Holy Grail for the Washington Park Police, due to their being able to temporarily confiscate an offenders car.

Confiscation meant having Tommy taking the offender's car to his tow yard. Which the car owner had to pay a stiff price to regain possession of his car. So, Tommy's arrangement with the Washington Park Police was a marriage made in heaven. Who gave Tommy a virtual monopoly on the municipality's towing business. Having his wife work for the Washington Park Police made the marriage a perfect union.

Chameleon was a one of a kind strip club. Being the only strip club in the area that didn't have a liquor license, Tommy could sell beer to his customers cheaper than anyone else could. Not having to have a liquor license was as simple as Tommy going down Highway 111 to the Clark gas station where he'd buy a few cases of beer, which he bought in cans instead of bottles. So, if the authorities came in to inquire about his liquor license, Tommy would tell them that the cans were his customer's beer. And that he was operating a private club for the benefit of his customers whose alcohol he'd keep in hand for a small membership fee.

I often did a few beer runs for Tommy, who would offer me free beers for my salary. But sometimes Tommy would have his wife run his bar for him. And when she did, things got almost embarrassing for me. Mary Lou would typically give me six, or eight beers every time I came in during her shift.

Chameleon soon became one of my favorite bars. While one of my best friends liked it just as much as I did.

Howard was a good looking young lawyer in his early thirties who was totally addicted to the Saint Louis Metro East strip clubs. So, it didn't take long for Howard and I to become great friends. Howard was a good talker who got a lot of his training arguing criminal law cases on the Missouri side of the river. It was Howard who gave Chameleon its real name. "The Whorehouse". Howard came up with it. I didn't. But both of us loved calling the place The Whorehouse. Which it certainly was, and which is one of the reasons Tommy could get away with calling his bar a private club.

In the back of the bar there was a large area comprising of several rooms. There's a Jacuzzi in full view in the main room. And one or two small bedrooms where Tommy's bar girls could do their tricks. All of which is a stroke of genius because Tommy never got a dime's commission from the girls.

The way it worked was each customer taking a girl into this back area had to pay a $25 towel fee. And that's it. Because it would be up to him and the girl how much he'd tip her for sex. Sometimes a girl might charge $200.00. While at other times she might ask only $40.00

depending how hard up she was for her drugs.

Because of this arrangement it would be nearly impossible for the authorities to charge Tommy for prostitution. Because Tommy could always claim, "I don't know what the hell they were doing back there. I only got a Jacuzzi fee."

At Chameleon the girls never wore g-strings. So they never looked like strippers, and although there was a small stage and a dancing pole, most of the girls preferred sitting around the bar talking with their customers. Howard came in looking dapper in his black leather jacket waving at me as he took a bar stool at the other end of the bar from me one of the girls took a seat next to him. “Can I buy you a drink, Tessie?” he asked the girl.

You most certainly can, How Weird.”

Tessie was obviously onto him. Although Howard had an engaging personality; he never made a secret of how he felt about things; and what came out of his mouth next proves my point:

“I love fucking whorehouses, he called out to me. Don't you Jack? And Tessie, you sweet little whore. Are you going to fuck me tonight?”

“Howard, I will drink to that. Here's to fucking whorehouses,” I replied. Both our voices carried throughout the bar as several of the customers looked away, being no doubt ashamed of being seen and having two men being very vocal about what everyone was doing there. While a couple others snickered at Howard's outburst.

Angie

One thing I have to say about Visions Gentlemen's Club: Is that the girls sure knew how to dance there. I started finding myself equally at home at Visions as I did at Dollies or Chameleon. I immediately started liking the new Manager there. Who liked the digital pictures I was taking in the other bars, and who had no problem whatsoever with my bringing my laptop into the bar, which he allowed me to boot up to show the club's dancers my website and the digital pictures I was taking.

Curtis was a slender good looking guy who looked every inch of being the quintessential ladies man. So obviously I wouldn't have any problems with him. I would continue to have a lot of problems with many managers in the Saint Louis Metro East Clubs. and would wind up getting barred from half the clubs here, and it was all due to jealousy Most of the strippers liked me a lot more than their bosses. I could write, and I could make them really look good with my digital camera While they understood and appreciated my totally off the wall sense of humor, which was a lot like theirs. So, a lot of the managers didn't like all the attention I was getting.

As I started to get to know him better I found that Curtis had the same off the wall sense of humor. And although he was very good at doing his job, he would be up for just about any prank my friends and I could come up with.

Visions had a new female bartender who I immediately got on well with. I would often come into Visions for lunch. And being a first class gentlemen's club, Visions provided food, which Lori would get for me. Lori was a tall, slender woman in her early thirties who could think and act quickly. She moved fast, while flitting around the club waiting on tables and returning to the bar to make cocktails, or pour beer into the glasses of her customers.

Charli soon joined me at the bar, and although she was the Assistant Manager, I bought her a drink anyway.

And then I spotted a slender dancer pole dancing at the far end of the room. I had observed Charli's twenty year old daughter pole dancing several times and found her to be quite good. But found the new girl I was now watching to be even better. Truth is most strippers cannot even begin to pole dance. So, finding the new girl to be a distant exception to this, I went back to her stage, and just stood there watching her. When she finally finished I spoke to her.

“You are excellent. One of the best I've ever seen,” I told the girl.

“That's because I'm from New York City,” the girl replied.

“What does that have to do with it?”

“New York’s the number one city in the U.S. It's got the best theaters. It's got the best restaurants, and it's got the best night clubs. So you have to try a lot harder in New York.”

“Let me buy you a drink. Because by God you've earned it.”

While we were having a drink together back at the bar, Charli approached us and said in her sarcastic Charli way: “You'd better be leaving Angie alone. She's a really nice girl and I don't want you corrupting her.”

Then I turned to Angie and told her, “I want you to watch me try to pole dance and tell me if I am any good or not.”

“No you can't, Jack. Not in my bar,” Charli added as her face broke into a huge smile.

“Why not, Charli? I just bought you a drink, so you owe me.”

"Because Jack, the last time I saw you trying to pole dance here, you fell on your ass.”

“That's because I was drunk. I'm not drunk now, Charli.”

“Alright then. Go ahead and kill yourself. It's your funeral not mine.”

Angie watched attentively as I showed her what I could do on the pole. I could do it. But not nearly as well as she could. But when she started laughing I asked her:

“What's wrong?”

“You are pretty clumsy. But really not all that bad. At least you are trying.”

*****

A few days later I took Angie home because she was working day shift and didn't have a car. Where I was surprised to find that she had a computer and an Internet connection. Once again I found that she was proud of being a New York City girl. But I didn't find her to be pretentious at all. Years later when I took my Thai girlfriend to New York I found out exactly what Angie meant. It is the Big Apple. And no other city in the world is like it.

Playing Julius Caesar at the Chameleon

I soon started doing a website for Chameleon. Tommy was becoming intrigued with my digital photography, and I had just found that Kodak had just come out with a new digital camera that was far superior to my DC-40. So, Tommy bought my DC-40 from me and started practicing with it.

“Tommy, I have the perfect idea for you.”

“What's that, Jack? Are you trying to freeload from me again to get me to buy you more free beers?”

“Really, I mean it. You have a great hot tub in your back room. We need to advertise it on your new website.”

“What do you have in mind?”

“We get someone to take pictures of me with one of your girls. The sexiest girl you have who's working for you.”

“And who's that?”

“Crystal.”

“Okay. Are you asking me to let her fuck you for free?”

“No. This is what we can do. I will be wearing my undies. Crystal will be totally nude. We fill up your tub with hot sudsy water and I will buy some grapes. I will be wearing a Roman headband so I will look like the Emperor of Rome. And then we will have Crystal feeding me grapes.”

“Sounds wonderful. When do we start?”

“As soon as I can get us a photographer and I can talk to Crystal about it.”

******

Crystal hadn't been working for the last few days. But as luck would have it I had her phone number and was able to get her to meet me at my apartment. Where we had a couple drinks while I outlined how I wanted the photoshoot to go.

But when I lined up my photographer, I chose Angie. Then I went out and bought several bunches of grapes and a headband that would be fit for a Caesar. I brought the grapes to Chameleon that afternoon where I told Tommy that I wanted them to be fresh and asked him to keep them in the refrigerator for me.

As soon as the day shift ended at Visions I picked Angie up at the club and took her to Chameleon, but when I asked Tommy for my grapes, Tommy replied:

"Those grapes looked so good that I ate them all myself."

Which came down to my having to go to a supermarket that was close to Chameleon. And my having to take Angie with me.

In general the girls at an upper scale gentlemen's club like Visions would look down on a roadhouse strip club like Chameleon, Dollies, or Miss Kittys. And as for Chameleon, it had long ago justified Howard's and my calling it The Whorehouse. Crystal was every inch a whore and being the best looking girl in the bar, she was able to get $200 from her customers for short time sex.

I'll have to admit though that I thoroughly enjoyed doing that hot tub with Crystal as Angie hovered above us shooting pictures. But, if the pictures seem to be showing Crystal and I having sex together, I can assure you that we weren't. Angie would never have respected me if we were getting it on. And she would have told all the other dancers at Visions that I was a real scumbag who was using my expertise as a writer and photographer to get a lot of sex from the girls. This policy would pay off in rich dividends for me later on. By not being a monger, I would continue to have more strippers as companions than I would ever be able to count.

Alex and my Hernia Operation

I once asked Kermit about hernias while he was farming.

“You can't go to the hospital when you are actually farming,” Kermit replied. “This is because when you are operated on, it takes a couple of months for it to heal. So, you can't be exerting yourself and do a lot of heavy lifting because you will screw the whole operation up. So, I just tuck in my gut and keep driving the tractor until I get done with the real farming. Only then when the workload gets much easier do I go in for an operation.”

I got lucky when I had to have my first hernia operation. I got the hernia from doing leg lifts in the gym. But it was winter, so I wasn't working that hard. And that meant for me that I was able to get operated on right away. But I was unlucky the second time. And had to wait it out a couple of months before I could go in for an operation. Like Kermit, I had to deal with that big swelling in my groin until I got a break from strenuous farm work around the 4th of July.

I dreaded the operation. But I found the best way to handle it would be to make light of the whole thing. Which is hilarious now that I think about it, and how I told the doctors while they were putting me under the anesthetic.

“Tonight I am going to celebrate getting this operation done by going to a strip club.”

Several hours later, Kermit's son and his wife picked me up at the hospital and drove me to my apartment. Kermit had been a tough old bird, but his son, Jack, was even tougher. I had seen Jack break his leg and his arm in the same accident. But he was back on his tractor the next day. Wanting to prove to Jack and Donna that I wasn't a sissy, I had them drive me that night to Dollies after dinner.

Donna, was an ex-stripper, Jack and I met,, at the Main Street strip club a few years earlier. Donna was about as good a drinking companion as one could find because although she had given up stripping, she still loved going to strip clubs. The hospital had given me Darvocet to lessen the pain I would be experiencing from the operation. I took one capsule in front of Alex after buying us two Budweisers right after my friends and I got to Dollies. While swearing to her that I'd get really trashed before the night was over.

Which was probably not a good idea for someone who'd just come of the hospital. But I had nineteen beers celebrating my first hernia with a good friend, so the precedent had been set. I could not wuss out this time. Nope. It turned out to be a bad idea. Prudence would have had me staying at home instead of partying until 2 a.m. Before the night was over, Alex caught me taking a second Darvocet, which was double the recommended dose. And when Alabama came up to me to ask me how I was feeling, I was so glad to see her that I picked her up off the floor. Now Alabama might have been a slim waif of a girl, but she sure was quite a lot heavier than 20 pounds, which is what the doctors warned me not to exceed.

We all got good and soused that night. But after one of the sexiest dancers in the place started crawling naked all over me I wasn't feeling any pain whatsoever and I am going to blame the Darvocet, which is a narcotic. Lesson to be learned. And one I would like to instill in all men being operated on for hernias. Don't be a pussy. The night after you get operated on, go to a strip club.

Taking Satin to Big Al's to Compete for Miss Nude Illinois

“Jack, I am hoping you can do something for me, and for Dollies,” Hawk mentioned to me as we went through some of my latest digital pictures together.

“Name it Hawk. I am up for just about anything.”

“Have you ever heard of the Miss Nude Illinois Pageant at Big Al's?”

“Yes. I remember Leah Layne winning it a couple years ago. I've been to Big Al’s a couple of times while driving through Peoria. And I have talked to Leah about it at the Exotic Dancer's expo in Las Vegas.”

“Big Al’s is one of the best known gentlemen's clubs in the Midwest. I want to put Dollies Playhouse on the map as one of the top clubs in this area. Thanks to your doing a website for us, and the Lost Angels chats, Dollies is becoming much better known outside the Saint Louis area. I want to have one of our dancers compete for Miss Nude Illinois in two weeks at Big Al's.”

“Who do you have in mind to represent Dollies, Hawk?”

“I have only one dancer who I think can represent us in a very positive light. And that's Satin. She's an excellent dancer, she's reliable, and she's very attractive. And she likes you, a lot Jack.”

“What does her liking me a lot have to do with her representing Dollies as a potential Miss Nude Illinois, Hawk?”

“Because I want you to take her to Peoria and look after her during the pageant. You will get your hotel room free of charge plus all your meals and other expenses. Since you are already staying with Satin and two of my other girls at the Best Western Hotel in Collinsville, I will put you in the same room together.”

“Why don't you take her, Hawk?”

"Because I have to stay here and run Dollies. And I can't hold up your jockstrap when it comes to taking pictures.”

“You run this by Nathan yet?” I asked.

"No. Not yet. But I think Nathan will agree to it and pay your expenses. But I can guarantee that you will have all your expenses paid for. Even if I have to pay them out of my own pocket."

*****

I have to hand it to Nathan. Nathan was a very progressive Club Owner, who had complete faith in his General Manager. I didn't even have to ask Dollies for reimbursement for our hotel room, our meals, my gas, or the few drinks Satin and I had together at Big Al's. Hawk simply handed me $400.00 in cash and Satin and I were off to our next adventure together.

Peoria was about 150 miles from Dollies. It is an industrial town that headquarters several large American companies such as Caterpillar, which has dealers all over the world. When I think of bulldozers, I think of Caterpillar. But recently Caterpillar had ventured into the agricultural machinery market. And had already begun production of large tractors that run on steel tracks instead of rubber tires. One of my best friends had bought one. But it didn't take long for the largest implement manufacturers in the United States to start building tractors running on steel treads that could successfully compete against Caterpillar.

I liked Peoria. And would return there many times to cover Pure Talent's Feature Showcases at Big Al's later on. Situated on the Illinois River, Peoria was far more scenic than I had hoped for. I found the city to be very well laid out, with the center of the city to be quite vibrant. And Big Al's? You just couldn't ask for more.

I know a lot of people might disagree with me, but I am sure a lot of others will back what I am saying. Big Al's is right off Main Street, in the very center of Peoria. It's been there for years. And it represents an enduring Legacy in its own right. There's a sign on the building that states "Big Al's World Famous." Which reminds passers by of Al Capone, the most notorious gangster the world has ever known.

An employee of the club seated Satin and me at a table for four that would give us an excellent view of the stage while the contestants competed against each other. We were soon joined by Vic and Kasey Karrington, who would soon be competing against Satin as the future Miss Nude Illinois. I found Kasey to be a very nice woman with impeccable manners. In startling contrast to the Kasey who had been recently sending me several insulting emails.

When I received Kasey's emails I couldn't remember what she looked like. All I knew was that she was a Visions dancer who obviously had it in for me. Her emails were articulate, but they oozed with biting sarcasm that called me an incompetent photographer and writer.

While Vic had been making a very conspicuous presence of himself at Visions, calling himself the club's photographer, who had been playing his part with his SLR camera and other photography gear.

It didn't take long for Vic to join our Lost Angels chat group. Where he constantly criticized my digital cameras. “They lacked resolution” he kept telling the Lost Angels members. And they would always be toys compared to film cameras that the real professionals (such as himself) were using.

But Visions soon forgot all about Vic. The new world of digital photography had arrived. My digital cameras paired with my laptop computer provided instant gratification. While the colors and flesh tones of my models came out nearly letter perfect.

Several months later, even Kasey, jumped on the digital bandwagon when she had Vic take her to Dollies where I could do a photoshoot of her with my digital camera. Which I found to be out of character for most entertainers from the best Saint Louis Metro East clubs who would have thumbed their noses at a "dive" such as Dollies.

But Dollies was no dive. In fact, it was well ahead of its time, and Kasey knew it. The Kasey who would do the photoshoot at Dollies brought several outfits along, so that I could do a variety of pictures of her. The Dollies dancers showed no sign of resentment. While Kasey showed not one trace of arrogance to the Dollies girls. Dollies had after all sent a worthy contestant to Big Al’s while being the focal point of the Lost Angels chat that was attracting a national audience. And as far as Vic goes, it would turn out that he was just one more of these guys trying to make a star out of his girlfriend. Who would be too late to grasp the future of the digital world.

Looking back at the Miss Nude Illinois Pageant at Big Al’s, I can't even remember who won. But I'd wind up returning to Big Al’s at least four more times to cover the Pure Talent Feature Showcases which Big Al would pay for, spending a bare minimum of $20,000 for all our hotel rooms, advertising the events on radio and television, and even more money to the owners of the Pure Talent Agency for bringing as many as 19 Feature Entertainers to put on their shows.

Prettiest Girl at Chameleon

Was Angel. Who had the distinction of being the only girl working for Tommy who would not allow me to take her pictures. I had heard a lot about Angel before from Crazy Czech. Who told me Angel was Mistress Mary's niece and that she was funnier than all get out. And although I had seen Angel working at Dollies before I had only caught glimpses of her. Looking very young and beautiful. But I had never said one word to her while she was working at Dollies because she never was there for very long.

But here she was at Chameleon where the girls did very little dancing. Who preferred talking with their customers at the bar where they could down a lot of alcohol and not have to do any meaningful physical work with the exception of the short times they were doing in the back room.

It didn't take long for Angel and I to gravitate to each other, which was because both of us liked to drink. So, I capitalized on Angel's weakness for tequila by always buying her a few shots. But Angel would nearly always reciprocate by buying me as many drinks as I was buying for her.

I can't recall how many times I'd sit at the front of the bar with Tommy before I'd hear Angel's loud voice calling out to me.

"Jack. Get your bony ass over here and buy me a fucking tequila."

By then Howard and I had become nearly inseparable. And Howard liked Angel every bit as much as I did. I said Howard and I were nearly inseparable. The keyword here is "Nearly." Because although almost every time I'd venture out to the clubs, Howard and I would usually meet or run into each other. This did not suggest that we held hands and went everywhere together. But almost every night we'd get in the Lost Angels chat room and compare our experiences that evening.

Howard and I started this little game where we would vote on who was the most memorable stripper we had met that evening. Who would oftentimes be Angel.

Since I was living alone in my Collinsville apartment I made a habit of eating in the restaurants that were near my apartment. Which was exactly 8/10ths of one mile from where Highway met the Beltline, which traveled up a high bluff to my apartment.

So, with Interstate Highway 55 crossing Highway 157 half a mile from the Beltline there were a lot of motels and restaurants in the immediate area. I'd have my choice between more restaurants than I could count. There was a McDonalds, a Hardee's, a Long John Silver, Arbys, White Castle, Steak and Shake, Denny's, and these were just the fast food restaurants. There was also an excellent Chinese Restaurant with an all you can eat buffet for $5.50 and a large Mexican Restaurant. Along with at least three steakhouses, an Applebee's, and a Ruby Tuesdays. And this didn't even count several more Chinese restaurants and Mexican restaurants if you drove East up the Beltline.

To my complete surprise as I was having lunch at Applebees, a very pretty girl came up to my table smiling at me. The girl had just done her hair, and she was very nicely dressed, but I couldn't remember where I had seen her before. Because all in all she looked like an eighteen year old High School cheerleader. We had a brief conversation and then her boyfriend suddenly shows up who takes her to their table. It took me over fifteen minutes to suddenly realize that the girl was Angel.

*****

I got a better look at her boyfriend a few days later as I was leaving the Chameleon where I found him close to the front entrance of the bar. He looked pretty young. In his mid twenties I thought.

"You fuck Angel yet?" the boyfriend asked.

I don't remember how I replied, and I don't remember all the things he said next, but I found him to be a very crude kind of individual who I had little in common with.

*****

A few days later, while I was in my apartment planning to spend the evening alone, Angel called me.

"What are you doing?" she asked me.

"Nothing much, Angel. I'm just watching the History channel on TV."
"Do you want to go out?"

"With you?"

"No. With my Aunt, Mistress Mary."

"When Angel?"

"Right now."

"What do you mean right now?"

"Twenty minutes from now, Jack."

"I don't even know where you live."

Then she gave me directions and told me she'd be waiting for me right in front of her house.

I was really surprised to find that Angel lived just fifteen to twenty minutes from my apartment. But there she was true to her word, standing right out in front of her house. To tell you the truth I don't remember exactly what we did other than my taking her back to my apartment that night. Because from then on Angel and I would be spending a lot of time together.

Angel Pepper Sprays Her Boyfriend

After we had been seeing each other three or four times, Angel decided to send her boyfriend packing, and locked him out of the house. But after David tried to break into her front door, I gave her a can of pepper spray. The next night when Angel opened the door and David tried to overpower her, Angel gave him a full blast of pepper spray in his face. Three or four days later, the police threw David in jail. David had just jabbed a screwdriver through his best friend's skull. Angel never saw David again.

Tommy Plays Baseball

“Ever play baseball, Jack?” Tommy asked me as I was nursing my first beer.

“A little when I was in Junior High, but I wasn't very good at it.”

“I played baseball last night, Tommy replied. “With an asshole's head.”
“Tell me about it.”

“You see this Louisville slugger,” said Tommy, as he pulled out his sawed off Louisville slugger. “I nearly broke it last
night. This asshole comes in here who wants to take his girlfriend out of my bar. Guy's a classic leech living off his girlfriend. So, he starts arguing with her and then I'm watching him slapping her around. So, I put my Louisville slugger behind my back where he can't see it and I ask him to leave. The guy's not about to leave and he calls me a fat motherfucker. So, I let him have it with this here baseball bat. And believe me, I sure made him a believer.”

“I hope you put him in the hospital Tommy.”

“I didn't land him in the hospital. I had him put in jail. You should have seen me, Jack. I kept bashing him in the head with it and then I threw him right through the door. But when his head hit the doorframe, it gets damaged. The police come right away, so I show the police how he's damaged the door frame. I was laughing my ass off watching the police seeing me ransack the guy's pockets. Got twenty bucks out of them. Then I told everybody that the asshole still owed me another thirty dollars,” Tommy added with a huge grin.

“What did you do about it?”

“I got it out of his bitch. By upping her tip out from twenty-five dollars to fifty-five dollars. She didn't have it straight off, so I got it out of her the next time she came to work.”

“You really are a scoundrel, Tommy.”

“No I'm not, because actually I was doing her a favor by fining her for keeping such an asshole for a boyfriend.”

Nathan Bites the Dust

If there's anything better than having a Nun working for a strip club, it's having two Nuns. So, I decided to make a Nun out of Marilyn Mynxxx.

When Marilyn first started stripping at Dollies, she bragged to me how she had once been a Porn Star, and that was the reason she added three x's to her last name. I found Marilyn to be very outspoken. When Congress tried to impeach President Clinton for perjury after having sex with Monica Lewinsky; which I found to be very ironical since Marilyn had become more enraged about Clinton's sexual misconduct than his lying; while Marilyn herself was quite proud for having been a Porn Star.

Feeling that Marilyn would be a perfect addition to our very popular Dollies Trendy Toilet Sex Internet skits; I went out and bought her a nun's habit; which she soon put to good use with two other girls. Pretending to be a no nonsense teacher every time Marilyn would turn her back on the other girls, they'd give her the finger. At the end of the skit, Marilyn, aka Sister Cuervo, puts one of the girls on her lap and paddles her behind.

We had just finished our skit and uploaded all the pictures into the Lost Angels chat when Marriah latched onto me and took me into the other room.

“They just found Steve's body, Jack. I was right all the time. Nathan murdered his partner. Can you believe it's taken the police a whole year to find out?”

“What happened Marriah?”

“Nathan's son suddenly turned chicken shit and turned his own father in. Nathan shot Steve in the head at a truck yard Nathan owned. Then he had his son help him bury Steve's body. I heard the son started having bad dreams and couldn't live with himself so he went to the police.”

“This means we won't be seeing Nathan here again, Jack replied. The police catch Nathan yet?”

“They already got him in the county jail,” Marriah replied.

“And to think that Nathan's been running Dollies for a whole year while Steve's been moldering inthe ground, Marriah. I would never have thought Nathan to be capable of murdering anyone."

"From what I heard, Steve's been embezzling money from the bar. So yeah, I can see why Nathan would get pissed off enough to shoot Steve."

Picture Collage I

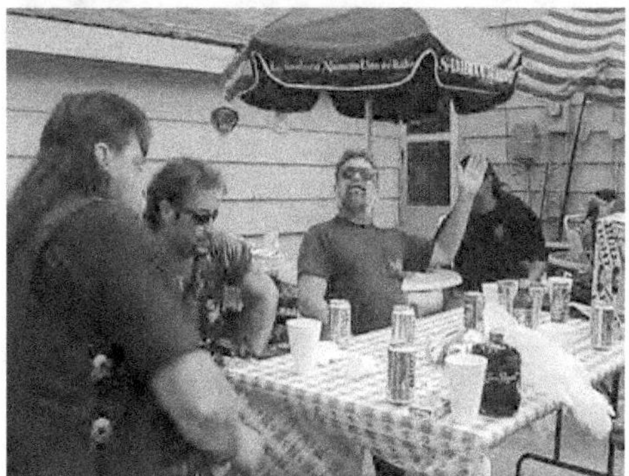

Dollies General Manager Hawk (third from the left) with friends at a Dollies weekend party for employees, dancers and customers.

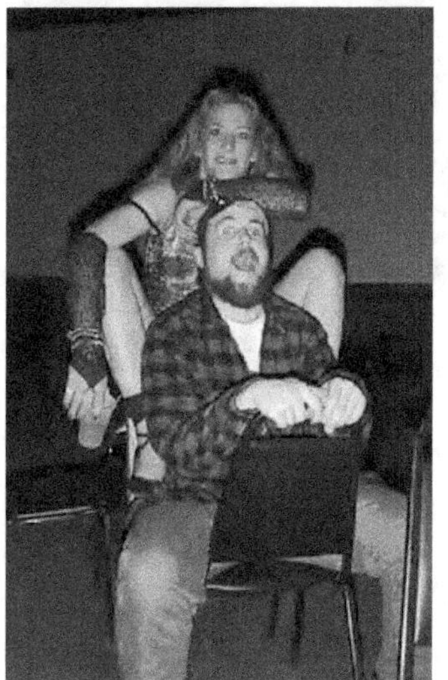

Marriah and Dirt. Dirt took over from Grey Ghost my web site design.

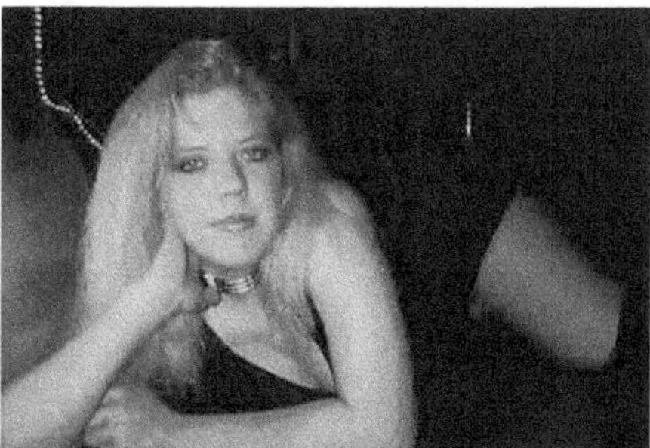

Jade

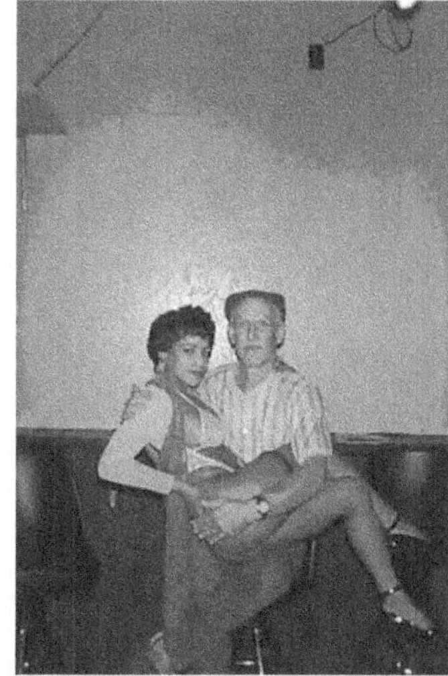

Satin and the author

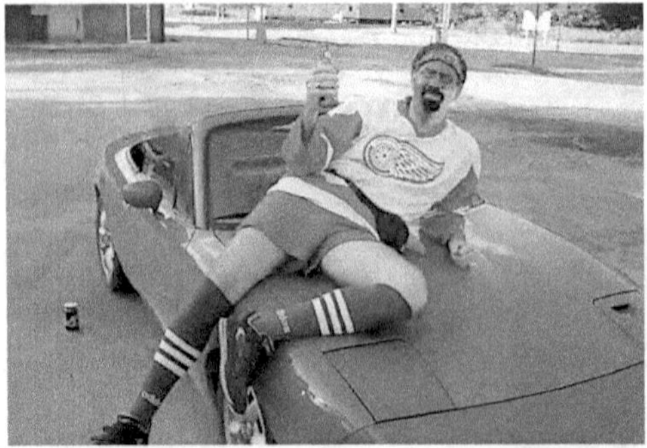

Crazy Czech, the founder of Dollies Trendy Toilet Sex and the author's supercharged Mazda Miata sports car.

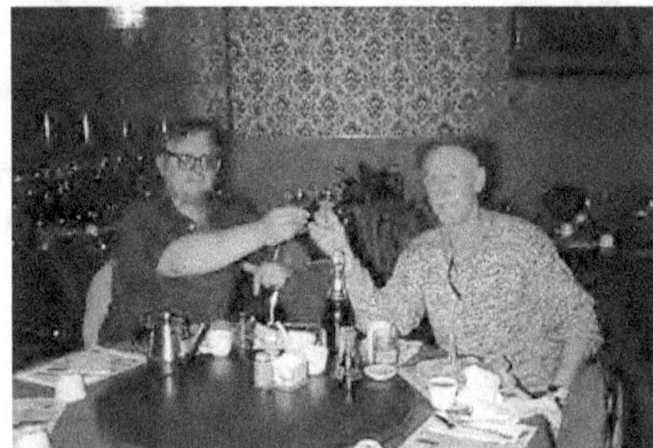

The Baron and the author

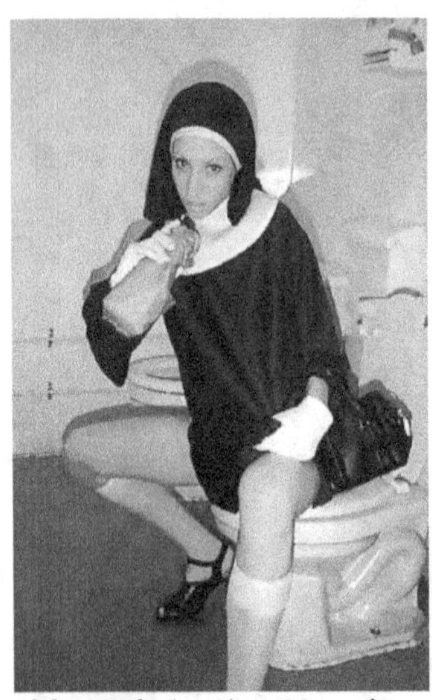

Alabama playing Sister Margarita in episode 1 of Dollies Trendy Toilet Sex

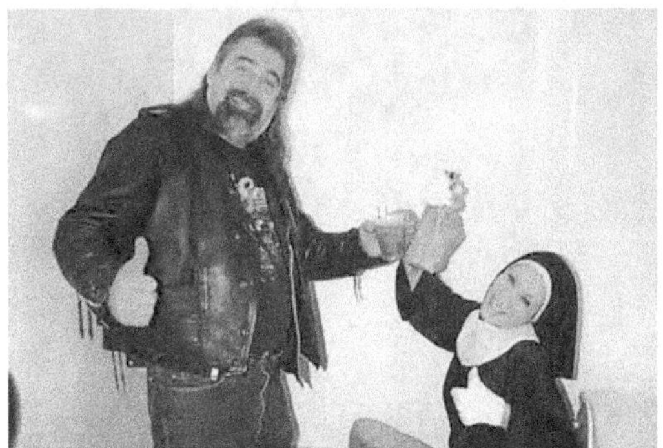

Hawk finally discovers Sister Margarita in the Dollies rest room.

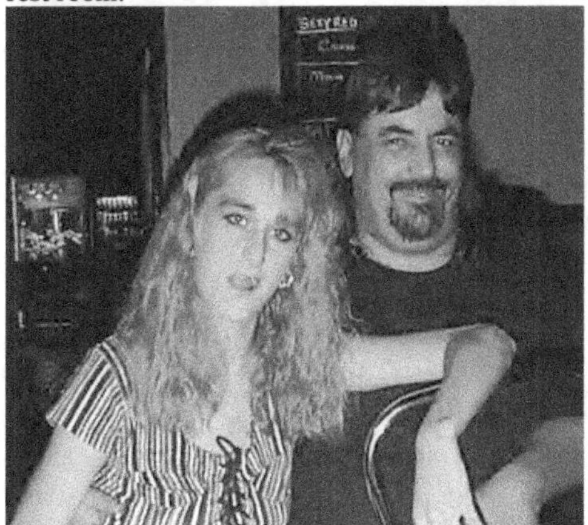

Dollies manager Howard, with Tori who Beater and Chid would take to Canada

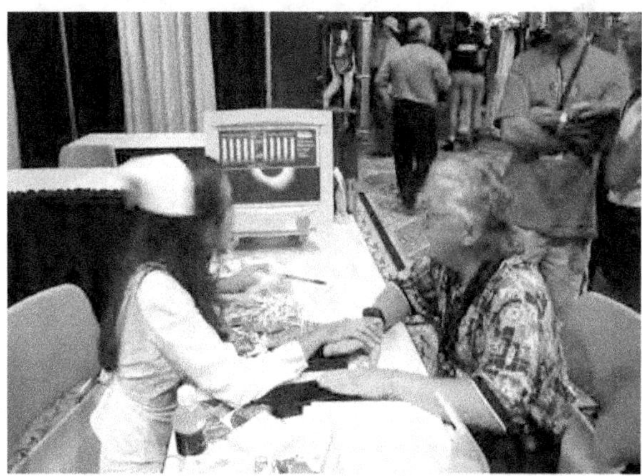

Stimmelators club owner Sam Stimmel at the Exotic Dancer Las Vegas Expo

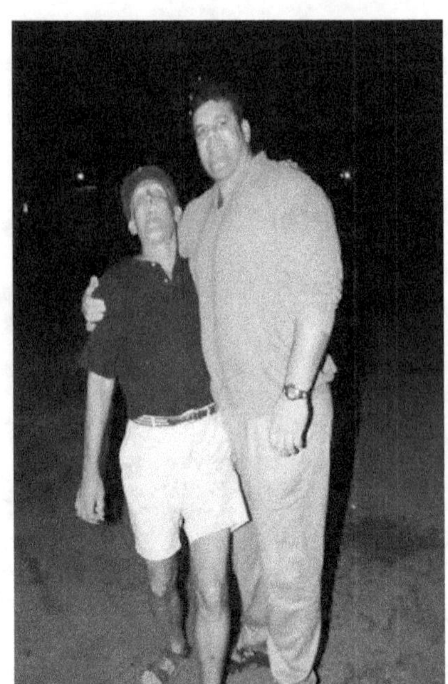

When Platinum Club General Manager Frank Marsala had the author cover club bouncer Leo, for a potential professional wrestling career, Jack didn't plan on sparring with the big man.

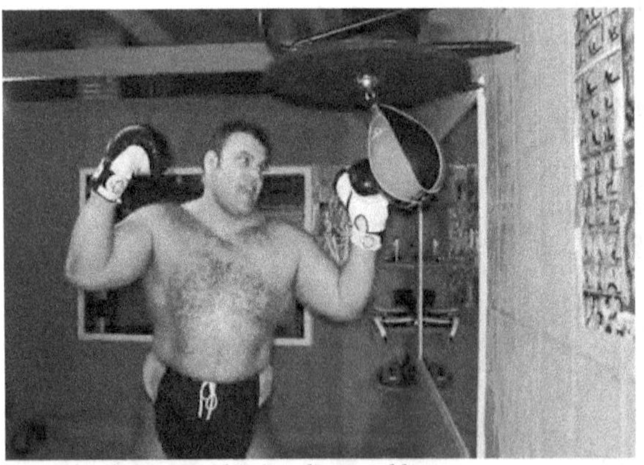

Leo in his home gym hitting the speed bag

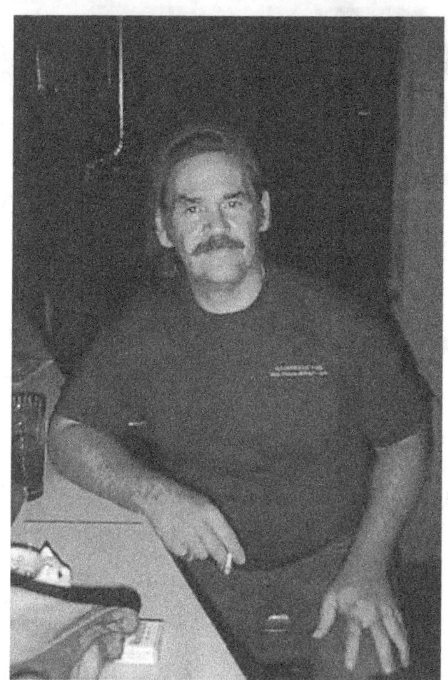

Doctor Doom

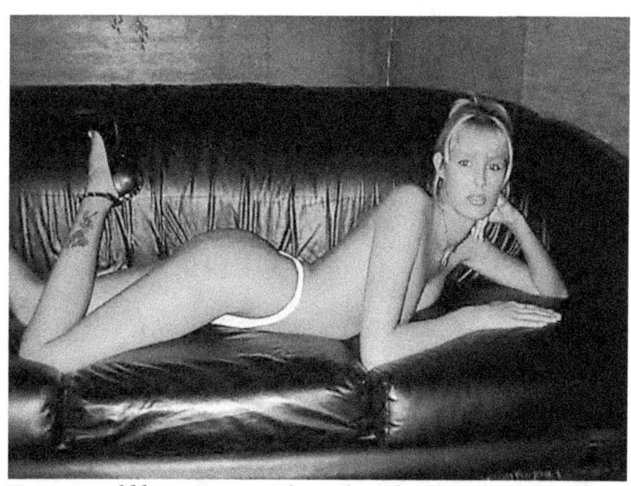

Heaven would later represent the author's booth at the Exotic Dancer Expo's trade show in Las Vegas with Dirt and Big Howard.

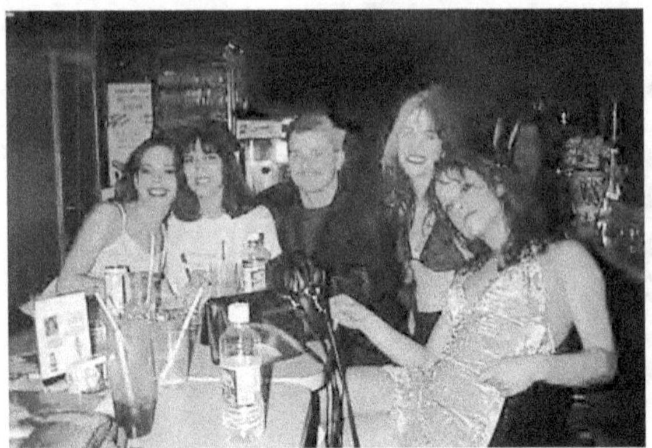

Left to right, Stimmelator's Marriah, Katt, RJ, Brandy (from Dollies), and Ruby. 10 of us including Doctor Doom, Brandy, Jade, Satin, Crazy Czech, and Baron went to Stimmelators for the weekend.

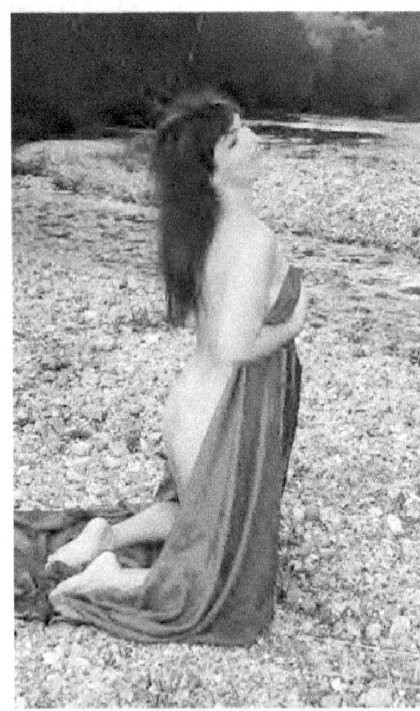

Alex was the first to read the author's first book, Death on the Wild Side. She also urged him to write his Dick Fitswell stories for Wild Times Magazine when he told her, "Alex, I can't write porn."

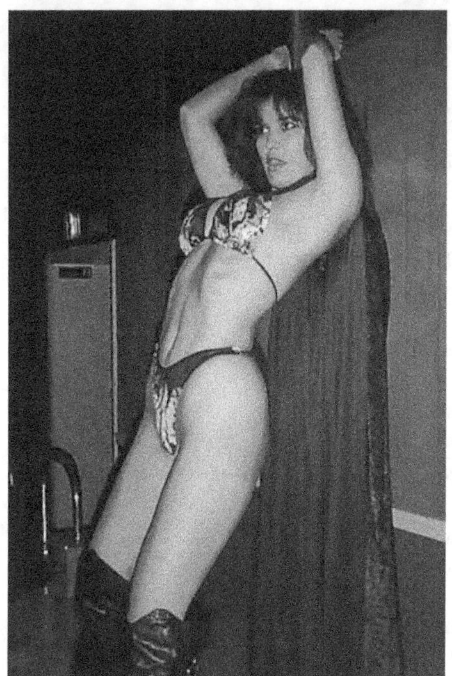

Kat

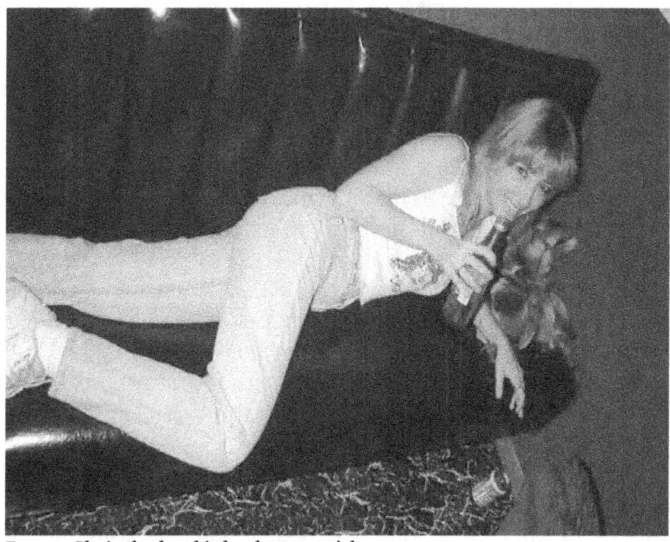

Renee, She's the book's back cover girl

Beat Off

When PlONe told me about a wild ass Canadian who was stirring things up in the Chez Paree chat group, I started to like the man already. PlONe and I had tried to link up with some of the Chez Paree chat members with no success. Two of the Chez Paree group members had even treated me with contempt. So, when I went to Beater's website and began to read about his antics in the Toronto area strip clubs, I immediately started to laugh my ass off.

Scott had started calling himself Beater, due to his ritual of visiting a strip club where he'd drink himself to oblivion, and then he'd throw up in the club. His drink of choice was Molson Ale, which was a Canadian brew that he claimed was far superior to all American beers. In his annals in which he described his experiences in every strip club he visited, Beater would write about his good friend, Chris, who had once been a strip club manager. In his accounts of his experiences in Canadian strip clubs, Chris would often have sex with one of the dancers in one form or the other. I don't know exactly why Scott used Beater for a nickname because now over twenty-five years later, I can't recall whether he ever beat off in a strip club, or not. So, I now believe that he should have been calling himself Barfaholic.

Most of the Chez Paree chat members detested Beater and often argued with him in their IRC based chats. So, one night while I was still living at the farm I logged into one of the Chez Paree IRC chats hoping to find Beater, and found him. I was alone that night in my farm house and I was in the mood to do some drinking. So, it didn't take long for me to find a new drinking companion in Beater.

IRC had a private messaging system in those days where a member could private message one person at a time or message the entire group in the chat room. Since my mission was to meet Beater rather than to chat with the other members I soon engaged Beater in a private conversation. Then I got him to try out our Lost Angels chat room and told him how he could log in as a new member with Beater as his user name. By the time Heaven and Katt started messaging him, and all three of us started posting digital pictures in our Lost Angels messages Beater was hooked.

Getting Beater addicted to the Lost Angels was a cinch. The IRC chat setup was drab and boring compared to what PlONe came up with in his revised version of the Lost Angels. The Lost Angels capability of displaying digital pictures alone would have put it at the head of the class. But once PlONe had programmed the ability to private message into it, the Lost Angels had become a real masterpiece.

PlONe had created a rectangular shaped window in its lower left corner, which displayed the user names of all members who were currently in the chat. But when a member left the chat, he had also built in a feature that showed how much time had elapsed since the member left the Lost Angels. The user names were normally in black text, but if a member should start private messaging another member the other member's user name would change from black text to red.

The finest feature of the Lost Angels were its female members. I can't remember seeing even one stripper while PlONe and I were visiting Chez Paree who was half as good looking as Katt and Heaven. We also had Brandy coming into our chats; not as often as Heaven and Katt; but often enough; then again, looks aren't everything. So even if this should be the case, our girls were much more entertaining than the women in the Chez Paree IRC chats. All three of them obviously having higher IQ's while being totally off the wall. But we also had other women coming to our chats on a regular basis, such as Alex, Jade, and Satin.

When I look back at our female members who stripped for a living, I still marvel over how intelligent most of them were. Then again, reflecting back to those years so long ago, we had a very intelligent group of men in the Lost Angels chat group as well. PlONe had a PHD in Computer Science while Howard was a successful lawyer. Baron was a very talented writer who would sadly never be discovered. While Grey Ghost had talents up the ying yang. Doctor Doom was hugely entertaining, and as I would find out later on, would surprise all of us with what he would later accomplish. Crazy Czech was a very savvy computer systems engineer who would later write five books.

And now we had Beater. Who I just had to meet and the sooner the better. So, I invited him to visit me in Illinois.

By then Beater and I were constantly baiting each other over which one of us could out drink the other. From my end, I kept bragging about how superior Anheuser Busch products were to any Canadian brew that had ever been bottled. While Beater kept informing us that Molson, being an ale was much stronger than any Busch, Bud Lite, or Budweiser beers the American chat members were drinking. And in his eyes made him the best drinker, due to the rest of us drinking Pussy beer.

I had Doc shoot several pictures of me sitting bare chested high up in a tree drinking a can of Budweiser yelling out to Beater, “When you come here I'm going to kick your ass!” Today we would have been shooting video, which would have meant my voice coming out loud and clear. But back then the Internet was God awful slow due to our having to use phone wires to use the Internet. So, I'd put my pictures up in the chat, and then I'd type the message, “Beater, I'm going to kick your ass!” beneath my picture.

By the time Beater arrived at the Saint Louis Airport, I had everyone prepared well for his visit. With the help of Five Star Graphics in Springfield, IL., I designed a special t-shirt which had a picture of a bear on it. But it wasn't exactly a bear. The picture was of a humanoid creature that I had dreamed up. Across the top of the picture Five Star Graphics had put lettering that read, "Beater Meat 2001" The gist of the t-shirt being that Beater was subhuman, due to his being Canadian.

I gave Beater Meat t-shirts to two Dollies Managers and five or six more to the Dollies dancers who were the most active in our chats.

We spent the first night after Beater's arrival at Dollies where Beater became an instant hit with the Dollies dancers. Beater and I had a pole dancing contest in the back room at the club. Where several of the girls later put Beater on the stage where they stripped him down to his underwear.

While Beater was still on that stage, I remember hearing Marilyn Mynxxx yelling out at him, “Before tomorrow I want you to be showing me your dick!” That night I drank nineteen bottles of beer. Which made me drunk enough to somehow drop my digital camera. Luckily, I was still coordinated enough to keep it from falling on the floor by intercepting its fall with my left foot.

I had gotten Beater and me an expensive room that had its own Jacuzzi. So, after leaving Dollies I ended up shooting naked pictures of Beater in the hot tub drinking his last beer. When I asked Beater to show his dick to the camera, he was just drunk enough to actually do it, and emailed Marilyn Mynxxx several pictures that showed his dick the next morning.

By Sunday, my left foot was throbbing from all the pain I was feeling. But somehow I still managed to walk Beater through the Saint Louis Airport all the way to the departure gate. Two days later the Doctor told me that I had broken my foot although the fracture only amounted to a crack.

Six Days in a Las Vegas Hospital

I had broken my foot, which was no big deal because it was just a crack in a single bone, but it took me three or four days before I got around to seeing a Podiatrist. Because I still had unfinished business at Dollies–more days of Tequila and beer business.

I had met my foot doctor at C-Mowes and later at Dollies. Who put a cast on my left foot and strapped on a walker that would immobilize my foot and gave me a pair of crutches. The fracture should have kept me from exercising had it not been for the deep pond on the old Route 66 that my family owned. With the help of Kermit, my surrogate father, I had built a dock out of Cypress, which is a wood that could stand up to a lot of water, and a raft floating on discarded barrels that I anchored out in the middle of the pond. I had created the ideal replacement for my exercise room.

The pond was so much better than any swimming pool, due to its depth that measured over forty feet in places and its being fed by underwater springs it was far cleaner. While my raft being 50 yards from the dock, allowed me to swim 100 yard laps. I'd swim a mile every day, taking my walker off on my dock, which I would put back on after I had finished.

My injury only got worse; however, and not because of the swimming, which is low impact exercise. I started having a lot of pain in my left thigh, which running might have caused. Except, I was no longer doing any running, and I had another Exotic Dancer Expo coming up in Las Vegas.

But I continued to wait until the day Dirt and I were to drive nearly 2000 miles to Las Vegas. My pickup truck was a 1997 Dodge Dakota four wheel drive sport with a short bed and an extended cab that had a small back seat. I had put what amounted to a lid over my truck's short bed that I could lock down from prying eyes while keeping its contents out of the rain. Dirt and I had already loaded the truck up with our luggage, computers, and a lot of promotional materials for our exhibitor 's booth. While I had even purchased airline tickets for (Dollies Manager) Howard and Heaven who would be joining us at the convention.

When we arrived in Belleville and went into the orthopedics's office, my doctor unloaded the bombshell on me:

"I think you have seriously injured your thigh and if I were you, I would be holding off on your travel plans," Mark warned me.

“How can that be, Mark? I haven't done anything that could possibly injure my upper leg.”

“I don't know. But I strongly recommend that you check into the hospital here so we can perform a few tests to find out what's wrong with you.”

“That's not an option, Mark. Dirt and I have to leave for Las Vegas this afternoon.”

“If I were you, I wouldn't get on that plane.”

“Airplane? Why hell, we are driving out to Vegas this afternoon.”

“I wouldn't drive if I were you. And if you do I'd let Dirt here do all the driving.”

“That's not an option either, Mark. Dirt doesn't have a driver's license.”

“What! You don't have a driver's license, Dirt. Why don't you?” Mark replied. “How can you be in college and not have a driver's license?”

“I take the bus to my classes. And in Springfield I've never needed a driver's license. I get rides with my friends. And I have a bicycle.”

“Okay then, I would definitely put off this trip of yours, Jack.”

******

I had no choice other than to attend the convention no matter what the cost. Not only had I already invested too much money in the exhibitor's booth, attendance fees to Exotic Dancer for Dirt, Howard, Heaven and myself, airline tickets, and hotel rooms, I would also be swallowing my pride.

By 2 p.m. Dirt and I were on our way. It would take us nearly three days to get to Vegas. While I was in severe pain the whole trip. Which I could alleviate at night by propping my leg on two pillows in our hotel rooms. While sticking my leg out my pickup truck's window in an elevated position whenever traffic permitted.

When Dirt and I finally got into our hotel room at Mandalay Bay, I got into the Lost Angel's chat where I started private messaging one of the women members. The woman lived in Saint Louis far from the Metro

East. She was a nurse, who enjoyed visiting us at Dollies where she became friends with Alabama, Jade, and Alex. When I told her that the pain in my thigh had gotten much worse after driving over 1800 miles, she told me, “Go to the hospital Jack. This is very serious.”

“I can't do that, Morgan. I have an exhibitor's booth to run here at the convention.”

“Go to the hospital Jack. If you don't have to stay there, you can still run that booth of yours.”

When I took the tests at the hospital the doctors told me I might die if I didn't stay at the hospital due to the blood clot in my thigh being life threatening which could travel into my brain and cause a stroke, or into my lungs, or heart. Leaving me with only one viable option, which was to stay in the hospital for a few days where the doctors could thin out my blood.

Although Howard, Dirt, and Heaven came to visit me once or twice, PlONe would visit me in the hospital every day without fail. Which speaks volumes for him considering he was the only one out of the entire crew whose expenses I wasn't paying. Although the hospital had hooked me up to an IV that tethered me to the IV cart that limited my mobility, I was still able to get to the toilet alone.

The IV was thinning my blood, which would go on for six days. Feeling no pain, and not having to be sedated, or having to take pain killers, my mind was like a steel trap. Spinning at top end to make a lark out of my predicament.

Although PlONe had a phobia against smoking I was still able to enlist him as an ally for my latest prank. Which would be a satire making fun of all the anti-smokers, anti-drug, and anti-alcohol fanatics wanting to legislate their own version of morality. Getting PlONe to agree to be my photographer, I took the IV stand with me into the toilet and sat on the thrown where I lit up a cigarette. After PlONe left, I wrote an essay glorifying smoking and drinking. The gist being that I was a secret agent who had infiltrated the hospital's computers where I found a digital database that proved drinkers outlived non-drinkers. And that those who lived the longest were those who drank Budweiser.

But before I left the hospital I showed one of the male nurses that I had smoked a cigarette in my hospital bathroom and that I was going to put my satire on my website. The nurse laughed his ass off when I showed him the picture of my breaking the hospital rules that prohibited smoking.

At the hospital I started learning how to do websites. Until then I was paying Grey Ghost and later on, Dirt, hundreds of dollars a month as my website designers. So, I owe it to that night I got drunk on my ass with Beater at Dollies and dropped my digital camera on my foot to my becoming my own website designer. Which proved I had been 100 percent right by writing that satiric essay extolling the virtues of alcohol.

While Howard, Heaven, and Dirt partied for six days and nights at the Exotic Dancer Expo at my expense, I wound up having to sit out the entire convention. On the sixth day, the doctors put me on Coumadin for an entire year to keep thinning out my blood.

Katt, Marriah and Ruby Visit Dollies

Everything was going well when Katt, Marriah, and Ruby drove four-hundred mile to my farm. I had a small room behind my kitchen that I had converted to an office. I had hung several Winchester rifles on the wall above my desk, which gave the room a lot of character. This is where I kept my desktop computer where the three Stimmelators girls hung around while one girl after the other took her turn chatting in the Lost Angels.

Katt had noticed that I had two Japanese replica swords on the coffee table in the living room. Taking the larger sword, she kept pretending to decapitate my penis with it while one of the other girls took our pictures. But once we drove to Dollies everything started to unravel. I can't remember what girls were at Dollies that night. With the exception of Brandy who we picked up on our way to the club.

I dimly remember Alabama working at Dollies that night, but I'm really not sure. Too many years have gone by. At least twenty and I've been living in Thailand too long now. Although I remember the three Stimmelators dancers sitting together at a table in the back room looking glum and miserable. Who, unlike Kasey Karrington, made it very obvious that they didn't want to mix it up with the Dollies girls.

Once we got back to the farm the Stimmelators girls started calling their boyfriends up, then all three of them went to bed, while Brandy and I continued to chat in the Lost Angels. In a way I could hardly blame the Stimmelators girls. Because as I've already mentioned, Stimmelators was a milk toast kind of bar whereas, Dollies was the epitome of sleaziness.

When we all woke up the next morning the Stimmelators girls told me they missed their boyfriends and that they wanted to drive back home. Swallowing my anger, I asked myself, 'How can they be missing their leech boyfriends?' While Brandy seemed perfectly content to stay another night.

I must now distinguish Joey from the Stimmelators girls' boyfriends. Although Joey never seemed to be able to hold onto a job for long, he was still working over half the time. Joey meant well. I had once recommended Joey to Dwight Rovey who was running two crews building grain bins and installing accessories such as fans and propane heaters, control panels, and conveyors at farm steads throughout the entire area.

Dwight often times worked 18 hour days. He was that busy selling and setting up grain drying systems for the farmers. Dwight had become so good at what he was doing and developed such an excellent reputation that he couldn't come close to handling all the business coming his way. So, he hired Larry Brown to run a second crew for him.

Larry was a lot like Dwight, moonlighting at night at a Farmersville tavern after traveling to farmsteads from 6 a.m. on. So, when Joey lit up a joint as soon as Larry brought his crew to a farmer's grain bin, Larry simply lost it, and fired Joey on the spot. Dwight wasn't amused either. Later telling me, “farmers have a lot of confidence in me and Larry. So as soon as they see one of my crew smoking marijuana, they have to ask themselves, '"what kind of assholes is Dwight hiring now?'”

But Joey was only twenty then. I think as he got older that he would have put away his childish ways.

Another good thing about Joey is, he never exhibited the control freak ways I would find later on in so many men. He enjoyed coming to my farm with Brandy and on at least one occasion, Joey, Brandy and I visited Stimmelators together. But there were a lot of other times when he'd just as soon stay at home than travel with Brandy and me.

As far as Brandy was concerned, she sure didn't like the airs the Stimmelators girls were putting on. Which came to a head when Marriah and Ruby kept scolding me for taking them to Dollies and criticizing me in a manner I didn't deserve. Yet Katt surprised the hell out of me by not joining in with the other two girls. On more occasions than I can begin to count she had badmouthed Heaven in the Lost Angels, so I knew how judgmental Katt could get. So, I took her silence to be her way of showing some loyalty to Brandy and me. Because even though Brandy had stopped stripping at Dollies the Indiana girls could always fault her for even thinking about working for such a seedy place.

Photographing Renee's Wedding

I must admit that it surprised the hell out of me, when Renee started messaging me in the chat that she was getting married and she wanted me to be her photographer. Because unlike Katt and Heaven Renee hardly ever came to the Lost Angels chat. Which disappointed Sam just as much as it disappointed me.

But Renee lived up in Michigan, which was another sixty miles farther for me than Stimmelators. So, I drove up to the wedding with Alan Nilman, who had become one of the newest members of the Lost Angels. Alan had tried to convince me to rent a new Single Lens Reflex digital camera that Nikon had just introduced to the market; telling me that it would make all the difference for us while shooting Renee's wedding. The damn thing cost over $6000. But neither Alan, nor I rented one. I think the reason why is there weren't any rentals available.

On paper the Nikon D1 camera that we might have rented didn't impress me much. Because I no longer was shooting with my Kodak Dc40 and had just upgraded to the Kodak Dc-280 which was rated 2 megapixels. So it could resolve over five times what my Dc40 could do. Had we been able to rent a Nikon D1 we would still only be getting a 2.7 megapixels resolution; but I would later be buying a Nikon D1X, which could do around 6 megapixels; but as I would later on be finding out there's a lot more that goes into a camera than how many megapixels it can resolve; such as a faster and better sensor and superior lenses.

But shooting Renee's wedding with the Kodak Dc-280 still wouldn't be the same had I been using top of the line film cameras real wedding photographers were then using. But Renee wanted me to be her wedding photographer, and she didn't care all that much what camera I would be using.

One couldn't ask for a better setting for a wedding. I remember there being a large fenced in area and lots of green grass. It might have been a school, or large club house for the lion's club, or some other civic minded organization. There was a very prominent gazebo in the middle of the large lawn. I was wearing a dark blue suit, which fit in well with the groom's entourage of close friends. I didn't see anyone in just his shirt sleeves, so it was obvious that everyone was taking this wedding seriously.

I found Lee, Renee's husband to be, as a very outgoing and genuine friendly kind of guy who was a little taller than me, making him about six-one or so. While most of his friends were wearing suits, Lee had rented a tux for the occasion.

When I asked Lee what he did for a living he told me that he was a truck driver. Which added to the impression that I was getting from him as being a good ole boy from the deep South, but certainly not a hick by any means.

Renee was dressed in a long white wedding gown–a Vivian Leigh while filming “Gone with the Wind” as Scarlet. But when it came to the brides father giving his daughter away to the groom, I was really surprised that Sam would be giving Renee away to Lee. And brother, did Sam look the part of a kindly father giving his daughter away to the groom.

But as I would keep finding out later on, most of the dancers working for Sam did regard him as a kindly father wishing the best for his daughters.

Once the wedding was over we all adjourned for dinner and some dancing afterwards. There I learned from Renee for the first time that although she hardly frequented the Lost Angels chat room, she had been checking my website out very thoroughly. And not just once, but often over a period of over a year.

From that point on, I would be calling her Mary instead of Renee. Because the real Mary never stripped for very long and from now on, she would be just your average small town woman, who lived a pretty normal life. Except as I would be getting to know Mary better, she was far more than the average woman you would ever be meeting outside the strip clubs.

Doctor Doom Gets a Job with Sam

I would get to know several more strip club owners in the future, but I would never meet anyone quite like Sam with his zest for new toys, a spare house or two, and other noteworthy items. There was the Porsche 928 and the Ferrari that Sam seldom used and a sailboat I never saw. But Sam's newest cash outlay wasn't just for toys. It was to start an entirely new business, and for this he needed an accomplice.

He probably had this new business in mind for a good while. And upon witnessing Doc's talent as a mechanic, let alone Doc's organizational skills, Sam viewed Doc as the right man for what he had in mind, and that was to get into the party limousine business. Sam had also seen Doc show off his Internet skill for sniffing out great deals that neither he, nor I had the patience for.

After getting Sam's phone call making good on his promise to hire Doc when the right time came, Doc told me he'd be leaving my farm for Indiana in a couple of days. Then he chuckled and said, "But I don't know if that hundred dollar car of mine will make it all the way up to Stimmelators."

But the car made it, and Doc started looking around for two limousines. Sam had already gotten one, which he showed to Doc, which was a used Lincoln stretch town car he bought for $12,000. In the next several weeks Doc found two more stretch limos. Including a gorgeous Excalibur Lincoln.

Then Sam put Doc in charge of a new company making Doc his limousine driver, mechanic, and salesman to sell Limousine rentals for weddings, corporate events, taxi service to airports, and school outings to zoos, museums, etc. And then to establish the image of having a successful new business, Sam bought Doc a chauffeurs uniform and hat.

After a month Sam kept pouring more and more responsibility on Doc, such as having him function unofficially as Assistant Manager for his club. Then Sam bought a second club in Peru, Indiana, which is about fifty miles from his main Stimmelators club inNorth Webster, and put Doc in charge of remodeling it.

In everything he did, Doc, was proving himself to be indispensable. So, feeling more secure than he had felt for years, Doc rented a nice house near Lake Webster, which was only a few blocks from the club. Then he moved Donna in with him from New Jersey.

I was very happy for Doc although I was missing his company at my farm. So, I visited him as soon as I could, and planned on staying the weekend with Doc and Donna.

When I got to Doc's new house, I was almost overwhelmed. Lake Webster is a very beautiful lake like many lakes in the area that had made the region a prime getaway for people living in the Chicago area. The house had been freshly painted and overall it had a very pleasant appearance that was fitting for a resort type feel. It was not a large house, and if I remember correctly it had two bedrooms and a comfortable porch. The yard was small, but it had a two car garage where Doc could keep his $100.00 car and one of Sam's new limos.

Inside there were a few things that Doc didn't care for, and that kept Doc and Donna pretty busy with carpenters tools Sam had lent them. I found myself very comfortable there with both Doc and Donna getting up early in the mornings, when Donna would brew a pot of coffee.

Although Doc had become an outstanding student of the Internet, Donna was no slouch. Which gave the couple a strong mutual interest they could share with each other.

Moving Off The Farm To Collinsville

I'm sure a lot of people are wondering why I moved off the farm to Collinsville. I had created an idyllic spot out of an 1865 farmstead that I had moved to when I was thirty. Although it had a 2.5 acre yard, my predecessors had fenced most of it in where they kept hogs, cattle, and chickens. Over the years, the animals had trodden and compacted the ground so much that grass could hardly grow on it and aside from the barn there were several other buildings on it that no longer served any useful purpose whatsoever.

There was a structure built from concrete blocks with a narrow hallway that had served as a small granary. And a small machine shed of tin that had become dilapidated and unsightly over the years. And two small structures for grain storage. One of them for eared corn with walls made from wire. The other out of thin sheet metal where farmers stored shelled corn.

It was cold as hell living in that old Civil War era farmhouse. The chief culprit being that the house had been built over eight by eight treated boards that had been placed over a concrete foundation. Through the years large cracks had formed between the foundation and the eight by eight boards.

When I moved into that house there were only four trees near the house. All four of them being old soft Maples that periodically had been nearly torn apart by strong prairie winds and lightning. Leaving huge branches all over the ground that I had to remove after cutting them into manageable segments with a chainsaw and axe. But since there had been only four trees to start with there was nothing to slow the prairie winds from rushing throrugh the gaps under the house and with winter temperatures sometimes getting to 20 below, it would get awfully cold living inside that house.

So, I got down to work. Borrowing an acetylene torch from a neighbor, I cut the two corn storage bins into pieces that I could haul down to the Litchfield city dump. Then I tore down the fences that used to hem in the livestock. This involved pulling out all the fence posts with a small tractor I had bought. Leveling the ground around the house turned out to be quite a chore. In some areas I could use a small tractor and field cultivator. But, I also had to use a rototiller in the much smaller areas I couldn't get a small tractor into. My rototiller was a small machine that had been designed for preparing seed beds for gardens. My rototiller had a 8 horsepower engine if I remember, which was enough to self propel it so long as I walked behind it and pushed down on its handlebars to enable it to pulverize the hard ground. But there were still spots that the rototiller couldn't penetrate. Where I had to loosen hard compacted earth with a spade. It took days to prepare a seed bed in which I could plant grass.

I still hadn't moved into the farmhouse when I started doing all that hard work, due to my still having a forty hour job in Saint Louis with the Hardy Salt Company. But I'd spend all my weekends there farming 53 acres while leveling the ground for a yard and planting over a hundred trees.

I got the trees from a number of sources. The white and Austrian pines and Spruce trees for my windbreak I bought from several nurseries in the area. While buying small pin oaks and fruit trees from Stark Bros, which was a mail order company from which one could buy a huge variety of trees, shrubs, and flowers. But I could not buy small white oak trees from Stark Brothers, or anywhere else.

White Oak trees are called the "Kings of the Forests" and for good reason. They can grow up to a hundred feet high. They are renowned for being able to branch out horizontally to an equal distance as their heights when you measure their diameter instead of their radius. They live for hundreds of years, are extremely hardy, but they will grow only a foot a year. But since they have large root systems equal to the spread of their branches, it's almost impossible to plant a small white oak and see it survive. My solution was to gather acorns wherever I could find them. I also bought a large number of black walnut trees from mail order outfits such as Stark Brothers and planted them in what would soon become my back yard when they were only two foot high and a third of an inch in diameter.

I planted a lot of trees, that would eventually number over a couple hundred, not to mention all the white oaks I planted as acorns around our large farm pond.

My neighbor and I tore down the two larger buildings on the farm with a log chain and tractor, which we burned and buried. You can't do that today due to the Environmental Protection Agency, which will end up costing a farmer thousands of dollars having the professionals do it. My Dad had renovated the house about the time I moved in. But the renovation was cosmetic only. Although my Dad had a modern fridge, new cabinets, electric stove, and new carpeting put in the kitchen and had put electric wires into the ceiling to heat the house, it still got awfully cold during the winter. Although the electricity heating the ceilings of the house was costing me over $350 a month, there was no stopping the cold prairie winds from coming up under the floors and gushing through all the cracks around the windows.

It would get so cold that I often had to wear gloves while reading books in my living room. My solution was to buy a 1930's coal wood burning stove that I put in the living room and to buy 5 tons of coal that I had a coal mining friend dump onto a concrete slab that had served as a foundation for one of the small grain bins I had removed. Although I had to keep hauling coal into the house to keep the stove going, it at least kept my living room warm.

Twenty years later, the Evergreens in my windbreak were over thirty feet high. Which were large enough to shield the farmhouse from the prairie winds. While my black walnut trees, pine oaks and pecan trees towered over my back yard. I had even built a small generator room on the back side of my exercise room that had a 300 gallon diesel tank and a ten horsepower diesel generator. I had figured that I could run the house for two months should a national emergency occur that would deprive me of electricity.

I had also wired my backyard so that I could light up my entire windbreak that surrounded my house on three sides. Did all the work myself although I didn't know much about electricity except for my hiring a trencher that cut a shallow trench around my yard where I put electrical wiring under the ground. Then I put six chemically treated four by fours in my windbreak and hung electrical light fixtures on top of them. But I took this one step further by hanging additional lights in my trees.

As for the large gaps underneath the floors of the house, I came up with an ingenious solution by hiring my two cousins to build a floor on top of the floor of the living room and kitchen. Then I had them nail two by fours in an upright position on top of the new floor. And had them put insulation between the upright two by fours, which they covered with drywall. A little plastering on top of the drywall, new wall paper, and that was that. I had what amounted to a box within the original walls and floor of the original house which the prairie winds could not penetrate.

The entire place ended up looking very idyllic. Here I would often have parties out in the yard and it would be all lit up at night. I also owned over thirty guns, which I could shoot anywhere I liked, while having lots of strippers visiting me.

So, what was there that was not to like? The Internet, which was so damn S-L-O-W. Because at the farm, my Internet was limited to what it could handle through telephone wires, and I still had to pay pretty substantial phone charges to access. While only 65 miles away Collinsville was now getting cable Internet. My photography was just starting to get into high gear while the Lost Angels chat group was continuing to grow. And although I was farming 560 acres, my Dad had just died leaving me and my sister's the landlord's share of all of our family's farms. So, figuring I'd be now making almost as much money off my new inheritance as I had been farming those 560 acres and constantly having to keep updating all my farm machinery, I decided to move to Collinsville.

******

Due to my sharing hotel rooms with Satin, Marriah, and Jade on Bluff Road, I had long ago started feeling right at home in Collinsville.

On my way back to the farm so many times when I was visiting my Dad in Saint Louis, and later on coming back from the Saint Louis Metro East strip clubs I had noticed a huge house 100 feet over the highway on top of a bluff and wondered what kind of man lived there. It looked like a Frank Lloyd Wright architectural masterpiece; a building like no other; which had to have an owner of impeccable taste.

But it so turned out that the unforgettable home was only one and a quarter miles from the hotel I was staying at with the Dollies dancers. So now, having resolved to moving away from the farm to Collinsville where I would be able to get Internet at blazing speeds, I decided to take a look at the magnificent home that stood alone on top of a bluff.

To my surprise, what I took to be a house wasn't anyone's home at all. Called the architectural building there were a few offices inside the structure. While directly behind it I found the Woodhenge apartment complex. I found the apartments there to be reasonably priced, but I still checked out a few other apartments in Collinsville and found that Woodhenge was exactly what I wanted.

Woodhenge was on the absolute pinnacle of the bluff surrounded by trees which had given it its name: Woodhenge. It had also gotten its name, due to its being so close to the Cahokia Mounds where the mound builders had built a wall out of logs that would later be called: Woodhenge. Causing me to wonder if some of the inhabitants of the Cahokia Mounds had resided right here in Collinsville where I would soon be renting an apartment.

Woodhenge was the perfect place in so many ways. The entrance and exit ramps for Interstate Highway 55 were just one mile away while Highway 55 itself ran just one hundred yards alongside Woodhenge, which one could barely see while driving by it. If one took Highway 55 another mile one could exit onto Highway 155. One could also get to Interstate 64 by driving just five minutes down Highway 155; or by taking the scenic route on bluff road while being skirted by 100 foot bluffs towering over the two roads that was also known as Highway 157.

Woodhenge was only 10 miles from Saint Louis and just 65 miles from my farm. Unless the traffic really got bad I could be at the St. Louis Airport in a little over twenty minutes, which was the same time it had taken my Dad to get there from his St. Louis West County home. And had I been getting my MBA at Saint Louis University twenty years ago and living in Collinsville instead of Saint Louis West County suburbia I could get to all my night classes just as fast.

All around me I had these wide six lane highways that could take me to Saint Louis, Chicago, or down into the Southern states without having to endure the much heavier traffic of the Saint Louis Metro area. While the rent was substantially cheaper on the Illinois side of the Mississippi. And once I had moved into Woodhenge and had gotten used to the Saint Louis Metro East suburbs around it I found that I could get to Southern Illinois State University in ten or fifteen minutes.

There were Chinese and Mexican restaurants close by, and as I've mentioned earlier, a huge assortment of all sorts of restaurants within one mile. Although Collinsville only had 20,000 residents it was part of the Saint Louis Metro East, which had over 375,000 residents. And as for Southern Illinois University, my ex-wife had gotten her B.A. in History there, but she had to drive all the way there from the farm. So, I was already acquainted with its campus and library where I would later on do some research for some of my gun articles I would eventually be writing for "Xtreme Magazine."

Although East Saint Louis was also in the Saint Louis Metro East, and East Saint Louis was widely known as one of the most crime ridden areas in the United States there were also a lot of wealthy suburbs here. Along with one of the best shopping malls in Central Illinois just six miles from Woodhenge.

So, I now understand why so many infamous gangsters from the Saint Louis area had lived on the Illinois side of the river instead of in Saint Louis. And why so many top managers and owners of the Saint Louis Metro East clubs had decided to live on the Illinois side when they could easily live over in Saint Louis.

But for me, one of the best things about Woodhenge is that it was only eight miles from Dollies, C-Mowes, Chameleon, Miss Kittys in one direction, and just ten miles from four of the PT's gentlemen's clubs in Centreville, Brooklyn, and Sauget. Because I had two vehicles, my supercharged Mazda Miata sports car and my Dodge Dakota Sport four wheel drive pickup truck parking at Woodhenge gave me huge advantages that I could not find anywhere. There were small parking slots with roofs overhead that would shield my sportscar from the rain and the snow. With each resident entitled to his own parking slot that still left a lot of room for me to park my pickup truck. The downside was one had to drive up a very steep curving incline to reach the parking lot. So whenever it would snow, most of the residents found that they could not drive up the snow covered incline. Or, if they had already parked up on the bluff, they'd find it very hazardous going down the incline. This had no effect on me whatsoever, because I could always put my Dodge Dakota Sport into four wheel drive.

Most of the apartments had their front entrances off the Woodhenge parking lot. While the front of their apartments opened up to communal balconies that they'd have to share with two or three apartments and other apartment renters. The balconies overlooked a very steep hill shadowed by high trees. My apartment had two bedrooms and a single bathroom measuring altogether around 800 square feet. I would live here for four years before moving into a larger 1,010 square foot unit that had its own private balcony and heated two car garage.

Mistress Mary's Friends Rob a Gas Station

Although I would never have a woman stay with me for a prolonged period of time (with one exception that I will write about later), I don't think more than two or three days went by before I would have female visitors. All of them working for strip clubs.

One night I opened my door after hearing the door bell to find five or six people looking for a place to party. Leading the group was Mistress Mary. There was another stripper with the group who I had done a photoshoot of before who had joined the group. There were three guys in the group who I had never seen before. All of them in their early twenties.

I don't remember what we all did other than the usual clowning around and all of us having a fair amount of alcohol to drink. Although I'm sure I was showing off my digital camera and how I could put all of my pictures into the Lost Angels. I still have pictures of our ad hoc party. What I do remember is Mistress Mary wanting to leave with the guys, and Barbie, who I had done a photoshoot of in my condo before not going with Mistress Mary and the guys. And Barbie calling me hours later to inform me that the three guys had robbed a gas station and been caught by the police. I still don't know if Mistress Mary had been part of the robbery, but if she had, she never got caught by the police.

Candy

One of the things we kept talking about in the Lost Angels was women who had been abused as children. Which later on, made them feel they were dirty, and that led many of them to become strippers and whores. Alex would talk about this often. And later Selena, an entertainer who I would soon be meeting at Visions, and so would Angel. But Angel would become a very special friend who would talk about anything.

When Candy sought me out at Dollies and asked me for help, I wasn't surprised because Candy had heard that I was a good friend of so many of the Dollies girls.

But I was even more surprised when Candy suddenly appeared at my apartment door. A short, slender blonde with a nice figure, Candy was the sort of girl that made a man almost cry to have sex with her. But here she was, calling out for help, and I am not one of those types of guys who is constantly preying on a girl's weakness.

"Jack, I told you at Dollies I need help. Some of the girls were telling me I could come to you and that I could trust you."

This inner voice kept telling me, 'Go for it Jack. She's yours for the taking. Just tell her how pretty she is and how you've always wanted to make love to her, and you've got it in the bag.'

But I couldn't do it. Which brings up my little secret that I will share with all of you who are reading this book. You won't take my advice though, and that's why I've got all these pretty women hanging around me all the time. And you never will unless you pay them a lot of money.

To really get to be friends with all these strippers you can't behave like a moron with your tongue hanging out with a big bulge in your trousers. There's a lot of truth in that old adage, "Treat a lady like a whore, and a whore like a lady." I get on the pole with the girls. I share pictures of them no one else is going to get. Because even if a man has a better camera than mine, and even if he's a far superior photographer than me, he's not going to get the best pictures. The girls have to trust the man taking their pictures. They have to see their photographer as a fun guy who they enjoy being with. And you don't try to fuck these girls unless they ask you to. And when that happens you are going to get it for free. So, here's Candy. Who's wanting something else from me.

"What is it Candy? How can I help you?"

“I am a drug addict, Jack. I do a lot of heroin.”

“So do a lot of girls at Dollies,” I replied.

“But you helped Marriah and Doc. You got Marriah to go to a drug rehab and you got Doc off the shit completely.”

"Yes, Candy. I did all I could to help both of them."

“Then can you help me? Can you take me to the drug rehab in Springfield Marriah and Satin went to?”

“When do you want to go, Candy?”

“Next month. In two weeks.”

“Okay. Then why are you with me now?”

“I am taking Methadone, Jack. I need a ride to the clinic where they give me the shots.”

Where's that?”

“East St. Louis.”

“When do you want to go?”

“Right now.”

Funny thing is, Candy directed me right down into the heart of East St. Louis only a couple of blocks from the police station. I had the top down on my Miata, but when I let her out close to the clinic, she disappeared from my view. There was parking all around me, but I couldn't see anything that looked like it could be a clinic. I didn't think much of it though, and Candy came back ten minutes later.

I took her home to an apartment she told me she was renting, but I never went inside.

A week later she asked me to take her to the clinic again. Which went the same as before with no surprises on a warm summer afternoon. But Angel busted my bubble a few nights later while we were chatting in the Lost Angels at my apartment.

“Where did you take, Candy?” Angel asked flippantly. “What kind of bullshit was she feeding you, Jack?”

“She had me drive her to East St. Louis right downtown real close to the police station.”

“How far from the police station?”

“A block, Angel, although I never saw Candy actually go into a building. So that clinic might have been two blocks from the police station.”

“Jack. There is no methadone drug clinic anywhere near that police station. Candy was having you take her to Johnny's. That's the drug dealer she's getting her heroin from.”

“How do you know, Angel?”

“Because I have friends who are heroin addicts. And sometimes I'd give them a ride to Johnny's.”

“So, you do heroin?”

“No. Never. I have enough problems of my own, and if I ever take heroin it might kill me.”

Marriah does two cartoons for the Death on the Wild Side Cartoon Strip.

When Marriah told me she had a great idea for our cartoon strip, Dirt was all for it. He'd still draw the cartoon and put it on my website and I'd still pay him fifty dollars. Knowing Dirt, I'm sure he was just as curious what Marriah would come up with as I was.

I would usually do the scripts for the cartoons, which I would fine tune for five frames, and leave it to Dirt to do the rest. With Marriah having a few beers with me at my apartment, I took out my notebook and started to write down Marriah's plans.

“Jack, we've got this Boner piece of shit asshole beating the crap out of Lori. I think it's time Boner gets his just desserts.”

“Keep going Marriah.”

“So, we have Boner getting into an argument with Lori and he beats her up. He's drunk on his ass and he goes out in her car to meet up with his friends. He's also doing a lot of drugs. He loses track of time and then he comes up to the state of Pennsylvania, but it's not Pennsylvania, it's Penis-avania. Put a hyphen in that Jack so everyone knows the state's named after a penis. He wanders out to this place that's called Amish Farms and he turns into this big penis. I want him to have the head of a penis for his head and a penis shaft for his body.”

“Sounds like my kind of cartoon already. And I'm sure Dirt will love it.”

"There's this young woman who comes out the door to greet him. She's got what looks like a black nun's habit on and she's wearing glasses. So, Boner goes in thinking he's going to fuck her. But as soon as he goes inside the Amish woman tells him that she wants him to follow her into the basement. So, Boner follows her expecting to fuck her in the basement. But as soon as they arrive in the basement the nun takes off her glasses, and then she takes off her habit. Which leaves her with only a g-string on. She's got this beautiful body and once she takes her glasses off, she's got a very beautiful face. So now she tells Boner, “I'm Dominitra, lick my boots.”

“That will be the end of the first cartoon, Jack. Now we start the second one. Dominitra puts a collar around Boner's neck, which she's fastened a leather strap onto. She has Boner sit on the floor and she announces to him, “Dog, you will see that you are mine.” Then she grabs a red hot brand and starts branding Boner right on his ass. His ass starts to hurt and you can smell his flesh burning. Then she tells Boner, “Get dressed, It's time to get dressed.” In the next frame you see Boner wearing a woman's dress. Then she tells Boner, “Tonight you will eat my shit. Tomorrow you will eat this dress.” By this time Boner's scared shitless, so in the last frame we will have Boner saying, "Fuck this, I'm out of here!" And you see him running right through a brick wall.”

Dirt does a great job drawing the cartoons. While obviously he likes Marriah's bizarre train of thought. I don't even do the script for his last cartoon. Boner finally rejoins Lori (which is Nipples’s real name). He sits on a couch with Lori, but he's still a penis. Lori asks him where he was. Boner replies, “I just come back from Canada. I was fishing with the boys of the Posse.” Who are the other members of Boner's imbecilic gang that is making money from stealing hub caps and dealing drugs. Dirt's cartoon image of Boner is still a penis, but now the penis has his arm around Lori. Boner now tells Lori, “I had to go. We are breaking in a new member.” While Lori's thinking, 'I should kick him out for stealing my money.’ Lori is also thinking, 'How many times have I heard that before?’

Then Boner tells Lori, "I thought of you the whole time," while he still has his arm around her. Then Lori tells Boner, “Alright, um, I believe you.” At this point the image of Boner changes from being a penis to his former self. In the last frame Boner's sacked out on the couch while Lori is telling herself, 'I guess life isn't so bad after all.’

He's only nineteen, but even Dirt understands that most women who get physically abused by their boyfriends nearly always go back to them. And that is why most policeman do not want to get involved in family disputes. Veteran policemen understand that if they physically intervene while a woman is being beaten up by her boyfriend, that the woman will oftentimes attack the policeman once he starts getting the better of the boyfriend who was just beating the hell out of her.

We were such a tightly knit group back then. With our stripper friends confiding in us about everything that had gone wrong with their lives. These were not just idle stories, the kind a lot of strippers might tell their customers to get more money out of them. Dirt and I were not paying the girls anything other than buying them a few drinks. We found the girls we hung around with to be splendid companions who had the same outrageous sense of humor we had.

I Am Warned I Will Be Replaced At Dollies

Nathan might have been a murderer. But he was a good businessman with a progressive outlook that enabled him to foresee the future. He had chosen and continued to back Hawk as his General Manager. Who was an excellent manager who could have transformed Dollies from a seedy hole in the wall into one of the most respected adult night clubs in the United States.

But Nathan was in jail, and Hawk's days as General Manager were rapidly coming to a close. Because Dollies had two owners, one of them dead while the other would soon be spending the rest of his life in Prison. Dollies soon fell into the hands of Steve's widow. Who didn't want to have much to do with the club, which most people could hardly blame her for.

From then on, I would not be allowed to shoot any pictures whenever Steve's widow was visiting the club. As for Hawk, from that point on about the only thing he could do was to keep on getting his salary.

A new manager was about to replace him–the widow's sister. Who until now had been working as a bar girl. I had always gotten along with her, and had even done a photoshoot of her. But it's a very tough and demanding job managing a strip club.

The widow's sister had a boyfriend. Who was a handsome affable fellow I had been getting along with until now.

There's a lot of truth to what I learned while getting my MBA at Saint Louis University. One of the things I would never forget is the Peter Principle. The Peter Principle basically states that people who work for a hierarchy will eventually rise to their level of incompetence. I will cite an example from the American Civil War.

Joseph Hooker, a Union General, had been an excellent combat commander. He was brave, he was smart, and he was aggressive. He had led a division of Union soldiers, and then a corps of 15,000 men or more. So, when several generals of the Army of the Potomac failed to defeat Robert E. Lee's Confederate Army, Lincoln appointed the aggressive Joe Hooker, to lead the Army of the Potomac. Having been given overall command, Hooker failed dismally at the Battle of Chancellorsville. Who Lincoln soon replaced with a new overall commander. Much later Hooker would redeem himself at the battle of Chattanooga by routing the Confederates at Lookout Mountain. The moral of this story is--Hooker was an excellent leader so long as he wasn't given command of an entire army. But when Lincoln promoted him to lead over 100,000 soldiers Hooker rose to his level of incompetence. Then much later he would perform brilliantly, so long as he was following the orders of his superior officer.

And so it was with the woman who replaced Hawk as the Manager of Dollies. Who had the bad judgment of allowing her boyfriend to have too much influence running the club.

It didn't take long for the boyfriend to corner me in the club's bathroom. Who had the temerity to tell me, “I will soon replace you here. Everything you are doing, I will soon be doing.”

Now this guy didn't know a thing about digital cameras, or website design. He didn't have his own chat community such as the Lost Angels. Nor, was he respected by the other Dollies managers. I don't even remember what he did for a living, but it sure didn't have anything to do with topless clubs.

The other two managers were Howard and Doug. Doug was a drinking pal of Howard's. The pair would often hang out at Killians, a bar on Bluff Road that was close to my apartment. I'm sure Killians would terrify a lot of guys, because the place had a lot of customers who could have been actors in a Hell's Angels movie. Howard would have easily fit the part of a Hell's Angel. And so would Doug, a tall long haired man who usually dressed in jeans and flanneled shirts. But I had always found Doug to be an easy going guy who short of being provoked never made problems for anyone. Now Howard, he was tough and big. The kind of man you'd never want to cross. Yet Howard had a gentle heart, which the Dollies girls fully appreciated. And Howard was gobs of fun. Howard was my kind of guy who was nearly always up for all my pranks.

Who Is The Greatest Studmufffin Of Them All?

Beater and I continued to be friends. And so did Howard and me. Howard would oftentimes come into the Lost Angels chats from the Dollies Web TV. But we were soon joined by still another new member, who lived in Toronto, Canada, a few miles from Beater. Who would long live in infamy as the Dirty Dawg.

The man's name was Marshall Shapiro, but all of us in the Lost Angels knew him by his user name, Dawg. Dawg was around 60 back then. Who had earned a living writing advertising copy. But somewhere along the line he had developed a strong interest in strip clubs.

It wasn't long that Dawg visited us on the Illinois East side just as Beater had a few months earlier. And got a hotel room in the same hotel Marriah, Jade, and Satin were staying at. So, it didn't take Dawg very long to become friends with the three strippers.

Most of us in the Lost Angels back then shared the same kind of whacky, I could care less what anyone thinks, sense of humor. Which Marriah had clearly exemplified when she thought out the scripts for two of Dirt's cartoons. To the men in the group, with the exception of How Weird, our lawyer buddy, the girls represented far more than sexual gratification. And that separated us from almost all the customers who frequent strip clubs. We loved them and they loved us because none of us took much of the world seriously at all with its thirst for keeping up with the Joneses.

And Dawg was fitting in so well with the group. Dawg kept glorifying his jetaime sex machine that he wanted to market all over North America. Although he showed me pictures of it, I can't remember exactly how it worked. But I would constantly refer to it as a dildo riding machine, and that Dawg kept bragging how he could strap a woman on his jetaime, which would give his victim an erotic massage that would bring her to orgasm.

While Dawg was visiting two other Lost Angels soon joined us. PlONe flew down from Oakland. While Philip21 drove his car over from Indiana.

Philip21 was one of the first active members in the Lost Angels.He was a farmer who was related to members of the Hardy Salt Company I had been working for before I moved to the farm. His father had drowned in a grain bin of corn and had left his farm to Philip. Having a farm in

Indiana Philip didn't live very far from Stimmelators where he had joined us several times for our parties at the club.

Since we had a big group in Collinsville, we decided to have a big party at the Chinese restaurant, which had a banquet room it used for special occasions. The place was ideal because it was right up Bluff Road from the hotel Dawg, Marriah, Jade, and Satin had been staying at. But the three Dollies girls were not able to make it, for reasons I've long forgotten about. But Alabama came, wearing her nun's outfit. And so did the nurse from Saint Louis who had become friends with Alabama and most of the Lost Angels guys.

Philip21 and PlONe had already met at one of our excursions to Stimmelators, so PlONe had already discovered that Philip21 was addicted to cigarettes. PlONe arrived at the banquet room wearing a hog's head mask to protect himself from Philip21's smoking. Which showed PlONe's phobia against smoking, which he regarded as being much worse than being thrown in a huge trough of pig shit.

We gave Alabama the honor of blessing everyone with a vial of methyl blue, which she invited us all to drink once she had mixed it in several glasses of water. I don't think anyone took her up on it, but Alabama and I certainly did. I still have a picture of Alabama and me together, our lips dyed a deep blue, that indicated that both of us would be pissing blue for the next few hours.

Later in the evening we all hooked up again, where Dawg met Big Howard for the first time.

Meeting Beater and His Pals in Toronto

Several weeks later, I drove my Dodge Dakota four wheel drive to Toronto to meet up with Beater and his friends. All of them living in Burlington, a suburb ten miles outside of Toronto. The first night I arrived I met Beater's ex-strip club manager friend, Chris. All of us got very drunk that night, with four of us driving to four or five Canadian strip clubs. We got down as far as the Canadian side of Niagra Falls with Chris driving us over 100 miles an hour.

The next day I met Dawg for lunch and then we went to a building where Dawg had told me they were shooting a lot of porn. But when we got there, we didn't find anyone shooting porn. The two partners were from Holland. Who we found to be pretty straight up guys. There were several bedrooms in the building where the Dutchmen would be shooting pictures of the girls having sex with men, other women, or masturbating. The concept was to sell video online to customers all over the world. But it didn't pan out that way for the two Dutchmen. Who told us the key to success was to get millions of hits on a website. Which would take eighty hour weeks of hard work to have any chance at getting those kind of hits.

Dawg had been looking for a suitable place he could rent where he could set up his own porn business, which as far as I know he never followed through on.

Dawg never cared much for Beater and his crowd of friends who he regarded as an immature bunch of ruffians. Whereas, Beater and his buddies no doubt felt Dawg was a pervert.

Chid and Beater Come to East Saint Louis

I had already written a few satiric short stories about Canadians such as: "Canada the Menace from the North," in which a Congressman is urging his fellow Congressmen to start a war with Canada on the grounds that the United States needed a war and that Americans could easily defeat Canada. The U.S. could then appropriate large sections of the Canadian Rockies, which were even more beautiful than our own mountains. I also had Canadians playing a prominent role in several of my Dick Fitswell short stories. In my Fitswell short stories, the Canadians were shorter than most Americans and they had shorter dicks. So, the Canadian doctors plotted to amputate part of Fitswell's penis to bring Fitswell's manhood down to a size that would convince Fitswell to stop bragging about his huge cock.

Our arguing about which country had the best beer, my satiric short stories and the comradery that continued to grow between my Canadian friends and the American Lost Angels members soon developed into our Studmuffin contests. Which pitted Howard against Dawg.

By now I had gotten to be reasonably competent doing my own website work. I was spending four or five nights a week drinking with Howard and the girls at Dollies. And after a few tequilas I'd start putting the Studmuffin Times up on my website. Using Wordperfect, I started doing web pages that looked like an actual newspaper. And although I never learned how to use Photoshop I had started getting pretty good using Paintshop Pro to do my graphics arts work.

Howard was of course my accomplice. And I had the digital camera, a laptop computer, and an online connection right in front of the Dollies stage. I'd shoot a lot of pictures of the Dollies Girls that I kept putting into the Lost Angels chats. From time to time we'd even have Crazy Czech driving over from Indiana to participate in all the craziness we were stirring up.

I'd have Alabama on a pool table with Howard crawling up the back of her legs wanting to have sex with her. While Alabama was crying, with actual tears running down her cheeks. I'd have Alabama and Howard in the toilet together pretending to be French Kissing each other. Or, having three other Dollies dancers pretending to molest Howard. I'd take pictures of Alabama and then I'd put Dawg's head on Alabama's body, so it would look like Dawg was using supernatural powers to control Alabama's mind. We would have entire groups of Dollies dancers and customers in the toilet playing with a rubber sheep fuck doll. And I'd have Howard blowing the sheep doll up with his mouth. The idea being that Howard was God and the sheep blow up doll was the son of God.

Doug played the Devil, and I had even brought a pitchfork over from my farm and had Doug wearing a black robe in the toilet while holding the pitchfork.

Eventually Alabama came under the spell of Dawg, and I'd write up the story in the Studmuffin Times. Then I'd have Alex denounce Alabama as a Canadian spy. Which left no choice other than to replace Alabama with Alex as the Chief Commissioner of the Studmuffin Times.

The Dollies girls couldn't get enough of our irreverent antics. While I didn't know quite what to think the Stimmelators girls thought of all of us. And as for Sam, who'd come into our chats every so often, I think he must have thought all of us were completely off our rockers.

Eventually Beater just had to come back down from Canada to set all of us Americans straight. Chris couldn't make it so Beater brought with him another one of his friends.

Chid was still in his twenties. He was a handsome devil, which got me to lying in the Lost Angels chat that Chid was my son. And that I had never realized that I had gotten his mother pregnant. I got a lot of the Dollies dancers believing this line of hog wash. And as I've mentioned, Chid was a really handsome guy. So, it didn't take long for one of the Dollies dancers to latch onto him.

Tori was one of the better looking Dollies girls, and being your typical East Saint Louis stripper she was out for new adventures. After several days of visiting Dollies and several of the other clubs in the area it was time for Beater and Chid to go back to Toronto. But they took Tori with them after promising her that she'd be making even more money in the Canadian strip clubs.

And this turned out to be a huge scoop for my Studmuffin Times. We already had Dawg as our villain, and Howard, the savior of all decent strippers. So what could be better than having one villain than having four or five villains?

So, the Studmuffin Times headlines now read, “Canadians Kidnap Dollies Dancer Tori. While Howard is trying to come up with ideas on how to get her back.” The article then continued to read, “Chid and Beater are keeping Tori chained up as their sex slave, while only unchaining her so that she can work for them in Canada's strip clubs."

And in a way was not all that far from the truth. Because after a few weeks of Beater and Chid, Tori had enough of the whole masquerade. Chid was doing a lot of drugs and alcohol on the money she was making in the Canadian clubs. And although she couldn't wait to come back to Illinois, she didn't have nearly enough money for her plane ticket. So, I ended up having to pay for Tori's safe return to Dollies and getting her out of the hands of those "CANADIAN CRIMINALS".

Howard Becomes Studmuffin of The World

Now that Beater and Chid had totally discredited themselves to the everlasting shame of their Canadian countrymen, it was Dawg's turn to turn Canada into the dust bins of History that most Canadians would want to forever forget.

The Studmuffin Times would continue to quote Dawg claiming that I was bribing all the Dollies dancers to vote for Howard as the greatest stud in the world. Which I couldn't blame Dawg for doing considering that I was Howard's campaign manager. And although Howard had the face of a man who had just come out of a knife fight, he was very popular with the Dollies dancers who saw him as a Hell raising rough neck who'd be up for any prank the rest of us could come up with.

But being both the owner and the editor of the Studmuffin Times I had the press on our side. Howard would wind up winning the Studmuffin Contest hands down. But I have to admit that articles such as this one ended up finally doing Dawg in:

Fantastical Non-Sense dreamed up from our Tequila bottle at the Dollies Playhouse Strip Club

Dawg Explains

And he sure has a lot of explaining to do.

In a move unforeseen by political analysts and students of the coming International Studmuffin Contest Dawg has jolted both his friends and his critics by calling in his opponents campaign manager, Jack Corbett, just to set the record straight and to belay any doubts about his honesty. The interview that follows shows the real Dog behind the man.

Jack Corbett: “Got a beer Dawg? I've come a long way to gaze at your carcass.”

Dawg: “Welcome to the Big City. Toronto's not like that little podunk place you seem to like so much...East St. Louis.”

Jack Corbett: “Yeah...but the girls are a lot prettier down here than they are up there, Dawg. Must be those Canadian ice storms they have up there that permanently freezes their faces into masks of putty.”

Dawg: "I called you up here to set the record straight."

Jack Corbett: "You can't do that with a crooked record. Even I can't do that for you Dawg, no matter how much beer you give me."

Dawg: "Go ahead and ask me any question. My integrity rests on my answers and I am fully prepared."

Jack Corbett: "Okay. Did you torture Sister Margarita into sending out all those emails that portray her as a Judas betraying her American friends?"

Dawg: "Sure I did. Why do you ask?"

Jack Corbett: "Why did you torture her?"

Dawg: "I like making young pretty girls squirm. Anything wrong with that?"

Jack Corbett: "I think there is, but I just can't seem to remember the reason right now. I had six tequilas before coming here."

Dawg : "Okay....You got it out of me. I asked her to do porn flicks a year ago and she wouldn't do them. She really pisses me off."

Jack Corbett: "Hey now, you are talking about my friend. Now we cannot even use her as the American commissioner. Her life's in danger. Ever since you sent those Plug agents out. By the way, can you explain exactly what Plug is?"

Dawg: "Plug is the Canadian equivalent to the American CIA. The name originated with the Canadian breweries: Labatt and Molson, and a few smaller ones. As everyone knows Canada's main claim to fame is its breweries, so the breweries pretty much controlled things around here. Of course now I control just about everything now that the beer quality has gone down and the breweries have lost most of their clout."

Jack Corbett: "Alright, we might just let you off the hook if you can call off your Plug watchdogs. Get them off Sister

Margarita's back."

Dawg: "I can't."

Jack Corbett: "Why not?"

Dawg: "I bribed all those guys w with 1000 cases of Creemore beer."

Jack Corbett: "No wonder you can't get them to stop stalking Sister Margarita. Those guys probably hate your guts. At least you could have sent them better beer such as Molson."

Dawg: "Creemore's the best. Every blue blooded Canadian knows that."

Jack Corbett: "It's horse piss and you know it, Dawg. Beater and I tried it one night. I almost got sick and he ended up throwing up all night long."

Dawg: "Can't call them off, Jack."

Jack Corbett: "Does winning the contest justify terrorizing a sweet young thing like Sister Margarita?

Dawg: "I will win at any costs. I will do anything to win. Howard must be stopped."

Jack Corbett: "Why? He's my buddy and drinks tequila with me all the time. Why don't you just admit it. That he's got you beat. Do you believe in self flagellation? Why punish yourself? No one can beat Howard? He's the best Studmuffin yet. Even Casanova was a piker compared to Howard."

Dawg: "I always win. I pull out all the stops and if you guys know what's good for you, you will get a new candidate. Someone who's easy to beat."

Jack Corbett: "Like who?"

Dawg: "Why don't you run? Hardly any girls will vote for you."

Jack Corbett: "Dawg--this whole thing is very important to the future of the United States."

Dawg:	"Why is it?"
Jack Corbett:	"Because you stand for pornography and making all women into witless sex symbols."
Dawg:	"Porn is good."
Jack Corbett:	"Okay. Let's get to it. What do you like about porn?"
Dawg:	"It makes me feel important. Because when I am behind that camera I am the one who is in control. Besides, it often makes the girls so horny when I'm shooting them that they want it right then and there."
Jack Corbett:	"Dawg-This whole Studmuffin Contest has become a country versus country kind of thing. You seem to have something against the U.S."
Dawg:	"Sure I do. The United States has become a land of perverts."
Jack Corbett:	"But you just told me you like to do porn. What does that make you?"
Dawg:	"I just shoot it. After that I am not responsible for what happens. These guys watching it makes them perverts."
Jack Corbett:	"Getting back to Canada. Why is it so important for you that Canada wins the Studmuffin Contest?"
Dawg:	"I think it is high time that Canada reaches its destiny as the finest country in the world. We have better scenery than the United States. Our women are nicer. We have a better health care system. Our cities are better kept up. Our toilets work better. Our sewers don't smell as bad. And our beer is better. It is time that Canada controls the rest of the world."
Jack Corbett:	"And why do you think your winning the Studmuffin Contest will achieve that?"
Dawg:	"The world needs a hero and I think it should be me. Look at all these guys getting these gorgeous babes pregnant: Guys who can't hold a job. Who won't work.

Who are whipped with ugly stick. Whose brains are rotted with stupidity. And these gals are fucking these guys. Can you believe it? We are truly living in a world of the anti-hero. The stupider you are and the weaker you are the more babes you will get. It is up to me to reverse that trend."

Jack Corbett: "What about that dildo riding machine you have. The one that you put women astride and that vibrates them to an electronic frenzy."

Dawg: "I think it's a good deal."

Jack Corbett: "Why's that?"

Dawg: "Because it is better that a woman ride that thing and stay with it then taking on the guys she's likely to end up with if she doesn't get off on the dildo rider."

Jack Corbett: "Can you please explain?

Dawg: "I would say that more than half the women in North America feel a lack of confidence with a real man...a man who is good looking, courageous, intelligent and a man of his word. So they end up going to the brain dead degenerates and create a race of retards. Far better for them to live with a machine like the jetaime machine. This is something they can feel confident in....that won't abuse them, and that won't go to other women. So, if they are too far gone to get a real man at least they can take comfort in a set of batteries."

Jack Corbett: "I guess I've had enough to drink. Thanks for the twelve pack Dawg. It was good going down and that was a great interview. I'd say I hope you win, but Howard is going to win anyway."

The Pimp Tee Shirts

By this time I had developed a regular business relationship with the owner of Five Star Graphics in Springfield, Illinois. My first order was for the Pink Giraffe shirt I had designed to promote my novel, Death on the Wild Side. Then I ordered the black Alpha Pro jackets for the most active members of the Lost Angels, such as Jade, Marriah, Dirt, Satin, Heaven and Katt. Then the Beater Meat t-shirt to honor Beater's first arrival in Illinois. Then came Beater Meat II, and Dollies Trendy Toilet Sex featuring Alabama drinking whiskey on the Dollies toilet in her nun's outfit. Then, I came up with my greatest masterpiece, the Pimp t-shirt.

I might have been an excellent photographer, but when it came to drawing or doing cartoons I was hopeless. But I came up with the idea for the Pimp t-shirt, and then I borrowed from two of my friends what really made the Pimp t-shirt a real classic. I had Five Star Graphics put a picture on the front of the t-shirt. Grey Ghost had done a lot of Boner cartoons. The one I chose for the t-shirt had Boner sitting in the weeds outside a strip joint waiting for his dancer girlfriend to come back from work. On his shoulder is a large rat, who is Boner's brother, Squeeky. Boner's out of money so he asks Squeeky, “When is the bitch coming back from work?” The back of the t-shirt reads in large lettering, “Pimp, the Pond Scum who lives off his girlfriend.” But I owe this one to PlONe who started calling the leech boyfriends of dancers, “Pond Scum.”

I ordered one-hundred Pimp t-shirts from Five Star Graphics for something like $4.00 each, and sold a number of them for ten to twenty dollars; others I just gave away; a lot of dancers bought them; while ironically a guy who was living off his dancer girlfriend also bought one, which I found quite amusing since he never considered himself a leech.

I will never forget my sitting at the bar one night at C-Mowes when a dancer told me she'd give me twenty dollars for a Pimp t-shirt. But the only one I had with me was the one I was wearing on my back. So, I sold it to her right off my back and walked out of C-Mowes shirtless.

I Have No Fingers

It finally came time to meet Audrie---though the wheels had been set in motion while I was still living at the farm. As another one of my jokes I had set a tip jar on a table at Dollies, asking the dancers to help pay my car expenses to Florida where I was going to meet Audrie, the owner of an English escort service.

From the farm it would have cost me close to a dollar per minute to call either England or Canada. But I had just obtained a new long distance carrier that had dropped its International phone rates to twelve cents a minute to either Canada or England.

I have to admit that there's something twisted in my brain. Because whenever something monumental happens such as dirt cheap new phone rates, my mind goes into hyper gear as it conjures up new wacky ideas.

Audrie had just been coming into the Lost Angels as Belnea. But after she had started being active in the Lost Angels, I decided to put her in the personality profiles. We used the personality profiles to introduce new members to those who were most active in our chats. This normally included the members' pictures.

Audrie had put a picture up on her profile that advertised her escort business. What she hadn't included was the phone number for her escort agency. I planned to pull a big joke on Audrie, but to be able to pull it off I needed her phone number. So, as the fearless leader of the Lost Angels group I emailed Audrie asking for her phone number, advising her to allow me to add her phone number to her personality profile that advertised her escort service.

After Audrie emailed me her phone number, I called it, expecting to hear the voice of a receptionist.

> "Is this the escort service I see advertised in the Lost Angels Personality Profiles?" I asked the voice on the other end.
>
> "Yes it is. What can we do for you?"
>
> "My name is Jim Rolly. I'm American and I am coming to England next week. I want good female company."
>
> "I'm sure we have someone with us who can provide that."

“What kind of services do you provide and where are you located?”

“We are in Manchester. As for services, you can expect the usual kind of thing. We start at $200 an hour, which can go up or down for extra hours depending on our arrangement, and as far as sex is concerned that will be up to you and your escort.”

“May I ask you what your name is?”

“Audrie. I'm the owner here.”

“Well Audrie. I have a problem.”

“What's that?” “I don't have any legs.”

“That's no problem. My girls are very understanding with men who have disabilities. What did you say your name is again?”

“Rolly. I call myself that because I'm no more than a torso on a skateboard and my friends have to roll me around.”

“Well Rolly. I am sure that whichever one of my girls goes with you that you will find her to be very empathetic.”

“Yeah, but Audrie. That's not the half of it.”

“What's that?”

“I don't have any arms either. The doctors cut them off just past my elbows after I had a car accident.”

“Well, Mr. Rolly my girls are very understanding.”

“But you don't understand Audrie. When I get sexually excited I can't help myself. Because my arms are no more than flippers and I start flipping them around when I am aroused, and then the girl who is with me starts laughing so hard that I lose my erection.”

“Oh my God. That's awful Mr. Rolly.”

“Yeah, it really is Audrie because my real name is Jack and you have really been had."

“Why Jack. Is it really you?”

“Yes, Audrie. Got you really going didn't I?”

“Why you bloody bastard. In one month I’m coming to the U.S. and I”m going to look you up and give you what’s coming to you.”

The Escort Service Madame's Villa

I can't kick much about how the Englishwoman treated me. Which, I'm now going to tell all of you whining Englishmen who keep complaining about English women now that I've been living in Thailand the past fifteen years.

In Illinois I was almost laughing out loud whenever Audrie started talking about a villa she would be renting near Disney World in Orlando, Florida. Until I actually got there driving my Miata sports car.

Audrie had a nice sized living room, so there was nothing extraordinary about that. And three bedrooms, one for her two children, one for her secretary who she had brought along, and one for herself. But what set Audrie's "villa" apart from most large hotel suites was that it had its own swimming pool inside the suite itself.

But after having an argument with her secretary, Audrie sent her back to Manchester.

I had arrived around 7 p.m. when Audrie greeted me at her front door. There were no surprises in her appearance because she turned out looking the same as the pictures she had inserted into our Lost Angels chats. Audrie had already gotten a pizza that she shared with her two children and me. Then she brought out a beer from her refrigerator.

"I bought a few bottles of Budweiser for you, Jack, because I keep hearing you and Beater arguing about which is better, Molson or Budweiser, in the Lost Angels."

"Thanks Audrie. That Molson isn't half bad, but you will never see me ever admitting that in the Lost Angels."

"That Beater's a twit anyway."

"Twit? What do you mean by that?"

"It's an English expression, Jack. It means Beater's a stupid, silly boy."

I wound up staying three days with Audrie. Who, in general didn't think much of most Englishmen. The first day I treated Audrie and her son and daughter to Sea World, which set me back $170.00 for four tickets. While Audrie paid for all of our lunches at Long John Silver. When we got back to her villa, she made steak dinners for all of us while I chatted in the Lost Angels with PlONe and several of the other members. Then we had several beers together that she had paid for.

The next day, Audrie treated her two children and me to the "Wide World of Animals," costing her $170.00. Once again, Audrie paid for my lunch and made dinner for everyone that night.

I found Audrie to be excellent company. She was funny. She laughed at all my jokes, and she didn't make up outrageous stories. While surprisingly she had a four year college English degree. Before I left, Audrie asked me if I might be interested in helping her relocate to the United States where she would startup a new escort service.

Starting an escort service in the U.S. was an exciting thought. And might have turned out to be very successful, as Audrie had years of experience running an escort service in Manchester. And obviously being very successful at it, due to her ability to buy plane tickets for her two children, her secretary, and herself and being able to rent her "villa" in Orlando, Florida, for several weeks.

But, I had my own agenda going to Exotic Dancer's annual Las Vegas conventions, getting up to Stimmelators in Indiana once a month, or hanging out with dancers, not just from Dollies, but also: Visions, Platinum Club, C-Mowes, and Miss Kittys. My plate was already full. In the coming months my plate would become inundated by even more strippers and strip clubs.

Leeches Get Me Kicked Out Of Dollies

The Lost Angels started a tradition it would continue every year. After all, if the Exotic Dancer Magazine can have an awards party at its annual Las Vegas Expos, why can't we? I had reasoned.

So, we had our 1998 awards party at Dollies. Our group had decided to award prizes in twenty different categories. I wound up buying 20 trophies from a shop in Collinsville that specialized in sports trophies that schools awarded to students who had excelled in football, basketball, and other extracurricular activities. With the help of Jade and Alex I was able to provide the shop owner with titles he should put on our trophies.

We ended up with 20 different categories the Lost Angels could vote on at our upcoming awards party at Dollies. Members of the Lost Angels could attend our awards party in person, or join us in the Lost Angels chat. Who would now vote for: "The Lost Angels Dancer of the Year, This Year's Most Promising Dancer, Best Female Bullshitter, Best Male Bullshitter, Worse Female Bullshitter, Worse Male Bullshitter, Most Photogenic Dancer, Most Unreliable Male, Most Unreliable Female, Biggest Female Drinker, Biggest Male Drinker, Most Obnoxious Female, Most Obnoxious Male, Most Derelict Female, Most Derelict Male, Humanitarian of the Year, and Leech of the Year, etc..."

The "Best Dancer of the Year" award went to Nipples who had been the inspiration for my main female character in Death on the Wild Side, even though none of us had seen anything, or heard anything of Nipples for several months. While the "Most Photogenic Dancer" award was a split decision between Heaven and Samantha. Samantha being a Dollies dancer who often drank with me, but hardly ever came into the Lost Angels chats. The "Best Male Bullshitter" trophy went to Dawg, who won a second trophy for being the "Most Obnoxious Male." Although technically we would have awarded the trophy to Dawg's Jetaime dildo fucking apparatus. But couldn't on account of the Jetaime being an inanimate object. We all found Mistress Mary guilty for being the "Most Obnoxious Female" in the group.

I got "The Best Prankster" award hands down largely due to the way I had duped Audrie with my "have no fingers, have no leg's" lies I had told her on the telephone. While Jade got the trophy for being the "Most Gutsy Woman" in the Lost Angels group. Jade got a second trophy, which she co-shared with her new boyfriend, Derf, who had become very active in the Lost Angels. This was for being, "A Match Made In

Heaven."

The "Most Unreliable Male" trophy went to Chid, for convincing Tori to go to Canada and then leaving her high and dry until I paid her airfare home. Leandra, a Dollies dancer who is hardly worth mentioning here received two trophies, one for being the "Most Unreliable Female," the other for being the "Worse Female Bullshitter."

Tommy, who ran Chameleon got the "Humanitarian of the Year" award, hands down. With his most humanitarian acts being cited by girls who had worked for him for his fining any girl who either didn't show up for her shift, or who came late. Tommy had two phone lines at Chameleon; one for his bar business; the other for his tow truck business. So, if anyone needed a tow or someone wanted to speak to him even about bar business, he would use the toll truck telephone number. But Tommy forbade his girls from ever calling him on the toll truck line, requiring them to use his club phone line. To use an example of why Tommy was considered such a humanitarian: suppose a girl was seeing a Doctor and her shift starts at 5 p.m. So, she calls Tommy at 4:45pm to inform him she's running a half an hour late. Tommy would deliberately not answer any calls on his club line in the time frame he believed dancers would be trying to call in late. And then he would charge the girls $100.00 for being late. While denying that the girls had ever tried to call in late.

I will have to admit that I felt such a warm tender feeling in my heart for Tommy that I personally went to Chameleon to give him his "Humanitarian of the Year" trophy, which almost brought him to tears as he took the trophy from me while pondering all the unselfish things he had done in his life.

By this time Alabama was almost nine months pregnant thanks to Rocci, her young boyfriend who lasted all of two weeks as a Dollies DJ. Now jobless, Rocci was living with Alabama who kept supporting him on her dancer earnings. By the night of our awards party Alabama was only a week from dropping her first child. Yet, here she was, still dancing and still collecting tips from her customers even though her once slender body had grown corpulent from her advancing pregnancy.

The whole situation was pretty repugnant to most of the Lost Angels. Who gave the couple the "Match Made in Hell" trophy. I had also gotten a "Leech of the Year" trophy from the Collinsville shop owner, but somehow Alabama must have caught wind of our plot, and stolen it from the bag of trophies we had put behind the bar.

Being a strong believer in Murphy's Law, that if something can go wrong, it will go wrong, I now put my backup plan into action. I had bought twelve live leeches from a bait and tackle shop near Alton, Illinois, which I put in a little jar that I filled with water. So when I found that Alabama had swiped the "Leech of the Year" trophy I went out to my car, and came back into the club with my jar of leeches.

Sidling up next to Rocci who was standing near me at the bar, I addressed the entire crowd:

"And here are 12 live leeches, which is a very special award I purchased for our "Leech of the Year." This leech has been living off his dancer girlfriend for the last year. And now here she is at Dollies with his child. She is 8.5 months pregnant and having to dance while he sits around her place drinking beer. I now proudly award Rocci who is standing right next to me, the Lost Angels "Leech of the Year Award."

I shit you not. Knowing that I could knock him down in a heartbeat, Rocci didn't know what to do. He actually accepted the jar of leeches I gave him and shook my hand.

Minutes later I pulled my Miata sports car next to Howard and Alex who had her car parked in front of Dollies. Sitting in the drivers seat she had her car window rolled down as she talked with Howard standing next to the car door. Suddenly, we saw a blonde come outside, advancing straight towards us. Although pregnant with her body bloated, she was still a striking girl. Which is one of the worse things about it----a girl who had been slender and still a very attractive girl reduced to dancing in an advanced pregnant condition, practically naked on the stage when she could have done so much better.

"Jack, I have something for you. (it was me she wanted, and keep in mind that my Miata was going topless). Here is your award for being "Fuckhead of the Year!"

Throwing her drink in my face, Alabama swung on me half heartedly as the liquid doused Howard's coat and got on Alex as she sat behind the wheel. I don't know if she meant to hurt me, but somehow I don't think she did as I pulled back my head and she missed by a mile. The three of us watched her go back into the club looking very much alone.

I laughed all the way home, my face still wet. I don't think it was tequila or a mixed drink but plain water. I came back to the club two days later, arriving at 10:15 PM on a Monday evening after a very important and productive business appointment. The girl who had gotten the awards for us and who had done such a fine job was sitting in a car when I pulled up in my Dodge Dakota four wheel drive. As I was getting out with my laptop and camera she came up to me saying: “I want to spare you the surprise and embarrassment, but you've been barred from the club, and I've heard you are never to be allowed back in.”

Selena and Sahara

In those days the strip club scene in the Saint Louis Metro East was dramatically different from what I had found in San Francisco. And from what many of my friends would tell me later, from just about anywhere else in the United States. It was the best, being the most fun, one of the least expensive, and raunchiest if that's what a man was looking for.

As I have mentioned earlier, there were a lot of good highways in the Saint Louis Metro East that were not heavily trafficked.
And some very scenic two lane roads such as Bluff Road. The area had a lot of excellent strip clubs and bars that might stay open as late as 8 a.m. While due to the area's light trafficked streets and highways permitted easy and quick travel throughout the area.

One has to stay here for a long time to be able to appreciate the areas virtues. That started with a 100 mile network of outstanding bicycle trails. Many of them had been created from abandoned railroad lines with asphalt paths replacing old railroad tracks. On which bicyclists could now pedal through all the old train tunnels. Both the Illinois and Mississippi Rivers were close by, providing some of the most spectacular bicycle trails in the country.

By now I had gained thirty pounds from all the drinking I was doing in the clubs. Finding an excellent bicycle shop in Edwardsville close to the university campus, I plunked down $1,200.00 for a gorgeous road bike from Specialized, a company that was selling bicycles costing as much as $7,000.00. The model I chose was the Allez, which means “Go” in French. My bike had a steel frame, which made it heavier than the new carbon fiber bikes that competitive bike racers were now buying. Even so, it still weighed just 22 pounds and was light enough to allow me to average 19 miles an hour over a one hour ride.

I could get on one of the bike trails from my apartment and not have to travel more than a mile on a public street to start riding on a smooth asphalt surface that converged with other bicycle trails. But since I owned a pickup truck I could put my bicycle into the pickup's bed, and drive a few miles to other trails. One of my favorites started at the old Chain of Rocks Bridge on the Mississippi River. This bridge was right on the old world famous Highway 66, which like the bridge had been abandoned to all motorized traffic. The old 66 had been replaced by Interstate Highway 55, which was now using a new bridge to cross the Mississippi one mile from the Chain of Rocks Bridge. The Chain of

Rocks Bridge was still being kept in good repair so that bicyclists, pedestrians, and runners could still traverse its one mile length. So, I'd take my bicycle to the old bridge and park my pickup truck on the Illinois side of the Mississippi; remove my bike from my pickup's bed; and ride it one mile across the bridge into Missouri. At this point where the Chain of Rocks Bridge ends on the Missouri side of the river there's a parking area for tourists that leads to another bicycle trail that skirts the Mississippi River all the way to the Saint Louis Arch. This trail is eleven miles long. My routine taking this route was to leave my pickup truck on the East side of the Chain of Rocks Bridge and pedal all the way down to the Saint Louis Arch. I'd then pick my bicycle up in one hand and carry it up the steps to the Arch where I would down a lot of water from a drinking fountain at the foot of the Arch.

This amounted to a twenty-four mile round trip. But I'd often take other trails throughout the area, which oftentimes took several hours to cover fifty miles.

Although there were a lot of seedy areas on the Saint Louis East side, I found much of it to be absolutely stunning.

So, by the time I had gotten barred out of Dollies I was socializing with a lot of dancers from clubs all over the area. From Visions I had already been seeing a fair amount of Angie and had even taken her to Shaw's Botanical Gardens on the Missouri side of the river. Then I met Sahara one night at Visions.

I already had become well acquainted with Sahara while she was working as a cocktail waitress at Visions when I used to take Nipples into the club. Back then Sahara was a very pretty woman, who I had always found to be sympathetic with me whenever Nipples was showing her violent side; but when I saw a slender dancer wearing a tight fitting tiger outfit; I didn't even recognize the woman as my old pal who used to commiserate with me about my latest misadventures with Nipples. This time I saw a different Sahara who must have lost 20 pounds to get into her tight fitting tiger getup.

By this time I was buying drinks for several of the Visions dancers. This included Charli's daughter although she would never become one of my regular drinking buddies. But about the time I was getting reacquainted with Sahara another dancer started hanging out with me at the bar.

Selena was one of the top money making dancers at Visions, oftentimes making $200 to $300 a night. By the time I was making Visions my second home after getting kicked out of Dollies, I had started bringing my laptop into the club. On several occasions Jade would accompany me with the two of us oftentimes winding up in the VIP Room. Sometimes I'd be pretty intoxicated, which made me a lot more aggressive than usual. This often resulted in Jade and me doing a lot of impromptu digital photoshoots that involved whomever we could get to join us in our VIP Room escapades.

Knowing I had been doing a lot of digital photography and that I was also a writer, Selena would often join me at the bar to ask me to show her my latest digital pictures. Or, if I was writing a new short story on my laptop what the story was all about. And oftentimes when I brought other dancers into the club with me, or a male friend or two, Selena usually wound up at my table.

A lot of times Selena would pass out on her bar stool during the middle of her shift. Sometimes she'd wake up to continue whatever she had been doing before passing out. While other times, Sahara would have to drive Selena home.

Then we got the good news that Selena was going to get married in Las Vegas. And that she'd soon be living over a hundred miles from Visions with a man, who had an excellent job with a bank.

So, although we didn't see anything of Selena for a few months, she'd still participate in the Lost Angels chat. Until finally she was able to talk her husband into bringing her back to the Saint Louis Metro East for several days. So, I offered Selena and Greg the 2nd bedroom in my apartment, a proposition they readily accepted. But it turned out that PlONe was going to visit us the same weekend.

Since I had recently been barred out of Dollies, young Howard and I had been meeting each other at other clubs in the area. One of the clubs was C-Mowes, which had barred me for life because I had beaten up Larry, its bouncer. However, I found my situation with C-Mowes to be reversed once Art Mowe discovered that Larry had been embezzling money from the club. I suppose Larry must have thought his boss to be easy pickings as soon as the Feds put Art Mowe in the penitentiary for tax evasion, but by the time Art Mowe got out, he had learned all he needed to know about Larry. Who took Art Mowe's place in the penitentiary while Art Mowe reinstated me in his club. And that pleased (lawyer) Howard and me to no end, due to C-Mowes giving us a good price on the macho mugs of beer the club was selling us.

So, now that Art Mowe started viewing me as a good guy who had knocked the teeth out of his embezzling bouncer's mouth, I asked for permission to bring Selena into C-Mowes, so I could do a special video and photoshoot of her.

I had already started doing a website for C-Mowes by now. While C-Mowes had redone its upstairs from being a seedy area where the dancers could do short times with their customers, to an entire second bar area. While the general atmosphere of the main bar downstairs was very ordinary and tavernish, the new upstairs was utterly delightful. Although it didn't have the cutting edge lighting and flashy overall appearance of a Platinum Club or Visions, the new upstairs had a very comfortable dance hall atmosphere that had a railing one could look over to view the main bar below, which appealed to me immensely due to my weakness for two level rustic bars that would allow me to view the action downstairs from an upstairs balcony.

I had bought a new Sony movie camera just for the occasion. So, after our group finished having dinner at Applebee's we found Howard and one of his dancer girlfriends' waiting for us at C-Mowes. But since C-Mowes had a fair number of customers upstairs and had several of its dancers scheduled to take their turn on the pole, we were allowed to shoot video of Selena for only two songs.

You can still see the two short videos of Selena dancing on the C-Mowes stage on my website, looking sad and forlorn. The shitty music the club was playing didn't help. But once we all got back to my apartment everyone's moods started to change. Howard was in rare form, making speeches about whores and timid men he viewed as pussies. And while Selena and Greg had been solemn while I was shooting her video at C-Mowes, both lightened up once Howard got into high gear.

I Start Writing For "Xtreme Magazine"

Everything started coming together for me in the second half of 2000. Grey Ghost and I had our annual exhibitor's booth at the Exotic Dancer 2000 Expo, but this time the Exotic Dancer convention layout had changed. Our booth was smaller than it had been before while it adjoined two other booths. Whereas, in previous expos all the booths were separated from each other by a few feet, which set them off from each other as totally distinct entities. One might say we weren't getting our moneys worth and accuse Exotic Dancer of cutting a few corners.

But being nestled right up between two other booths was the best thing that could have ever happened to me. For one thing, both Allan and PlONe had joined our booth at this convention. I also had Lori, from Visions with us, whose room and airfare I had paid for. So, our booth was a pretty lively spot compared to many others at the Expo.

Tina Toy's booth was to our immediate right. Tina was sexy and vivacious. So, our having a busy booth and Tina Toy's booth being right next to us, our little section of the trade show drew a lot of visitors.

This is where Leah Layne and I became well acquainted.

I had seen Leah Layne a few times before at one or two of the Saint Louis Metro East Clubs. At Miss Kitty's someone pointed her out as Miss Nude Illinois. I can't be sure now, but I think she had just won the Miss Nude of Illinois title at Big Al's, and then she had gone to Miss Kitty's to celebrate. Miss Kitty's being one of the first clubs Leah had ever stripped at. Although I never met Leah that night at Miss Kitty's I got the overall impression that she was inaccessible to unknown photographers such as myself.

My impression of Leah did a complete one-eighty once she started visiting our booth, however. Gone was the haughty veneer of her Miss Nude Illinois title, which had been replaced by a super friendly, totally unpretentious woman, who was obviously enjoying our little corner of the convention.

At the Exotic Dancer Las Vegas Expos there was always a favorite bar where all the conventioneers hung out at. This year the expo was being held at Mandalay Bay, while the previous year it had been held at Caesar's Palace. But it didn't matter where the convention was held. Because all of us associated with the Expo would eventually find each other at the same bar. So, when Grey Ghost first entered the bar, Leah

Layne, ran up to us and invited us to join her at her table where she was having a few drinks with several other Feature Entertainers.

I'm sure that Leah was pretty impressed with Grey Ghost, who had this cocky air about him and the personality and expertise to back it up. But by now I was getting the impression that Leah liked being around me, and that I had been the main reason for her seeking us out. Over the upcoming years my experiences with Leah would prove that I had been correct in my initial assessment of her.

By this time I had already published several of my Dick Fitswell short stories with "The Wild Times." Since most of the strippers from the Saint Louis Metro East clubs found Fitswell with his 18 inch penis to be hilarious, I set out trying to get my Fitswell stories published in other adult magazines. I found the representatives for several adult magazines at the trade show who I sought out to see if they were interested in carrying my Dick Fitswell short stories.

Foremost among them was "Xtreme Magazine," which has its own exhibitor's booth, which it was not sharing with any other vendor. Even more impressive was the presence of three or four men who were all wearing their "Xtreme Magazine" tee shirts. But the most striking thing that I found out about Xtreme, was the fact that it was an East Coast adult outfit that was circulating its magazines throughout the New York, Tri-State, Mid-Atlantic & New England areas.

Now let's face it. When the East Coast is mentioned, and especially New York City, you have to be impressed. Now I'm not about to contend that you are going to have a favorable impression. But you will be impressed one way, or the other. The New York Times is probably the best known and best financed newspaper in the world. You might hate it. You might think it's too liberal. But you are going to have some opinion or another simply because the New York Times is the Big Apple of newspapers. And as far as people from the East Coast are concerned you might think they are snooty, that they are pretentious snobs, or that they lack good ole fashioned Mid-Western common sense. But you are going to have an opinion of them one way, or the other. So I made it my mission to get over to the "Xtreme Magazine" booth as often as I could without making myself appear too solicitous.

I found the owner of "Xtreme" to be a man of few words who had the uncanny knack of being able to size people up he was meeting for the first time. This was a man who could be very abrupt with people who he felt were wasting his time. I almost felt that way when I first met Andy, who seemed very busy talking to two other men. But when I mentioned that I was a writer who was already publishing articles for another adult magazine, Andy politely told me to talk to his editor who was quietly sitting alone at the booth in sharp contrast to the tall, burly owner who obviously preferred standing to a sitting position.

Andy preferred standing to sitting, due to his aversion to being unnoticed by people around him. Whereas I found Jeremy, his editor with "Xtreme" to be far more quiet. But who could still sell himself whenever it was required of him.

When Jeremy started reading my Dick Fitswell stories his face broke into a smile.

"I'm not only the editor of Xtreme. I do a lot of articles myself. Let me show you. I couldn't help laughing out loud when Jeremy start ed showing me the horror scope he was writing for Xtreme. To the right are examples to show you how whacked out Jeremy was in those days.

Jeremy was also writing his "Letters from the Back Door Man" series of short stories for Xtreme. So, if some people reading my Dick Fitswell stories might have felt I was completely demented I found Jeremy to be right up there with myself

Deja Vu had its own stage at this year's Exotic Dancer Expo that had its own

Scorpio - "With summer in full swing you sense freedom in the air like you never have before. Face it, you've always wanted that Harley. Buy it now and don't ever look back because you are getting older. This will help make up for the fact that your penis seems to be slowly atrophying, or the women you used to be able to attract are now starting to look at you like canned tuna."

Libra: "It is time for a fat bitch. Yes, it is your turn to pull the weight. "Fat women need love too!" Should be the next bumper sticker for your car. (I'm betting this sticker will get you laid all month long!) Besides, it's good for your biceps! You ever wonder why you see a fat chick with some skinny dude? That's because he's doing the Tae Bo, Bowflex and Jane Fonda workout on that big ass! Live out your inhibitions."

Taurus: People of your sign are truly special. It is a little known fact that those born under the sign of Taurus can have incestuous relationships and get away with it. For you, this is the year to capitalize on that. For as for all of us death marks the extinction of the individual, that unique blend of chromosomes that make you what you are. However, if you can mate with someone in your family, say a brother or a sister or first cousin, you can truly become immortal by generating offspring whose abilities and dispositions are closest to yours. Go for it. Now is the time for you to unleash that raging bull within you.

dancing poles.

At the time the Deja Vu franchise had over sixty strip clubs in the Deja Vu organization, and if you fast forward a bit just for some new info, the Deja Vu organization as of 2021 owns over one hundred and thirty strip clubs, including International clubs! Seeing that none of the Deja Vu dancers were on stage. I decided to demonstrate how I could pole dance with the worst of them to anyone who cared to watch. Since the Deja Vu stage was smack in the middle of the trade show I'm sure there must have been at least twenty people watching me make a fool of myself while PlONe took my pictures.

I don't know if Jeremy saw me pole dance or not. But I made damn sure to show him the two digital images PlONe had gotten of me later on. By the time I left the convention Jeremy agreed to give me a shot at writing for Xtreme.

Nudes-A-Poppin

Although I would soon be writing for "Xtreme Magazine," another great event soon opened up for me through Sam Stimmel. Sam wanted me to create publicity for a young House Dancer of his who had been crowned "Miss Nude Galaxy" at "Nudes-a-Poppin" a month earlier. Doing my own photoshoot of Devin was easy, due to Sam's encouraging Devin to do it the next time I came to Stimmelators. But the real key would be to cover Devin competing at "Nudes-A-Poppin" the next month.

For years, "Nudes-A-Poppin" had been earning an international reputation as the largest outdoor Nude Beauty Pageant in the world. The pageant was being held twice a year at the Ponderosa Sun Club Nudist Resort in Roselawn, Indiana. The "Nudes-A-Poppin" event was a very prestigious event in the American Adult Entertainment Industry that would attract one hundred entertainers who would compete against each other for awards such as Miss Nude Galaxy, Show Stopper of the Year, Best Breasts, Best Show, Best Legs, Rookie of the Year, and so on. The credits were trophies that "Nudes-A-Poppin" awarded to the winners of events that were being held on a long outdoor stage in front of an audience of several thousand men and women who were willing to pay $50.00 a ticket.

The "Nudes-A-Poppin" trophies were among the most treasured credits adult entertainers could use to advance their careers. Who could earn even more credits by being featured in such adult magazines as Penthouse, Playboy, Hustler, Cheri, and Xtreme Magazine.

For example: Let's suppose there are 3000 strip clubs in the United States with perhaps half of these having the financial resources to be able to hire Feature Entertainers. By definition the difference between a Feature Entertainer and a House Dancer is a House Dancer normally works for a single club. Whereas, a Feature Entertainer travels extensively across the country to do special shows for strip clubs that had hired her.

On the low end a Feature Entertainer might make $100.00 a show in a club that expected her to do 4 shows a night. This would amount to $400.00 a night, plus she could keep whatever tips she made, or monies from any private dances she did. This same Feature Entertainer would have entered into a contract with the club to do 2 or 3 nights of shows, amounting to between 8 and 12 shows per contract. So, in this low end example if the Feature Entertainer contracted for 12 shows over three nights she'd make $1200 for three nights (plus the tips she accrued). The club would also have to pay the feature's hotel and travel expenses along with what it was paying her for her shows.

On the top end a well established star might be making $400 per show, which would amount to $4800 for three days of work. While a notorious Porn Star might command as much as $1200 per show.

Sometimes the Feature Entertainers represented themselves, but from what I've seen most of them were represented by talent agencies such as Pure Talent, Continental Agency, or Universal Talent, which were the top three talent agencies of the time period. These talent agencies would get 15 % commissions from all the bookings they made for their feature entertainers.

The name of the game was for entertainers to get as many credits as they could at such events as "Nudes-A-Poppin," Exotic Dancer's annual expos, or being featured in well known adult magazines. The Feature Entertainer's market value would then be largely dependent on how many credits she had earned and the quality of these credits.

However, not just any wanna be adult photographer or writer can get into "Nudes-A-Poppin" free of charge. The main focus of "Nudes-A-Poppin" is a large swimming pool and the long outdoor stage. Around both and their immediate environs is a fence. This fence divides the insiders from the outsiders. The outsiders are paying customers who are allowed to shoot pictures, but they must do so outside the fence. While the insiders are writers, photographers, club owners and managers who have gained the approval of Scarlett, who is the owner of the "Nudes-A-Poppin" Festival.

Sam had told me straight off that Scarlett's a tough woman to deal with. Who won't suffer any fools and will only give free admission to those individuals and organizations that can advertise her event, so that it can make even more money in the future. But Sam had two things going for him: Devin had already won a title at "Nudes-A-Poppin" as a promising rookie; the second thing he had going for him is he had developed an excellent reputation in the American Adult Entertainment Industry; and his club was in Indiana; which wasn't far from the Ponderosa Sun Club in Roselawn, Indiana. Which is the family nudist resort that hosts the "Nudes-A-Poppin" pageants. So, Scarlett already knew a lot about Sam and Stimmelators.

The deal Sam made with Scarlett was, "If you let Jack get into your event free, he will do his best to write an article about your event and also about Devin, who's already won an award from you, in "Xtreme Magazine," or other adult magazines he's writing for."

When I got to the Ponderosa Sun Club, I had to drive my Miata sports car through a security check point, where two or three employees checked my credentials. I then joined three or four other photographers in a small building where there was a long line of entertainers signing up for the pageant.

Each participant in the "Nudes-A-Poppin" pageant had to produce two full color picture ID's to be allowed to compete. After satisfying Scarlett that she was of age, each contestant had to have her ID photocopied and stapled to a release that she had to sign along with a lot of personal information. Then, each contestant had to deal with me and the other photographers in the sign up shed. I had brought my own releases with me. While Bob Ferguson, for example, who was one of my fellow photographers had all the contestants sign releases that had been printed by Cheri Magazine. I wouldn't be using the "Xtreme Magazine" releases until the following year, so I used a standardized release format in which I inserted the Alpha Wolf logo from my website.

The last step was for Bob, myself and the other photographers to take pictures of each entertainer holding up our releases and the identification number "Nudes-A-Poppin" had given her that she would use while performing her shows.

There were other photographers inside the fence, so it wasn't just us who would be allowed to take pictures of the entertainers in the pool and stage area. I have no idea what they were doing for releases. But there were only four or five of us in the sign up shed being required to methodically process every entertainer in the building before she was allowed to exit the sign up shed.

The credibility our little group of photographers had earned in the sign up shed was through the roof due to our being officially sanctioned by Scarlett to participate in "Nudes-A-Poppin's," very strict sign up process. Which amounted to our having enormous prestige with all 100 entertainers who had signed up for the event.

One of the "Nudes-A-Poppin" participants was Heather, a House Dancer from an Iowa Club who would play a huge part in my future projects. I found Heather to be one of the most attractive and aggressive women at "Nudes-A-Poppin." By 11 a.m. after we had gotten through the sign up process, Heather invited me to join her and some of her friends at the Olive Garden restaurant.

“Behind the Public Image of Nikki Lynn”

Allegedly, she had been in Penthouse, but wherever she had performed before, Nikki Lynn, was now in my neighborhood performing as a Feature Entertainer at PT's Sports Bar. When I called Jeremy McTeague over at "Xtreme Magazine", I knew I was on with Nikki, when he said, " Nikki Lynn. Why hell yes, I've heard of her. Get an interview with her, and I'll put your article in Xtreme."

I brought Angel with me to PT's that night. Where the bar was serving its $1.00 a beer Monday night specials. Larry was tending the bar tonight, so I had decided to give him a treat by giving him the real Angel experience.

After watching Nikki Lynn perform one of her shows I was ushered into a small dressing room PT's reserved for visiting Feature Entertainers. Although I had been able to introduce Angel to Nikki after she finished her show, I had to do the interview without any outside interference that would distract me from my game plan.

I had seen a lot of interviews of such up and coming stars as Nikki before, which for the most part had left me cold. In these interviews the interviewer would be asking the entertainer her bust size, how she felt being viewed as a superstar, and then the interviewer would keep making inane comments about how beautiful the entertainer's body was, and how much she turned him on. I had something more in depth in mind. Such as: “What are you dreams, Nikki?”

To which Nikki replied, “To have more Harleys, I already have four of them.”

I got a lot out of Nikki that night. Finding out for example that she had been a Registered Nurse and a Certified Teacher and that she felt American schools did not stress teaching History enough. Then I got Nikki going about boyfriends who went jobless to help their entertainer girlfriends with their careers, and sugar daddies, and a whole lot of other subjects that Nikki obviously enjoyed talking about.

A year or two after “Xtreme” published my Nikki Lynn interview, Nikki told me I had done the best interview anyone had ever done of her–and then she asked, “Can you get "Xtreme to publish another interview of me" I tried, but couldn't. Not that Nikki wasn't a terribly interesting woman, it's just that Jeremy and I had too many other stars lined up.

“Secrets Behind Adara Michael's Scandalous”

When I found out that Scandalous would be featuring at Diamond Cabaret I was on the horn with Jeremy right away. This was right after I interviewed Nikki Lynn. It was to be the night the World Trade Center went down on 9/11/2001. My interview to take place at Diamond Cabaret, PT's Sports’s even more upscale sister club in Sauget. I wrote this for "Xtreme Magazine"

"Who is the number one feature act in the U.S. today?

Although many might rightfully claim this distinction, I believe the frontrunner is Scandalous which has charted a course that is unparalleled, with its dazzling display of lights, its highly original concept of promoting itself, and the originality and raw impact of its shows. For the average patron Scandalous is Adara Michaels and her "twin sister;” two utterly, unforgettable blondes, nearly identical in appearance, who are renowned for their innovative dual acts. Each show is different, with its own choreography which the twins follow in nearly perfect synergy resulting in a stunning performance that literally propels the audience into another world. A trip to Adara Michael's website gave me fresh insight about the Scandalous team. Scandalous began with Eddie Marshall's, an ex-Chippendales dancer, and Adara Michael's vision of a traveling troupe of performers. Adara and Eddie lost $40,000 when their investors and tour operators fell through. Greedy promoters and unscrupulous agents destroyed the couple's second attempt at making it big. After losing another $60,000 Adara nearly went bankrupt. Their next attempt became the world famous dual act of the “Scandalous Twins,” which led to Adara's endless quest for her other half of the Scandalous duo.

Fourteen or fifteen past "twins" have either succumbed to drugs and alcohol, greed, lack of ambition, or just moved onto other things. Her latest twin, Anne Marie, would do her first Scandalous performance last Monday night at Diamond Cabaret, a PT's owned club in the St. Louis Metro East. But the first questions I'd ask Adara would be all about Eddie Marshall.

The interview took place the same day as the Twin Towers massacre that had left over 3,000 Americans murdered in a mass grave of rubble. All day I tried to shake it off. With the country in a somber mood, Diamond Cabaret would undoubtably have a disastrous turnout that would continue for the rest of the week, I decided. Undaunted, Adara Michaels and Anne Marie put on a dazzling show amidst an incredible array of special lighting effects.

After the first show, John, Scandalous's stage technician shot Polaroids of the very few customers posing with the two blonde entertainers. Gregarious and cheerful the twins seemed unaffected by the small crowd. I had just witnessed professionalism at its very best, a professionalism that transcended the sense of tragedy and loss affecting nearly all Americans, Scandalous included. When I was ushered into the dressing room, Adara and Anne Marie were already sitting by a table relaxing with a half gallon bottle of Absolute Vodka."

Xtreme: “Who is Eddie, and what does he do?”

Adara Michaels: “He created Scandalous. It was all his idea. All the shows are his ideas.”

Xtreme: “It wasn't both of you?”

Adara Michaels: “Well, yeah. But he made me a Feature first. That lasted three weeks by itself. But he felt two girls are better than one. This girl was nearly identical to me, which is why we started the “Scandalous Twins.” Even Eddie couldn't tell us apart. The funny thing is we were ten years apart in age.”

Xtreme: “Your website mentions that you spent $100,000 in lighting alone?”

Adara Michaels: “The lighting, yes. This show is a little reduced. We have at least $30,000 of lights sitting at home we don't even use.”

Xtreme: “Your website also suggests you do your own bookings instead of relying upon agencies?”

Adara Michaels: “Every now and then we have an agent who steps in if we have a good booking.”

Xtreme: “Why don't you go through an agency?”

Adara Michaels: “Why have an agency if I do all the work? If the agents would say, 'I've booked a show and I want it to be here,’ I'd say "great," but I'd end up calling the club, I'd send out the promo, I'd find out if there's a dressing room, I would send them the contract, I'd make sure how many shows we had and what time they were, and how to get there. The agent did nothing. They'd call me and say, 'This club wants you,' and that was it. And I'm supposed to send them 15 %? No."

Xtreme: "15 %?"

Adara Michaels: "15 %. If you work for your money I don't mind giving you 15%, but I'm sure as hell not going to give you a cent if you don't do any damn work." Adara suddenly notices I am tape recording our conversation "Are we on a recording?" she asks, as she breaks out laughing.

Xtreme: "I just did the Platinum Club website and I put this girl up and compared her to a thoroughbred racehorse. I told her on the phone she's got great legs, a perfect waist, flat stomach and a great ass. And how she's got the perfect body. So she's mad and says: 'You just called me a horse!' and both twins break out laughing.

Adara Michaels: "Oh no!"

Xtreme: "Would you feel insulted if I called you a thoroughbred?"

Adara Michaels: "Of course not." Still laughing. "I've been called better and worse things. I understand what you mean. There's a finely tuned machine and everything's working and a lot goes into it. That's us: Scandalous works like a machine. I bring in someone new here, like Anne Marie, and I tell her we are unlike any normal Feature Show. Most Features, bless their hearts, have their theme shows. They have beautiful costumes and you've seen our costumes. It is nothing fancy. We don't pride ourselves on our costumes. We pride ourselves on our lights, our production, our choreography; how we handle ourselves on stage, off stage, in public; and the whole persona of Scandalous. That's what we are about. So I bring someone in and they think, 'I just go dance on stage and look pretty and dance around to whatever theme and make tips?' No, that's not it. The girl often asks: 'There's so much money out there and we can't even take it?' We just have one song at the end of each show where we take tips and then we play games on stage with the guys, or by doing private dances, so the guys can give us money there. Whereas, other girls nine times out of ten make a lot more money than we do. But that's not what we are about and hopefully we will make our money in other avenues."

Xtreme: "What motivates you to work so hard?"

Adara Michaels: "The person behind all that is Eddie. We call him

Hitler." Both Adara and Anne Marie, sitting to my left start giggling. "Today we are calling him, General Marshall. He's tough. He's hard. Any of the 14 or 15 partners I've had will be the first to tell you that, but he's dedicated to a cause, which is "Scandalous," and he believes in what we are doing and he doesn't want it to falter like everybody else. He wants it to be unique all the time and that's why he never lets his guard down."

Xtreme: "Tonight's first show is different than last night's. I expected to see the same gig."

Adara Michaels: "Every show is different. We have twelve choreographs."

Xtreme: "Don't you ever get tired of all this? There's waterfront property for sale down in Belize in Central America which has the best scuba diving and snorkeling in the world. You see 50 feet in the water, you have the Caribbean Trade Wind in your face, and you have your deck facing the sun setting soon across the water. You can be there barbequing with a little sailboat at your private little dock and just kiss all of this goodbye. Ever think about doing that and just disappearing?"

Adara Michaels: "Of course everybody has dreams." Anne Marie echos Adara with an ethusiastic "Yeah." "You think of great things like that. Something for the future and it motivates you even more. But we never could "DISAPPEAR," although I took six months off and just went bass fishing everyday at Lake Okeechobee, Florida. People would be saying, 'Scandalous is just fading away. And Adara Michaels is just fading out.' "NO. You are Adara Michaels and we are "Scandalous." We've always been huge.... we can't fade away. We have to tell everybody we are leaving. We would have to have that final hurrah."

Xtreme: "You can start your own strip club there."

Adara Michaels: "I haven't taught Anne Marie to do the pee thing yet. She has to go to the bathroom...."

Xtreme: "I know a couple dancers who have asked to go to the bathroom with me. I'm serious."

Adara Michaels: (cracking up) "I taught Christy Lake how to pee. Ok. I taught everybody how to pee."

Xtreme: "You look more attractive here than you did out there."

Adara Michaels: "What? I have my hair in a bun."

Xtreme: "You are more animated. More natural. And drinking vodka."

Adara Michaels: "I am more relaxed. You know we have to have Absolute. Well, we don't have to. We enjoy Absolute. Besides that, we've had a rough last few days. The World's Trade Center got trashed today, so we are going to get trashed too."

Eddie: (Hitler walks in) "We have things to do."

Adara Michaels: "This is Hitler. He's right behind me."

Xtreme: "Hi Hitler. Can I call you Hitler in the article?"

Eddie: "Nobody cares about me."

Xtreme: "Well, I do. You were my number one question. I've researched your website and I want to know more about you."

Eddie: "I'm pretty easy going." The entire dressing room breaks out laughing, especially John, their stage hand, who's followed Eddie into the room. "I have one motto and she hates it. It's–'When that job first has begun, Leave it not till it is done, Be it a matter of big or small, Do it well, or not at all.' Adara chimes in with Eddie on the last four words, "Or not at all." "So, if we are going to do a show, we are going to do it right. And I'm going to be Hitler if it takes that to get it done right."

Xtreme: "What do you think it takes to be a successful Feature Entertainer?"

Adara Michaels: "Live with Ed Marshall."

Xtreme: "What do you guys want to do when you retire?"

Adara Michaels: "Fish."

"It had to have been a disappointing week for both Diamond Cabaret and Scandalous as the whole country remained in shock over the Twin Towers atrocity. Americans would stay home pondering an uncertain future. On Thursday a dancer interested in featuring accompanied me to Diamond Cabaret to see the Scandalous shows. Whether performing on stage or mingling with the audience, Adara was all eyes, magnetic and charismatic. As the twins mixed with the audience, Adara's eyes met mine, greeting me as Anne Marie came up to our little table and clasped both my hands warmly in hers. Business wouldn't pick up until Saturday when I watched Eddie standing in front of a control panel intensely manipulating the switches and buttons that controlled the dazzling array of lights and other special effects occurring at the stage. I watched Eddie and the two entertainers take their audience from a stage performance to a consciousness of another time and place–where two blonde Goddesses cavorted in a dream world of surrealistic fantasy. As the chemistry grew between the entertainers and their audience the whole mood of the place changed, from one of somber meditation over the tragic events in New York City and Washington to a rampaging, partying mood. I had seen and experienced professionalism at its very pinnacle. Anne Marie, Adara's new twin, I found to be consistently warm and engaging. John, Scandalous's stage technician proved to be a very friendly and helpful Virginian when we discussed the pictures needed for this article. Enough credit cannot be given to Eddie, who can best be described as Scandalous's main mastermind. As for Adara Michaels herself, there's not enough superlatives to describe the warmth, wit, and sense of humor I found in this exceedingly, talented gem."

Shooting My First Feature Showcases

Later on, I would be shooting pictures of Feature Entertainers at the most expensive night clubs in Las Vegas. But it didn't matter. A fifty million dollar club, or even an eighty million dollar club like Sapphires. The most sensational strip club I'd ever visit was Platinum Club in Brooklyn, Illinois. Which was the sister club to Visions out in Centreville. And while I had found Visions to be top shelf, it could not begin to compare to Platinum.

In 2000 both clubs were owned by Jim Lictey who was living in Kansas City. Jim owned about four or five clubs at that time, including Club Cabaret, near Kansas City where I'd soon be shooting the Miss Nude Great Plains Pageant.

The Platinum club was something very special. To begin with, its ground floor was an odd shape that was neither rectangular, nor circular. Its upstairs is difficult to describe other than calling it a wide oval walkway that surrounded a large open space that looked down into the club's ground level. There were artificial plants and small trees all along the walkway, a couch now and then, and a large VIP Room adjoining a well stocked bar.

The Platinum Club's VIP Room became my favorite watering hole of all time. It was completely first class, with an unsurpassed view of the entire walkway, the bar downstairs and several stages surrounding it. The club had its own kitchen where I could buy sandwiches for five to six dollars and complete dinners for around seven dollars and fifty cents. Less noticeable to the average club goer was the fact that it was expertly managed.

The General Manager's name was Frank Marsala. While his wife, Sherry, managed the club during the day, Frank could usually be found in his office upstairs. I don't recall anything ever getting by Frank. Every credit card the club ever ran had to go through Frank.

I used to bring my nephew to Platinum whenever he'd visit me from Arizona. Only nineteen, my nephew was still underage according to Illinois law. So, it was oftentimes difficult to get him into my favorite clubs, which were very careful at carding their customers.

The reason why most clubs in the Saint Louis Metro East were so strict about checking ID's is many Americans have it in for titty bars, which they view as being immoral due to the strippers taking their clothes off. Because of this negative image so many people have of adult night clubs, the adult clubs have to be even more careful about who they let in and how their employees treat their customers. If a club makes one mistake the authorities and politicians will be using every possible excuse to shut it down.

The one thing my nephew and I had going for ourselves was by now I was getting a reputation as a photographer writing for adult magazines. And that meant I would very seldom have to pay cover charges again, due to many club owners and managers viewing me as good potential publicity for their bars. So, whenever I'd take my nephew to Platinum, I'd tell the doorman that I wanted to talk to Frank, the club manager. And Frank would invariably reply, "Send Jack on up to my office."

In his office I no doubt oftentimes found Frank bored shitless. This was because Frank was often manipulating a mouse that he used to zero in on all of the club's security cameras.

One time my nephew and I watched a customer come into Frank's office to complain that a dancer had stolen his wallet. Frank politely asked the customer to wait outside his office while he investigated the customer's complaint. The customer had been doing a private dance with one of the strippers in the VIP Room. As Frank zeroed in on the small table next to the couch where the couple were doing their lap dance, we saw an object that was about the size of a man's wallet.

"That's gotta be the guy's wallet," said Frank. "Let's see what happens to it."

We watched Frank go over the video footage over and over again. By the time the dancer rose off the couch and started walking to the bar, the object had not moved off the table. Which seemed to indicate to us that the customer waited until he had finished his private dance, and once the dancer left him, had retrieved his wallet.

"Why that son of a bitch!" Frank exclaimed. Nobody even touched his wallet. He's just trying to stir up a lot of trouble for me and the club."

"What are you going to do about it?" I asked Frank.

"I'm just going to let him come back in here, and then I'm going to apologize to him that we have found no evidence of theft, but I'm going to buy him a drink anyway. That should appease him because in his pygmy sized brain he's going to think that he's gotten the best of me."

I soon started becoming well acquainted with one of the more attractive girls at Platinum. She had a great shape; and that's something that gets my instant attention; so right off I buy her a drink–well, maybe two drinks because as I just said, the woman had a great body.

But the next time I visited Platinum, she was nowhere to be found. So when I described her to Sal, the bartender downstairs, he replied, "You must have met Zoey. She's a bit strange Jack."

One day I'd find Zoey working, while the next time I'd visit Platinum, someone would inform me that although she was supposed to work her shift that night, she never showed up for work.

Ironically, Zoey wanted to become a Feature Entertainer, which I found a little odd because Feature Entertainers have to be reliable; because if they aren't no club owner's ever going to book them; while Zoey was failing to work half her shifts at Platinum.

Zoey's dream aside from becoming a Feature was to get a tit job. But when I told her I thought she already had a great body, she explained to me: "I'm cross-eyed. So whenever I first meet a customer he's looking at my eyes. And I'm really pretty ugly when it comes right down to it. Now, if I get these big silicon tits the first thing he's going to look at are my breasts. Which he will keep looking at as he starts to get horny."

As far as I was concerned the two biggest agencies representing Feature Entertainers at Exotic Dancer's Las Vegas Expo were Pure Talent and Continental Agency. But when I went to "Nudes-A-Poppin" I saw no signs of Anne Marie or Jim from Pure Talent at the large outdoor nude pageant, but I did run into Ken Shinkle from Continental at "Nudes-A-Poppin."

Shooting over a thousand pictures a day in the hot sun is a lot of work. By 5 p.m. the picnic tables outside the sign up building were already starting to fill up with some of the contestants, several club owners, and several other photographers. By now several Ponderosa Sun Club employees were serving free picnic dinners inside the sign up shed. Although I still had to drive several hundred miles back to my Collinsville apartment, I went inside for a plate of food and a couple bottles of beer, and returned to a vacant table where four or five newcomers soon joined me.

Ken Shinkle was a curly haired, good looking guy who appeared to be in his early forties. Although he was not the owner of the Continental Agency, he was to all intents and purposes "Mr. Continental." This was due to the owners of Continental pretty much giving Ken, carte blanche on how to run their agency.

At first we made small talk as we had a couple of beers together. Then Ken asked me, "Do you want to shoot our next Feature Showcase two weeks from now? We are having it in Lafayette, Indiana. You will have to get yourself down there somehow, but once you get there I will make sure that your hotel room is paid for."

The showcase took several days. But I wasn't shooting yet with my Nikon D-1 X, so my pictures didn't turn out nearly as well as they would later. I can't remember all the names of the Feature Entertainers I took pictures of other than Carrie Bare who I'd later often meet when she started participating in most of Pure Talent's Feature Showcases. I also remember Jada Deville who in my opinion did the best shows at the showcase. But I also got the impression that Jada Deville had a very high opinion of herself.

My biggest mistake was taking Zoey along with me. Although she was not on the list of scheduled Feature Entertainers, Zoey insisted that the club allow her to dance for its customers, which ended up infuriating both the club's House Dancers and Continental Agency's Feature Entertainers.

Zoey was certainly no Feature Entertainer, nor was she a House Dancer working for the club. So, when Zoey started shooting off her big mouth, demanding that she be put on the stage, right now, and not later, the House Dancers felt that Zoey was getting into their pockets while the Feature Entertainers were thinking, 'Who is this loud, foul mouthed upstart?'

The way a lot of these Feature Showcases work is the Feature Entertainers are given so much time to perform their shows. To give you an example, let's say that Ken had nine Feature Entertainers representing Continental Agency for this particular showcase. The club would allocate ten minutes for each Feature Entertainer to do one or two shows. After the first three Feature Entertainers did their ten minute shows, the club would then have an intermission that might last for half an hour while its House Dancers took their turns on the stage. Then the next three feature entertainers would start performing their shows until another half hour went by when the House Dancers would once again take their turns performing on stage.

So, I cannot blame Jada Deville for being a bit of a snot that night. Because at the end of the showcase, Ken told me, “Jack, you are okay , but I don't want to ever see you bring that bitch anywhere near me again, or any of my girls. And if I can have my way, I'm going to call up Platinum Club and do my damnest to make sure that she never works there again.”

Shooting my first Pure Talent Feature Showcase

With Grey Ghost doing the website for Pure Talent, it was a no brainer for me to approach Anne Marie and Jim about my shooting a Feature Showcase for their agency.

“You just did the Feature Showcase for Ken Shinkle, Jim replied. "Of course you can shoot one of our Feature Showcases. We have one coming up in two weeks in Springfield, Missouri for Reginas. Reginas has over a dozen strip clubs over four or five states, but they are having their Feature Showcase in Missouri, which isn't too far for you to get to."

“No, It's only several hundred miles from Collinsville, Jim. There's, Silver Dollar City, a very popular resort area on the way to Springfield I can visit and in what is now Springfield, there's a Civil War battlefield. I think it's called Wilson's Creek, and a lot of men got killed there. So, I will really look forward to driving my sports car to Springfield.”

Zoey wanted to go with me to Springfield in the worse way. But I was going to shoot pictures; not play games or to babysit a House Dancer who couldn't even show up for half her shifts. While remembering how badly she had screwed up at the Continental Agency Feature Showcase I had handled for Ken Shinkle. I gave Zoey my conditions for her joining me at the up Upcoming showcase. First, she had to follow me in her own car. And second, I would not share my hotel room with her. So I told her, "you can pay for your own room or if you can get one of the Regina's House dancers to let stay with her, you can save some money."

With my room already being handled by Pure Talent, I got down to Reginas around 7 p.m., where one of the Eubank Brothers started introducing me to all his brothers and cousins and several of the House Dancers working for the club. I don't remember which Eubank it was because there were so many of them, but I think it was Terry.

The first night was what Pure Talent called a "Meet and Greet". This would set a pattern for many Pure Talent Feature Showcases I would be shooting over the next few years. The Meet and Greet is an informal event that Pure Talent had built into its Feature Showcases, which were two or three night affairs in which the Pure Talent features competed against each other in front of an audience of visiting club managers and owners. This was the main reason for a club to sponsor a Feature Showcase, because it provided visiting club owners the opportunity to decide which Feature Entertainers they would like to book to perform special shows later at their clubs. The second reason was to entertain the average kind of customers who liked strip clubs, but who also wanted to watch a superior level of adult entertainment that he or she normally could never experience in their day to day visits to their neighborhood strip club.

Pure Talent's sole purpose for having its Meet and Greets was was to get all their Feature together in one place where Anne Marie and Jim could go through the rules of the upcoming give the entertainers an idea of the restaurants near their hotel. While also getting everyone in a relaxed state of mind in an environment where nothing was expected of them.

Of course, well established Feature Entertainers such as Aspen Reign and K.C. Cannons had long ago become familiar with the Pure Talent way of doing things. And it was here, at Regina's, where I met K.C. and Aspen for the first time. But several of the Pure Talent girls were house dancers who were hoping to become Feature Entertainers. It would be these House Dancers entering Featuredom that Anne Marie and Jim felt could benefit the most from the Meet and Greets.

Two of the new girls were Heather Monroe and Natasha Stone. I hit it off immediately with Heather Monroe who was a wise cracking ball of energy who would later on demonstrate first class dancing skills. And as for Natasha, I got the impression that she might have been an European immigrant who had recently become a stripper. And with a name like Natasha, she had to be Russian. Of course much later on I'd be getting to know Natasha a lot better. Nevertheless, my first impressions of Natasha were of an enigmatic woman who had a very different exotic appearance that set her off from most of the other Feature Entertainers.

After having a few beers with my new acquaintances I just had to show off my pole dancing skills. But I was nowhere close to a Heather Monroe, or a Natasha Stone. Let alone an Aspen Reign or a K.C. Cannons who were two of the best known Feature Entertainers in the country.

Zoey was able to latch onto one of the House Dancers, which got her out of my hair. Although I still hadn't bought my Nikon D-1 X that would later on make all the difference in my photography.

Obviously, I was shooting the entire event for Pure Talent, and although there were a couple of other photographers shooting next to me, I was making quite a spectacle of myself darting all over the room, or stooping to one knee to get the best shots of the entertainers on stage.

One of the House Dancers kept getting eye contact with me. Who I encountered after midnight later on. By the time the Features performed all their shows, most of us had gotten hungry. While I was desperately thirsting for a few beers. The Lamplighter restaurant was next to the club, and it seemed that practically everyone went there after the club started shutting down.

The woman was one of the prettiest House Dancers I saw that night. And by the time she joined me while I was sitting with a group of Feature Entertainers I found her to be very flirtatious and full of herself. A few weeks later she joined me at my apartment, so I could do a photoshoot of her. She brought a male friend with her, so I took them both to the Platinum Club the first night. And then I featured her pictures on the Platinum Club website I had started creating.

But all this happened so long ago that I can't remember all the details that led me to make a big impression on Big Daddy. I had already met Big Daddy's brothers and cousins and Ishmael, the owner of the Lamplighter. And taken a lot of pictures of them at Anne Marie's insistence. But Anne Marie brought me over to the big guy, the DJ, who as far as I was concerned was just another one of those Eubanks.

The part I don't really remember is a little detail about one of the strippers and I wanting to get together outside Springfield to do a special photoshoot. We were to meet at some hotel or another, whose name I long ago forgot. And I wound up driving a hundred miles, had gotten lost, and to make a long story short after finding the hotel, found out that the stripper had never showed up. I can't remember hardly anything about it now, other than my calling Regina's and finding out that I could inquire about the strippers whereabouts from Big Daddy. So, I wound up driving all the way to Fort Smith, Arkansas, where I found Big Daddy in his office.

As General Manager of thirteen strip clubs in five states, Big Daddy had to move around a lot. I still don't remember what we talked about; but Big Daddy never forgot about me.

Selena Moves In With Me

The phone call hit me like a jolt out of the blue. But at least I had some consolation that Allan was staying with me that weekend when I got the distress call from Selena. Allan lived over sixty miles away from me, but every now and then he'd come to the Saint Louis Metro East out of either boredom; or to join forces with me on matters that could benefit my Alphapro website; or that had some chance of being profitable to either one of us as photographers.

Selena needed a place to stay, and not for just a night or two, but for a week or perhaps even months. Because she was either getting kicked out, or was leaving her husband.

"Be sure to bring your pickup truck and not that little sports car of yours," Selena told me on the phone. "Because I've got a lot of my stuff out in my yard in all these boxes."

Oh shit, Allan. This is really awful. I like Greg and I thought they were getting a long together so well."

You are lucky to have two bedrooms, Jack."

"Thanks for your consoling words of advice, Allan."

I had never been out to anywhere near where Selena had been living, which was close to Marion, Illinois. Allan and I would be driving close to Shawnee National Forest, which is often called the Illinois Ozarks. So, the terrain was bound to be hilly in sharp contrast to the flat prairie where I had lived at my farm for twenty three years. The bad news was we drove the hundred and twenty miles to Marion at night where we never got to see much of the picturesque scenery I had heard so much about.

We found Selena out in her yard waiting for us. There must have been over fifteen boxes of her clothing, kitchen utensils, music tapes, and all kinds of odds and ends. Knowing that she'd soon be moving in with me I felt really odd having to deal with Greg.

For all I knew he might have been beating the snot out of her. I never figured him out to be a woman abuser, but one never knows who's going to turn out to be a wife or girlfriend beater and who's not.

But, when he came to the door to observe our progress, I went up to him and said:

"Greg. I have no idea what this is all about. Selena just called me up about two hours ago and told me she was moving out of your house and needed a place to stay."

"I don't understand, Jack. I can't understand this woman. I caught her tonight raiding my medicine chest of drugs. And I caught her taking a lot of my Coumadin."

"I used to take Coumadin, Greg. It's an anti-coagulant."

"I don't know why she wants to take that. But it's dangerous if you take too much of it. Anyway, she's going through all these mood swings, and she's even swung on her own daughter."

"Her daughter. Where is she now, Greg?"

"Staying with me. She's here with me right now. But she doesn't want to stay with Selena anymore."

"I don't know what to do, Greg. I am just a victim of this cry of distress, and I have no idea of what's going on. But...if she stays with me, I'll keep you informed about what's going on at all times."

Two hours later, we were almost in Collinsville. So, Allan and I decided that since it was still pretty early that we should all go out to Chameleon for drinks. Which seemed to be a great idea because it would take the edge off of all of us.

Selena took an instant liking for Angel once we got her to Chameleon. For the first hour it was looking like she had become the life of the party. With several of the girls gravitating towards her. And then, on her way to the toilet she took a header.

Allan's deceptively strong and he's a good six foot two. So, it didn't take much for us to get Selena into the backseat of my Dodge Dakota Sport. But once we got her into my apartment once again Selena collapsed onto the floor. When we finally managed to get her upright, we both noticed that she had this dark black encrusted stuff all over her lips.

Selena stayed with me three or four weeks. We watched a lot of television together. After the first week she wanted to go to the local tanning salon where I took her every other day. On at least one night I took her to a man's house who lived pretty close to me in Collinsville where she would spend all night and then I'd pick her up the next morning. She claimed that he was an old friend of hers who she had known since High School. But I never managed to figure out the real nature of their relationship.

Here she was staying with me for nearly a month and anyone seeing us out in a restaurant, or bar would likely have thought we were boyfriend and girlfriend and that we were having sex together.

But we never had sex together. I would oftentimes call Greg, or receive calls from him. Among other things Greg and Selena were having financial problems. And it was not because Greg wasn't making a good salary. It was because like so many other strippers Selena had never learned how to budget her money. So, here I'd be on the phone with Greg helping him devise various budget plans while promising him that I'd put it on a spreadsheet and try to teach Selena how to use it to plan a monthly budget.

I don't know whether or not Selena was doing drugs, but she sure started having a lot of problems with headaches and periods where she would actually pass out. So, I started calling Sahara for advice, who had somewhat of a nurse's background and who had once worked in a hospital.

Sahara and I finally concluded that she was in a far better position than I was in having to deal with Selena's medical problems and other issues. And that resulted in my finally getting Selena and all her belongings over to Sahara's apartment in New Athens.

The Strippers of New Athens

New Athens is a small town on the Kaskaskia River in Southern Illinois, that's roughly thirty miles from my Collinsville apartment and from Visions in Centreville where Selena and Sahara were stripping. By the time Selena moved in with Sahara there were four girls from the Saint Louis Metro East clubs who had moved to New Athens.

Sahara had just recently moved into a bottom level apartment in a two level apartment building. The apartment building was no ghetto by any means. But it wasn't a place where the affluent would choose to stay either.

Another stripper who I kept calling Sexy Jessie was living in a house one mile from Sahara and Selena with her boyfriend who was a member of a rock band. I had met Sexy Jessie once or twice while she was dancing at Dollies, but I never got to see much of her, because she never seemed to be working a regular shift. Once I started to get to know Sexy Jessie and her boyfriend better it all started to make sense to me. Although Bob did not have a steady job and didn't have a steady income he still was getting money from the rock band's gigs. While his girlfriend would work for one strip club, or another for a few days and then she'd suddenly disappear.

Sexy Jessie would spend a lot of time on her desktop computer where she started to learn how to design websites. I would often visit Sexy Jessie in her home where we would exchange ideas about website design and how to format digital pictures and other subjects that interested us. It didn't take long for me to borrow Sexy Jessie's DVD of Microsoft Front Page Internet Design Software, which I copied onto my computer's hard drive. We both had been using Dream Weaver with mixed results that finally convinced both of us to convert to Front Page.

Living right next door to Sexy Jessie and Bob were Lori and Ron. Lori was my favorite bartender from Visions while Ron was Lori's handsome boyfriend she kept calling a leech. Ron was a roofer. Whose business had its ups and downs while also being subject to the weather as one cannot install a new roof during a heavy thundershower.

Lori and Ron had two children who lived with them, their oldest being an eight year old boy. It didn't take long for me to really start liking Ron. Who might have had a few leech credentials. Perhaps he didn't work as hard or consistently as he might have. I don't really know one way or the other. But Ron did a lot of the cooking that needed to be done in the house. And he would never let the dishes go unwashed for more than thirty minutes whereas Lori would. So, when it came down to who did the most household chores, I would put my money on Ron every time.

Both of them had outstanding personalities. And one thing I found that they had in common was ---- both of them were always up for my outrageous pranks.

Although I was still hitting the Saint Louis Metro East clubs pretty often, New Athens became a second home. Smitty's was a very nice Marina right on the Kaskaskia River where both Lori and Sahara moonlighted as bartenders. And I could even get Selena and Sexy Jessie to meet me at the Marina for drinks. Which made that New Athens Marina even superior to most strip clubs I had been frequenting. For one thing all four of the women were pretty good lookers compared to most strippers in general. While the drinks at the Marina were a lot cheaper than I was paying at the higher dollar clubs such as: Platinum, Visions, PT's Sports, or Diamond Cabaret.

The overall ambiance at the Marina was first-rate as one might expect to find at a Marina on a laid back river such as the Kaskaskia. So, I was surprised to learn that it was a 325 mile long tributary feeding into the Mississippi.

I might have been kicked out of Dollies, but I was more than making up for it by becoming close friends with the girls at both Platinum and Visions, while still being on the good side with Chameleon and C-Mowes. But I was also starting to become a regular photographer for Pure Talent's Feature Showcases while writing for “Wild Times,” “Xtreme Magazine,” and “Exotic Dancer.”

Renee

When Renee found out I would be going back to Indiana to visit Stimmelators, I found her messaging me in the Lost Angels wanting to meet up, posting, "That will work out well for me, because I have to go to Indiana to help a friend out with her computer."

Renee was living in Michigan at the time, and when I arrived in North Webster, Doc told me right away that "Renee is waiting for you at the club. She says it's urgent that you please come see her."

Renee had agreed to help a girlfriend troubleshoot a computer Renee had sold her. So, I drove Renee to a little town called Warsaw, which was fifteen miles from Stimmelators. We were on time. Her girlfriend wasn't. After having lunch together Renee and I got back to the house her friend Erika was renting and we found that Erika had gotten home late, and not finding us waiting for her had accidentally locked us out of the house. Renee tried to open the lock with a credit card. And when that failed had me boost her up to an upstairs window sill where she was able to pry open the window.

When we finally were able to get inside Erika's house, I understood what had happened when Sam had provided Renee with a house rent free for several months. Like me, Sam had always had a soft heart for Renee. But after he checked up on the house where Renee had stayed for several months, his ardor subsided when he saw that the house looked like a pig sty. But the fly in the ointment would soon be resolved as I kept remembering Sam's telling me that Renee had moved a girlfriend in with her.Erika had been the same friend who had moved into Sam's house with her. And when I questioned Renee about the incident, she told me she had moved out on Erika after the first month who continued to live there for another two months until Sam kicked her out.

It all made sense to me now, because Erika's house was a total mess; dishes had gone unwashed; while most of Erika's clothes littered the floor. Which amused Renee to no end as she kept pointing out one example of bad housekeeping after another. Like a little child, Renee went from room to room pointing out to me one mess after the other. "Take a picture of these dishes, Jack. Isn't this disgusting." And then when we went into the living room, "Look at all these unwashed clothes. Yuck."

Renee finally got busy taking her girlfriend's computer apart. When she exchanged the defective part for a new one, she was able to get the thing to boot up.

“Erika owes us one, Jack. Did you see that six pack she had in her fridge? I think we should drink it, don't you?”

A couple of cans each was just enough to get our minds working on how we could get back at Renee's friend, who had stood us up and locked us out of her house. I won't take credit for the initial idea, which was all on Renee. Most of us were on Yahoo messenger back then. While each user had the option of creating his own profile much like Facebook does today. Since I had already shot a lot of pictures of the Stimmelators girls and had done a website for the club, Renee and I had a lot of weapons at our disposal.

I started out by finding the absolute worst pictures I had ever taken of the ugliest Stimmelators dancer I had ever shot with my digital camera. So, as soon as Renee had started preparing a new profile for Erika, I used Yahoo Messenger on my laptop to send the pictures to Renee's laptop.

"Damn is she ugly," Renee commented to me with a huge grin on her face. "I never saw you take pictures of girls that ugly before."

"She's no looker. That's for sure," I replied. "But Renee, Yahoo is now asking us what Erika's doing for a living and what her life long ambitions are."

"That's easy. I am typing it into her profile right now." 'I am working as a prostitute as a street walker.'

“That's great, Renee. Now put in what Erika wants to do when she gets older.”

“How about: 'I want to fuck an average of twenty guys a week, so I can buy a nice house on Lake Syracuse before I reach thirty?'

“That's perfect Renee. Erika ought to love what we've done for her.”

“All of this won't be worth a shit, Jack, unless we start messaging some of the other Stimmelators dancers who know Erika, and Erika herself of course. If we don't do that, she will never know that we've played a trick on her.”

By the time we were driving back to Stimmelators, Renee came up with a suggestion that I could not refuse.

“I know Jack that you are planning on spending tonight with Doc and Donna. But why don't we go back to my house in Michigan? You can spend the night there, then the next day we can do some photoshoots together.”

South Bend, Indiana, is a famous University Town. Notre Dame's there, which makes South Bend the home of the Irish. And so is Holy Cross, and Saint Mary's. All in all the drive from North Webster to South Bend is a pleasant one. But Renee was a Michigan girl, who now lived with her husband in a small southern Michigan town, which was roughly seventy miles from Stimmelators.

Although Lee had not gotten home yet, Renee's four children were, so I went out to buy pizzas for the entire household. By the time I got back with the pizzas, I found Renee looking at the latest messages in the Lost Angels chat.

“Come look at this Jack. That damn Doc. I told you I never liked him much.”

“What's Doc up to now, Renee?”

“He's found out what we just did to Erika. And he's talked to Sam about it. And now Sam is saying that you won't be allowed to shoot pictures anymore in his club. Because you were being very unprofessional and that you posted pictures of a Stimmelators dancer and then we told everyone that she's a prostitute.”

Lee finally got home about 8 p.m. that evening after having to do a long trucking haul all the way down to Chicago and back. After having a few beers together we all went to bed. I had to sleep on the couch, but I slept very well that night due to my feeling good about myself, and about Lee and Renee who I felt made a very good couple.

The next morning, Renee made breakfast for me, and coffee, and then we started planning our day together.

Her daughter was eleven or twelve then, so we took her with us in my Miata sports car. I took a few pictures of mother and daughter together, which shows that the daughter would soon grow up to be a very beautiful woman. While Renee, was looking better than I had ever seen her before. I took a lot of pictures of Renee in my Miata, or lying across its hood near a lake. And then after we all finally returned to her house,

Renee asked me to do a totally nude photoshoot of her.

“I've never done one before. But I've always wanted to. So, I want you to shoot me completely naked, Jack. I trust you completely, and even if Lee finds out he will understand also.”

I did the photoshoot in the basement, which had been being used for a bedroom, so we had everything we needed for the shoot. But it was the weirdest photoshoot that I remember ever doing. Renee was my friend, and my partner in crime, and now I had to shoot her purely as a sexual object. I can't explain it. I just felt so odd doing it.

Xtreme Weapons

I was writing a huge variety of articles for "Xtreme Magazine" when Jeremy threw the big one right into my lap. Nearly each month I'd do a dancer profile. And to this day I don't think the women I wrote about have ever forgotten me. How could they when I came up with catchy titles such as “Aspen Reign, Magician in Pursuit of Excellence,” “Samantha Starr, Soul of a Champion,” “Devon Lee, Headed for Super Stardom,” and later, “Arianna A Del, Louisville Spice,” and “Leah Layne, Twenty-Four Hours in Leah Layne Land.” And these titles were no bullshit. Because each title captured the essence of the woman I wrote about.

Take Aspen Reign, for example. Aspen's shows were pure magic due to the huge number of hours Aspen devoted to - Excellence. When I was shooting the shows of up to nineteen Feature Entertainers a night, there was Aspen, and then there was everyone else. Or Samantha Starr? I saw her get injured badly enough to put her on crutches, but she came back onto that stage and put in an incredible performance that gave her first place at a Pure Talent Showcase. I wasn't writing bullshit, and the women knew it.

I was writing a few odd ball articles also, such as “The Lure of the Leech,” in which I offered my opinion on why so many beautiful women choose scoundrels for boyfriends. But when Jeremy wanted me to write a gun article about my .454 Casull, I went over the moon.

Adult magazines do not ask their writers to do gun articles. But most adult magazines don't have a Jeremy McTeague for their Editor. I loved guns, and Jeremy did too being an ex-military man specializing in Field Artillery. So, when I told him I had bought a .454 Casull the most powerful handgun in the world, Jeremy must have started having dreams of elephants and cape buffalo being knocked on their asses by a single shot from a .454.

Andy, the owner of Xtreme and the guys working with Jeremy must have loved “The .454 Casull, One Handed Buffalo Stopper,” because Jeremy soon asked me to write another gun article, which I titled: "The Israeli Soldier and His Uzi." For my Uzi article I had to spend many hours in the Southern Illinois University library reading up on the 1967 Seven Day War when Israel defeated three Arab nations. I loved History and I loved Guns. So, what could be better than getting paid to write gunarticles that I could embellish by putting the History behind the weapon into each article?

Babes. That's the only thing that would put even more fun into my writing about guns. Jeremy and I came up with the idea of adding models posing with weapons for my "Guns and Babes" gun articles, based on his growing up reading the Adult Magazine, Club & Club International, which would sometimes feature articles on some badass military equipment, but those articles did not have babes posing with weapons in them. So, between Xtreme Magazine and all the strippers and Feature Entertainers I was meeting, there would be an unlimited supply of beautiful women I could write about and model with the weapons.

I have already explained the difference between a Feature Entertainer and a House Dancer. Until now, I was pretty much limited to writing about Feature Entertainers for "Xtreme Magazine." Feature Entertainers are the Ferrari's of the adult entertainment world. They have to be in splendid physical condition to perform at the professional level that is expected of them. They must be willing to work at least 50 hours a week doing their shows, exercising, planning their shows, marketing themselves, working on their websites, shopping for new outfits in their acts, etc..... Most of them are smart, and they are high powered. But there's a lot of House Dancers who are absolutely gorgeous. Who are fun to be with. And smart. Who for whatever reason do not want to live the life of a Feature Entertainer.

I could now write about any gun I wanted to write about. And I could choose any woman to be my model. So long as she was attractive enough to satisfy Andy and Jeremy. So what gun am I going to write about next? How about the M-1 Garand, "The American Infantryman's Battle Rifle" that General George Patton called "the greatest battle implement that had ever been devised." I think I want one.

Skie

Was the most beautiful stripper working for Platinum. And since she's the front cover girl for this book, you can only imagine how terrific she was. But I never spoke to her until I walked into my favorite Chinese Restaurant. And there she was. Sitting with a guy, but her eyes lit up when she recognized me as the photographer for Platinum.

She was only twenty then, but she had the poise and good manners of a forty year old lady who had been brought up in a well to do suburb. And I thought she was as cool as all get out when she invited me to her table.

Skie only lived about three miles from me. So, it didn't take long for us to become very well acquainted. She would oftentimes stop over at my apartment where we'd play around with my computers. We had many lunches together. While we did a lot of drinking together at night too.

But Skie was a nobody that I could never write an article about for "Xtreme." Until now. But I needed to get my hands on an M-1 rifle first.

My solution was to go to gun shows to buy my very own M-1 Garand. And the biggest and best gun show of them all was right in my backyard. All I had to do was to go down that big hill from my apartment at the top of the bluff and cross over to the other side of Highway 157. This is only 8/10ths of a mile. While another half mile would take me to the Collinsville Convention Center where I would find a gun show featuring over two hundred tables run by conventioneers selling guns to people like myself.

I found M-1 rifles in various states of condition at several booths. Several of them had been taken right off the battlefields of World War II, and because nothing had been done to them, some of them were going for as much as $2,000.00. But I found one that I really liked that I bought for around $1,000.00.

I bought it from Vic Meyer, who worked in Saint Louis as a computer programmer. But as I would later be finding out, Vic was no normal kind of guy working at an office job. I would soon be visiting Vic and his wife at their sensational home out in the foothills of the Ozarks a good forty miles West of St. Louis's West County suburbs.

Vic had altered the M-1 I had just bought from him. Putting a new stock on it and a new barrel my rifle was as good as my getting a new one fresh out of the factory. But it did not wear the scars of combat, so in a historical sense, it wasn't the real deal.

I took Skie with me to the Belleville Gun range that was only ten miles from my Woodhenge apartment. The M-1 fires the same cartridge as my Springfield 03 that Marriah enjoyed shooting so much. But it's a heavy rifle weighing over nine pounds. Skie probably would have enjoyed shooting it, but I wanted to keep that new rifle to myself. So I'd just rent an inferior weapon to keep her busy.

I chose a Walther MP-5 submachine gun to keep Skie occupied and out of my hair. The gun range had three submachine guns I could choose from. Starting with the Uzi that I had already rented when I was writing my Uzi gun article for "Xtreme." There was a Thompson look alike. That fired full auto just like a real Thompson, but was nowhere close to a Thompson in quality, or appearance. The MP-5 was the latest state of the art submachine gun most people are not allowed to buy. It's German, and it's got that German quality feel about it. And, unlike the Uzi which fires from an open bolt, the MP-5 utilizes a closed bolt system that makes it much more accurate than any Uzi or Thompson.

It fires a 9 mm, so it doesn't recoil nearly as much as a 45. And while the MP-5 is very light for a submachine gun, it still packs more mass than any 9 mm or 45 pistol, which also lessens the recoil. This made Skie a very happy camper as she continued to blaze away on full auto at a target that had been placed 25 yards away.

Me? When it comes to guns I don't like play toys. Not that the MP-5 is a toy. Far from it. It's the most effective short range fully automatic weapon you can buy unless you compare it to an American military M4 firing the more powerful .223 round. But the MP-5 is far more compact than any M4.

From the first round on I fell completely in love with my new M1 rifle. Firing the same rounds as my Springfield, you can shoot right through 30 inch diameter trees with one. I found it to be just as accurate as my Springfield with far better sights. While shooting at a man sized target at 25 yards I could get off one shot a second and keep all eight rounds within the head of the target. In fact, the gun range would not allow me to shoot the shells I had brought with me, due to their being actual steel tipped military rounds that would shoot through all the steel backstops the gun range was using. So, I had to buy much higher priced ammunition from the gun range using softer bullets.

Skie would keep coming back with me to the gun range several more times. Where she would shoot 45 automatics, 9 mm pistols, and even .357 Magnums.

Arianna a Del

After 140,000 miles the transmission on my 1993 Mazda Miata finally crapped out. I would have expected it to last 300,000 miles. Mazda Miatas are that reliable. But that transmission had been built to handle only 116 horsepower. Whereas, I had supercharged the car and changed the header and exhaust to bring over 180 horsepower out of its small 1600 c.c. engine. After blowing three engines, I finally took the supercharger off, but I think all those rampaging ponies had already damaged my transmission.

My solution was to treat myself to a brand new 2002 special edition Miata that came with 143 horsepower stock. It was a gorgeous charcoal silver color with a light brown leather interior.

I had four nights ahead of me at Big Al's in Peoria, Illinois, where I'd be shooting another Feature Showcase for Pure Talent. But this time I had THE CAMERA, a new 6 megapixel Nikon D1x camera with a 28 by 70 mm 2.8 Nikon zoom lens. The camera set me back $5,000 with the lens adding another $2,000 to my cost. I had also brought along three Nikon professional flashes at $400 a pop. I had gotten three flashes just in case one, or even its backup would crash and burn on me.

I was ready for anything and confident that I'd have the best camera equipment in the house. No matter what the other photographers were using. And now I had "THE CAR" with less than 500 miles on its odometer.

Nineteen Feature Entertainers attended Pure Talent's Meet and Greet that night. Big Al's had two large main rooms. We got the second room while Big Al's House Dancers went about their normal nightly routine in the other room entertaining their customers on several small stages. In the center of the room was a large table where I seated myself between two Feature Entertainers. There were still more Feature Entertainers sitting on chairs, or other small tables close by. Nineteen Feature Entertainers in all who would be competing against each other over the next several nights. With each entertainer taking her ten minute turn each night.

Over the next twenty minutes Anne Marie explained the ins and outs of the upcoming Feature Showcase, that included what she expected of each girl, and the rules and operational procedures that had been laid down by Big Al. Who wasn't very big at all, and most certainly did not look, or behave like Al Capone. I had found Big Al to be the complete

opposite of what most people might have expected. He was a short man with a handsome, youthful face and a pleasant air about him.
After Anne Marie finished, Jim stood up to address the Feature Entertainers:

"Ladies. Anne Marie and I have invited a special guest here tonight. He's sitting right across from Anne Marie. Now some of you ladies have been with Anne Marie and me for a long time so you know what's going on. Whereas, some of you other ladies are new to Pure Talent. For several of you this is the first time you are meeting the other Feature Entertainers Pure Talent represents. Especially for you newcomers, the most important thing is learning how to maximize your income. And the best way to make money is to get a silicone breast job. The man we have invited here tonight is Dr. Alvarez. Dr. Alvarez has a new clinic that does plastic surgery, specializing in breast jobs. I will now turn this meeting over to Dr. Alvarez."

"Thank you Jim for inviting me here tonight. And for all of you ladies with us tonight, our average price we charge for having your breasts enlarged is $3,000.00. Now I know some of you can get it done cheaper. Just keep in mind that you get what you pay for. And when it comes to your breasts you cannot afford to compromise. And our clinic has a two year guarantee, so that if something happens to the breasts we make for you, you can come back and have corrections made at 50 % off."

"Wow, I thought to myself. Here's this quack telling everyone that the breast jobs his clinic are offering will likely last only for several years after which his customers will end up having their tires refilled at 50 % off. And how can all of you people even think of convincing women to harm their bodies by having a tit job? God, I hate artificial breasts.'

Then the doctor asked: "Is there anyone here in this room who hasn't had a breast job yet?"

Only two hands went up. Which meant that the other seventeen Feature Entertainers had all been siliconized at least once.

I soon found myself talking with the prettiest girl in the room. Well, at least I thought she was. And like the other sixteen women she had grown an oversized set of breasts. She had a trim little body, which is exactly what I like in a woman. With a narrow waist and slender legs. She was blonde and showy looking, and had a youthful sounding voice one could hardly say no to.

"Hey Jack. I have to start doing my shows tomorrow. And I don't exactly know what I am going to be doing. You wouldn't mind going shopping with me now, would you?"

And just as I said, the girl was not used to having people say no to her. Besides, now I had THE CAMERA and THE CAR. So now I will just have to have THE GIRL.

I'm not going to tell any of you what her real name is, because we still are talking to each other even though I'm now living in Thailand. But she was going under the stage name, Divine Dame, although later she would be using Arianna a Del. So, we went out shopping that night while her blonde hair and young face matched the paint color of my new sports car perfectly. The other entertainers got to watch us drive out into the night together.

She had bought one of those cheap plastic inner tubes little kids use in swimming pools, some makeup and a whole lot of paint. Which she now used during her show while I took over a hundred and fifty pictures of her ten minute performance. Most of the other photographers were using Nikon SLR's. But they were using film, so they could go only 24 to 36 pictures before they'd have to stop shooting to put a new roll of film into their Nikons. Whereas, I had three memory cards with each one of them good for up to 500 pictures. All of us were wearing on our belts these flash chargers that operated on a single very large rechargeable battery. This enabled us to take one shot a second and to be able to keep shooting for very extended periods of time.

This leaves me shooting more than three times as often as the real pros using their film Nikons. So, guess who got the best pictures?
Of course I did, because I had the competition completely outgunned. Out of the gals, I got the most dazzling pictures of Aspen Reign, whose shows are always totally spell binding. But overall, I got the best pictures out of my new friend. With most Feature Entertainers doing their shows on stage, I'm lucky to get one out of ten decent pictures. But with Arianna (from now on I'll be using her new stage name), I was getting over 60 percent, which is an astonishing success rate.

I did have a little incident happen during the showcase that everyone should pay close attention to if they ever have any hopes of becoming a successful adult photographer. I will refer to the Feature Entertainer as Nina_____and not her full name she had been using as a Feature. Anne Marie suddenly looked me up to ask a favor of me during the showcase. And when I asked Anne Marie what she wanted me to do for her, Anne Marie replied:

“It's Nina. She's had way too much to drink tonight. So, would you mind taking her back to our hotel and see that she gets inside her room?”

“You can count on me, Anne Marie.”

Our hotel was two or three blocks from Big Al’s, so I must have been putting my arms around Nina as I walked her back to the hotel. And when I took her to her room, she looked at me as if she wanted to kiss me. She would have had a roommate, because Big Al was paying for all the rooms, but only if Pure Talent doubled up on the girls. But .... where was Nina's roommate that night? Most likely, she was still at Big Al's, which would have left me alone with Nina.

Now here's the lesson. “You don't fuck the girls.” Because if you do, the movers and shakers of the adult entertainment world are not going to have anything to do with you. This means people like Anne Marie and Jim Hyatt who sponsor over a hundred Feature Entertainers and reputable club owners like Big Al. If you play this game like a gentleman, you will be getting to know hundreds of beautiful women, and in the long run have pretty much the pick of the litter.

Picture Collage II

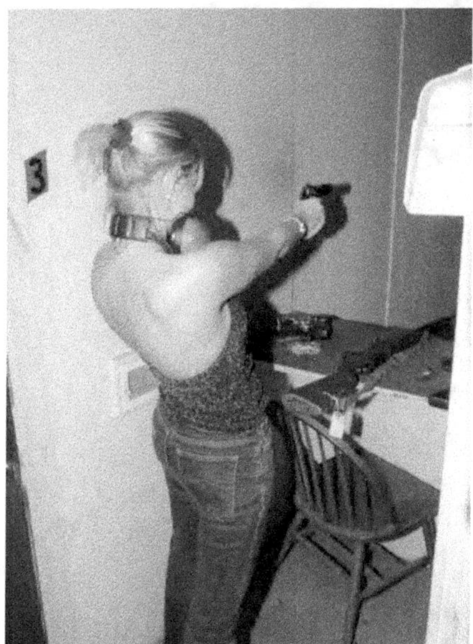

Skie (she's on the book's front cover) shooting guns with the author.

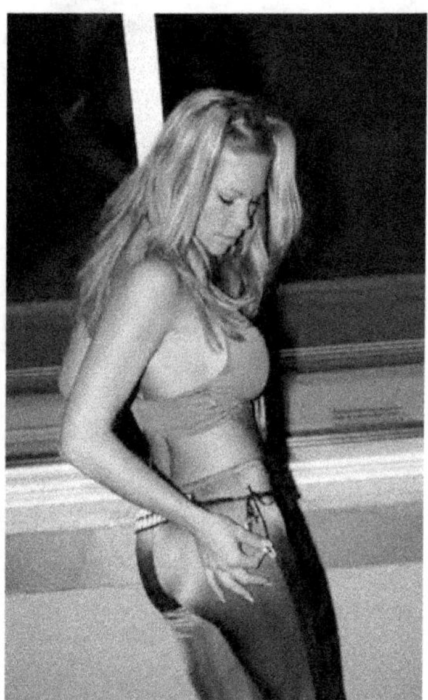

Leah Layne doing a photo shoot for the author at the Luxor Hotel and Casino in Las Vegas.

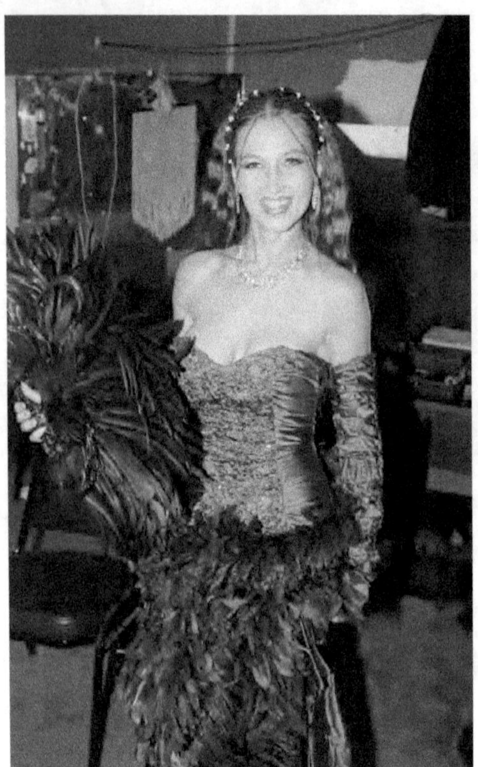

Feature Entertainer Darien Ross who would be the author's model for two Xtreme Magazine Gun articles

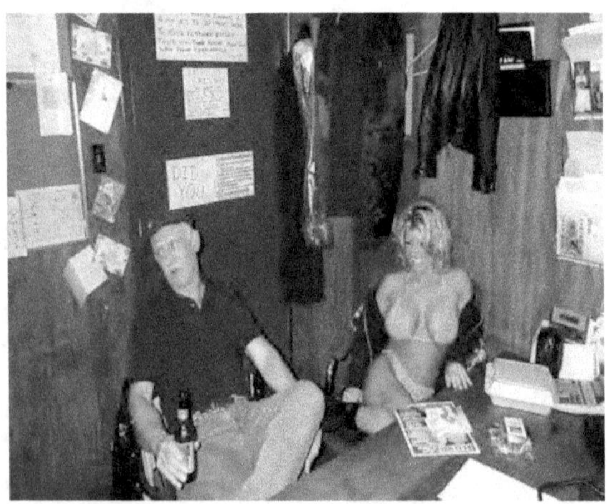

The author interviewing Nikki Lynn at PT's Sports on the Saint Louis East Side for Xtreme Magazine.

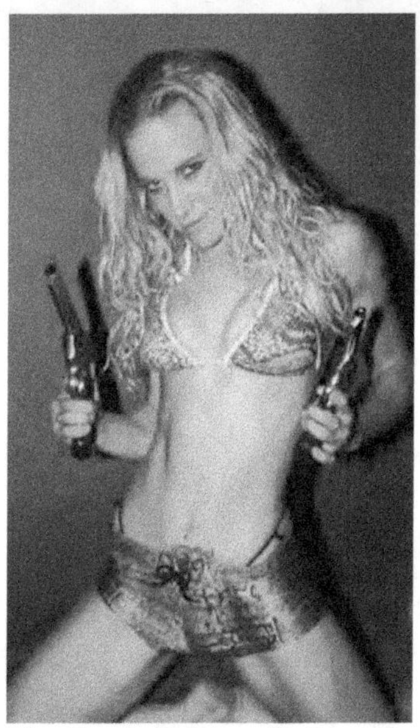

Dirty Heather posing with the author's Colt Python for his Xtreme Magazine article "Dirty Heather and the Colt Python. 357 magnum". Dirty Heather would soon wrestle Killer Kloey at Big Daddy's Cabaret in "Death Match 1" which started off S.P.E.W., Sexy Professional Wrestling between the Iowa and Missouri strippers.

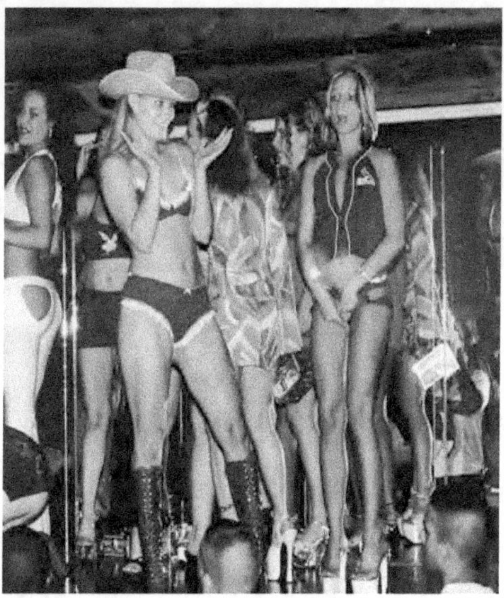

Dirty Heather's nemesis, Killer Kloey at Big Daddy's Cabaret. To the right is Carmen who would be the model for the author's "Xtreme Magazine" article on the 50 caliber machine gun.

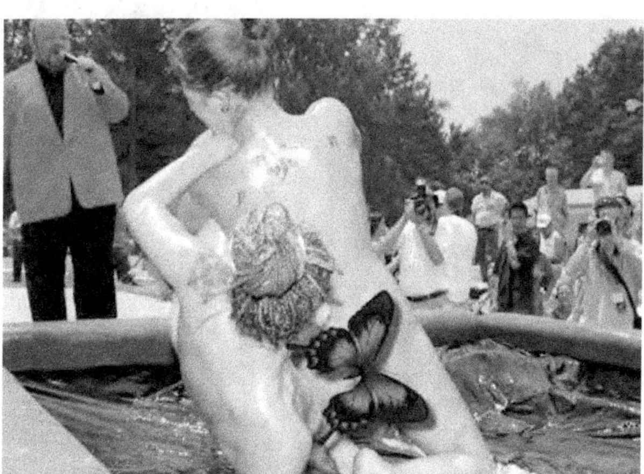

Big Daddy, the founder of S.P.E.W. MCing at Nudes-A-Poppin in his favorite red tuxedo.

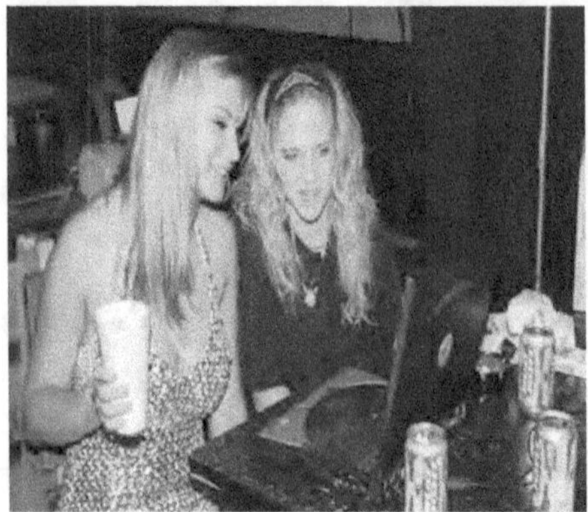

Dirty Heather on the right shows Feature Entertainer Brandi Morgan the pictures the author just took of her at a Pure Talent Feature Showcase at the Lumberyard.

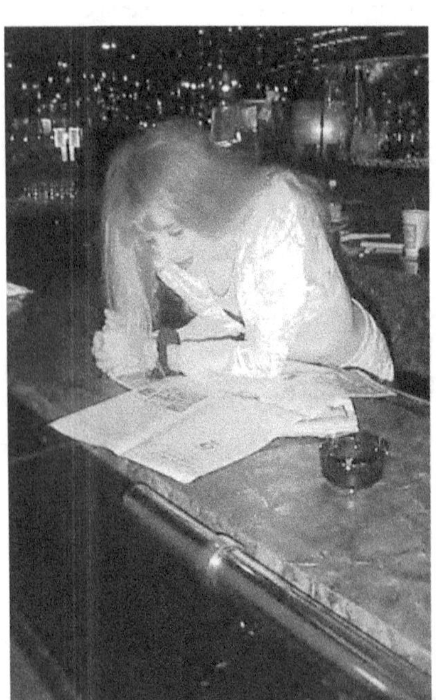

Lori, World's Best Bartender at Visions.

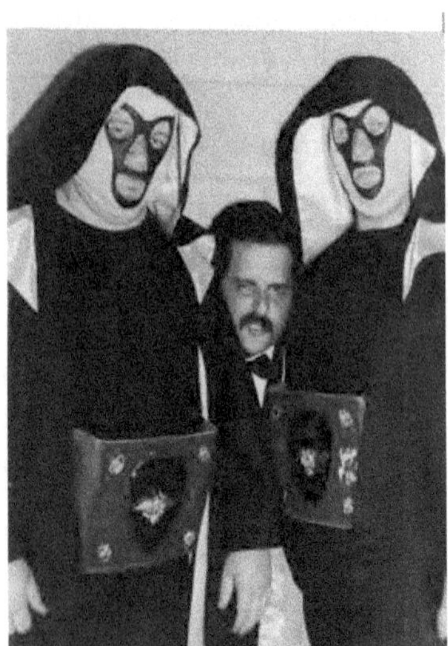

Big Daddy (on the left) wrestled three times as one of the Masked Assassins on television before his injuries forced him to halt his professional wrestling career.

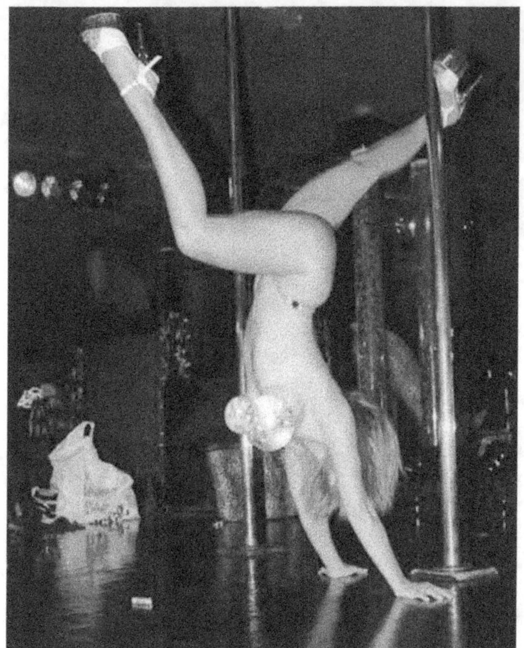

Lolly Tops competing for M.S. Texas at Club Maximus.

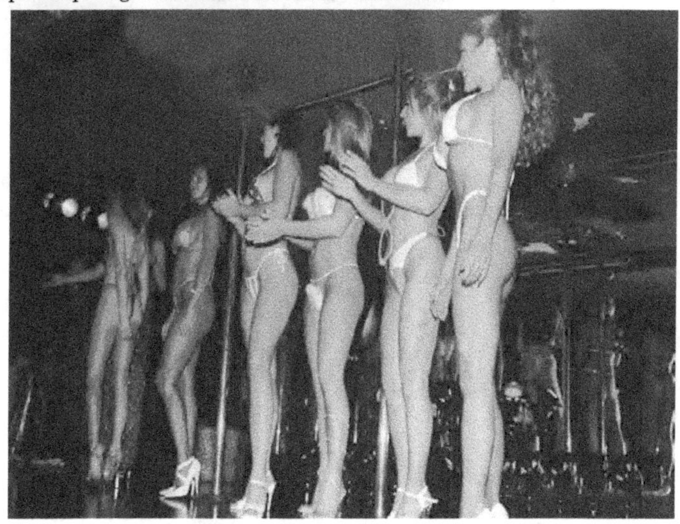

Contestants competing for M.S. Texas at Club Maximus

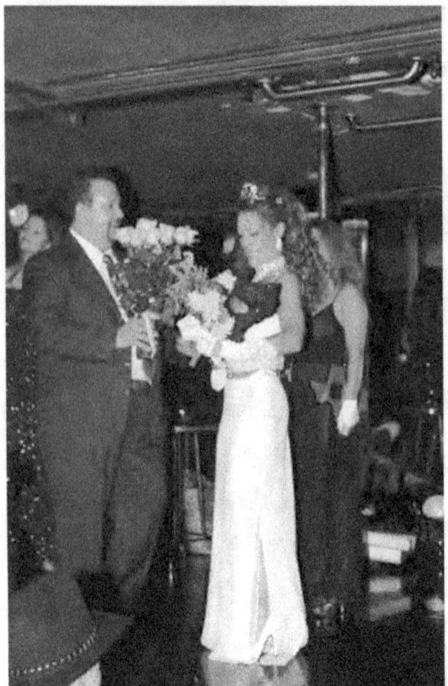

Vic Robinson, General Manager of Maximus congratulates Montana Steele for winning M.S. Texas

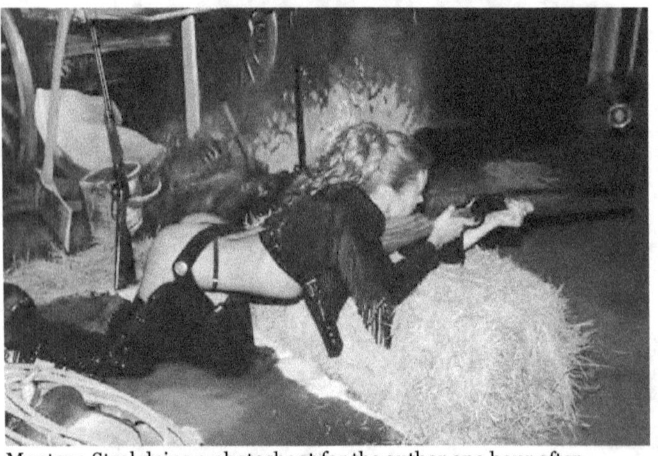

Montana Steel doing a photoshoot for the author one hour after winning M.S. Texas. The author had brought 3 of his lever action Winchester rifles to the club for his upcoming author "America's Gun the lever action Winchester."

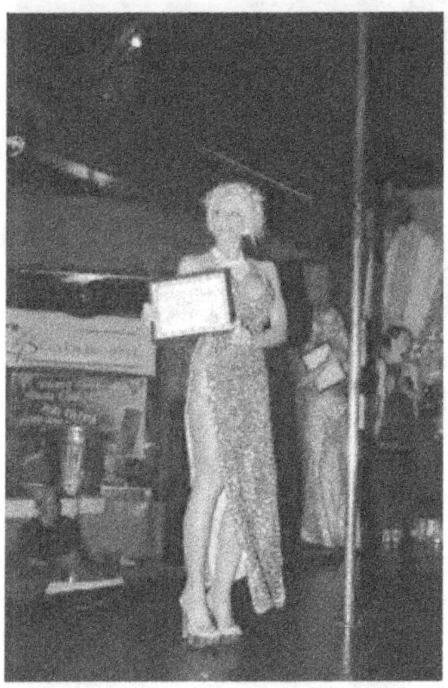

Aspen receives her award for Best Show at Big Al's By 2012, she would win Miss Nude World for the 5th time. No other Feature Entertainer has done that, and big surprise, once again Miss Nude World was held at the Lumberyard in Des Moines, IA.

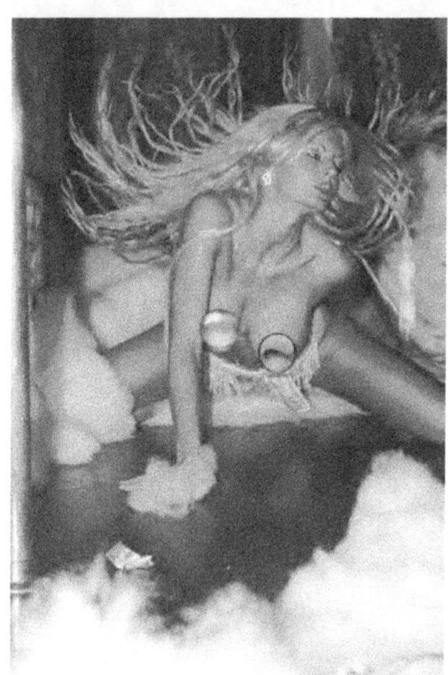

Aspen Reign performing at a Pure Talent Feature Showcase at Big Al's in Peoria, Illinois. Aspen in the author's opinion is the best Feature Entertainer he ever photographed.

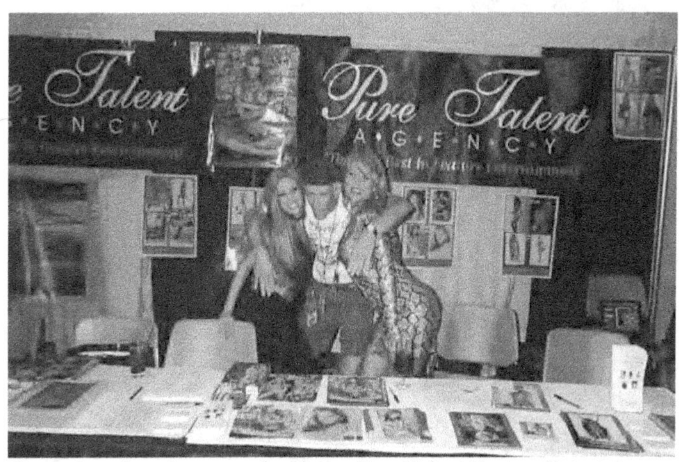

The author clowning around with two Pure Talent Feature Entertainers at the Exotic Dancer Expo in Las Vegas (to his right XXX porn star Gina Lynn).

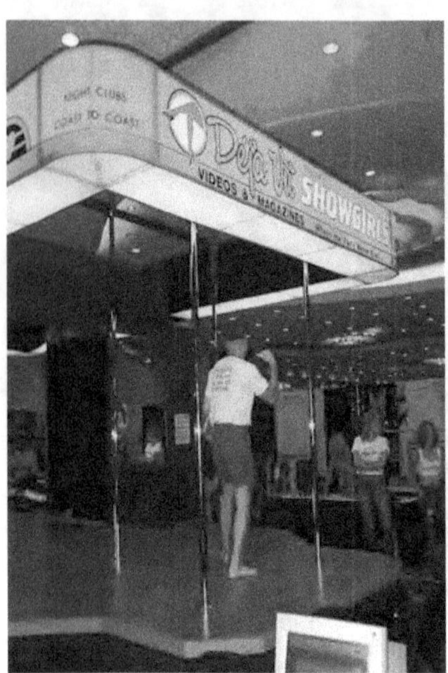

Wearing the pimp tee shirt he created, in a few seconds the author will do a pole dancing exhibition at the Exotic Dancer trade show at Mandalay Bay. It wasn't pretty but he did it.

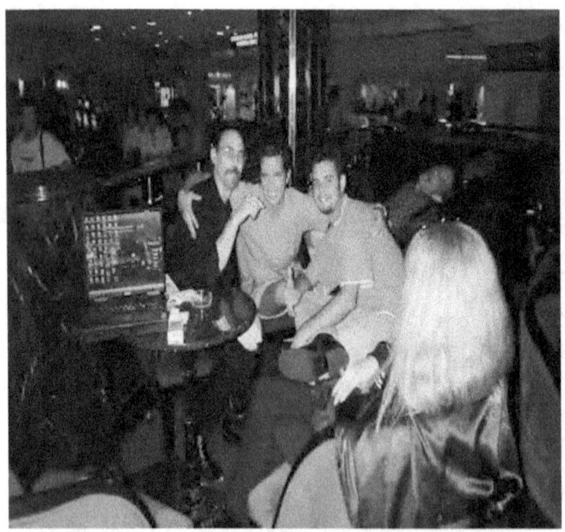

At the Exotic Dancer Expo at Mandalay Bay in Las Vegas. To the right, Lori, World's best bartender, who was representing the alphapro.com booth. To the far left Grey Ghost.

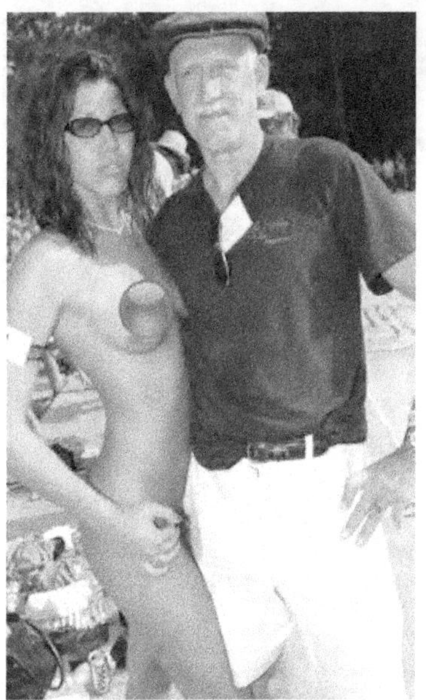

The author wearing his "Looking Glass Magazine) tee shirt with one of the contestants at Nudes-A-Poppin.

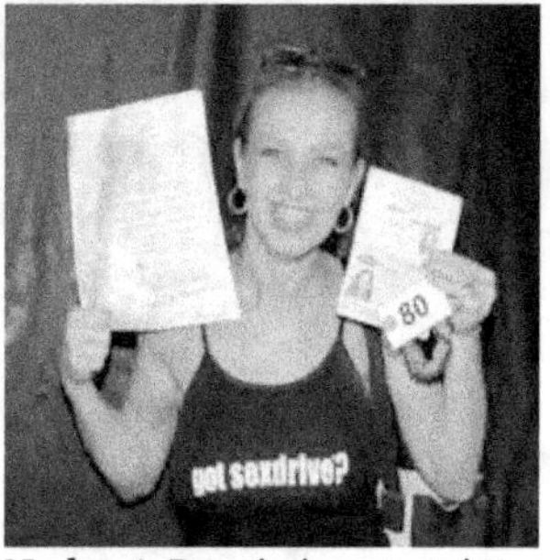

Nudes-A-Poppin is very strict when it comes to requiring contestants to provide their credentials. The author is photographing Feature Entertainer Darien Ross holding up her driver's license and his own release. Nudes-A-Poppin also required all contestants to sign the Nudes-A-Poppin release. Darien would do two photoshoots for the author for two of his gun articles for Xtreme.

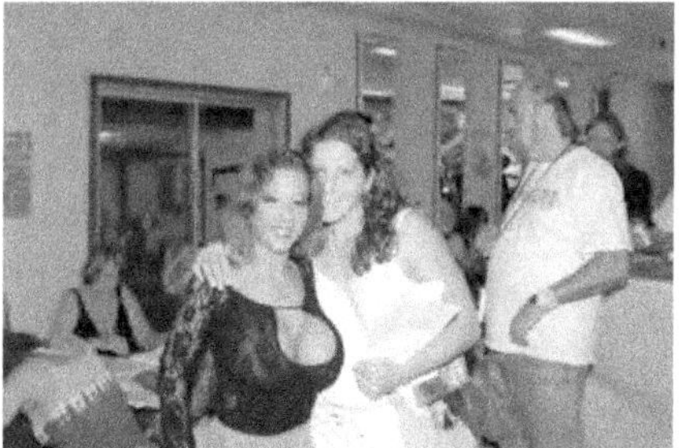

Lolly Tops on the left. To the right is ace photographer for "Cheri Magazine", Bob Ferguson.

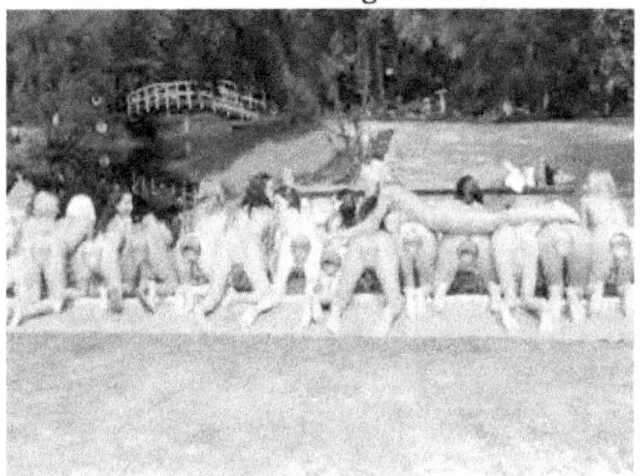

Contestants at Nudes-A-Poppin

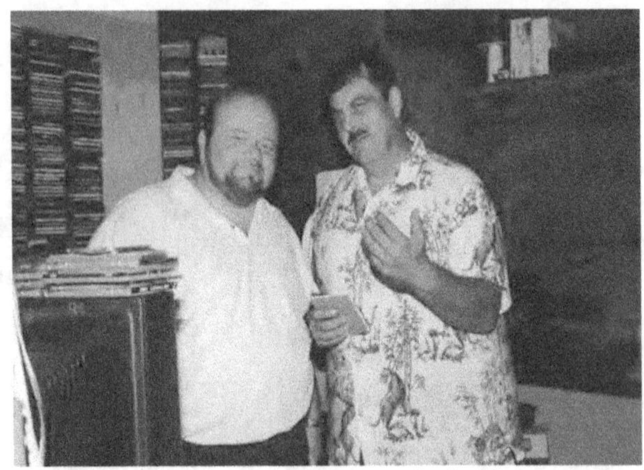

Big Daddy and the late Ken Grossman who had been one of BD's disk jockeys, and later a good friend of the author's. Due to his family being deceased Kenny once told the author that Big Daddy and BD's brother, Terry is his only family.

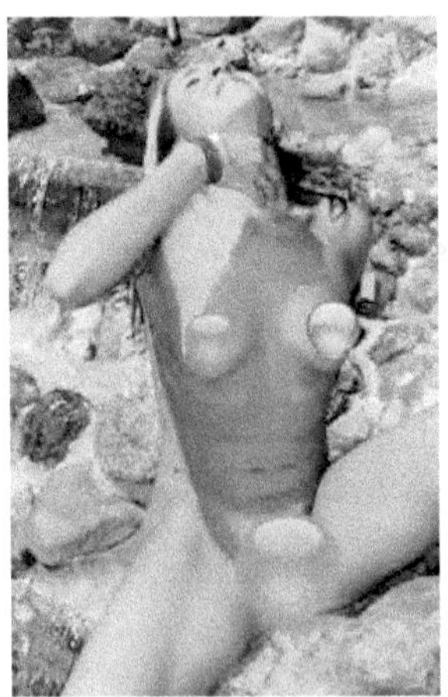

It is very difficult to be accepted at Nudes-A-Poppin as a photographer (to be allowed inside the fence serving as the perimeter for the swimming pool where the contestants compete). The 4 or 5 photographers who get to have their releases signed in the sign up shed gain enormous prestige with the entertainers.

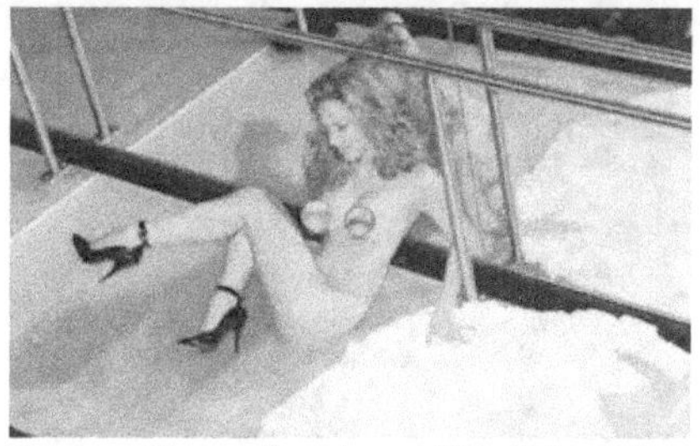

Serenna Star performing at Ritz Cabaret in Baltimore, Maryland at a Pure Talent Feature Showcase. Before being crowned Miss Nude World Serenna would be featured in one of the author's gun articles for Xtreme after posing with an FAL assault rifle

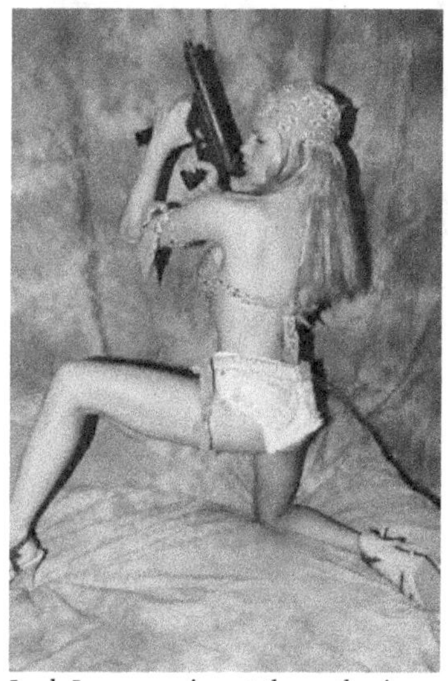

Leah Layne posing at the author's apartment for an upcoming gun article in Xtreme Magazine

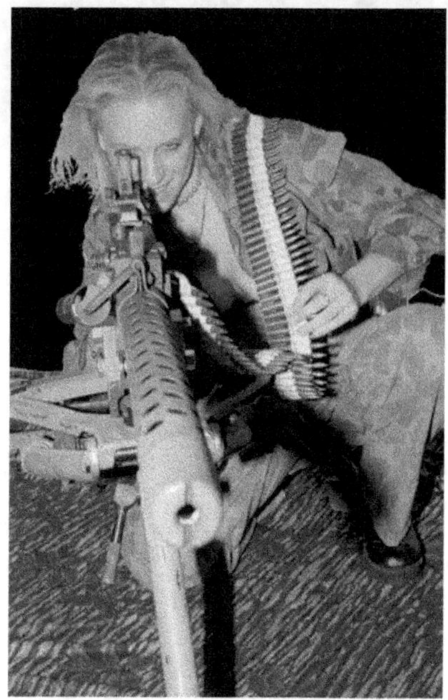

Heather as "Machine Gun Heather" in my series of Guns and Babes articles for " Xtreme Magazine". The series would continue for over two years and later be the foundation for Exteme Guns and Babes for an Adult World which is now available world wide in full color paperback, black and white and ebook editions.

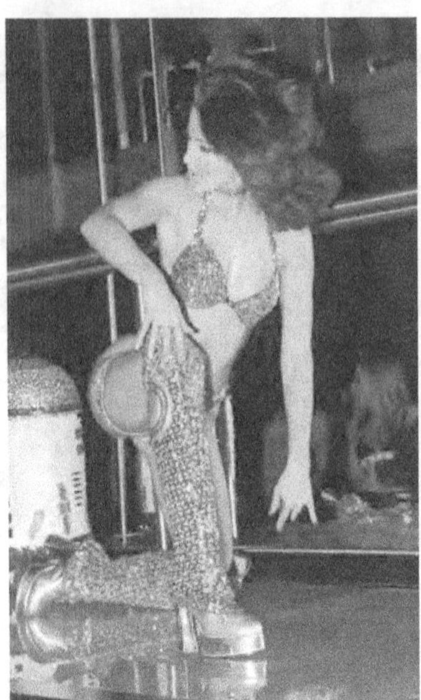

Lauren Kaine performing at a Pure Talent Feature Showcase at Ritz Cabaret in Baltimore, Maryland.

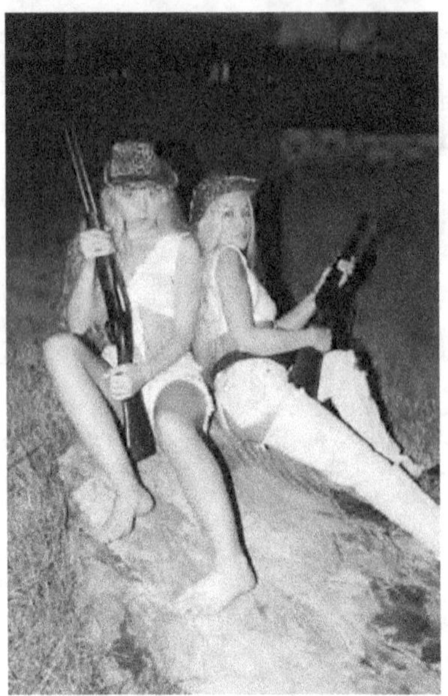

Pleasure and Pain as the author's models for an upcoming Xtreme Weapons gun article. Pleasure on the left. Paine, Pleasure's mother on the right

Tits

I have never been a big fan of breasts, one way or the other. I like women with nice slender legs, a firm belly and a nice shapely butt–with no exceptions please. But lately I've had tits on my mind. Starting with Zoey who's been calling me as often as ten times a day.

She just couldn't keep her mind off becoming a Feature Entertainer and getting a silicone job that will keep men looking at her bosom instead of her cross eyes. And she's always coming up with places she wants to drive to where she thinks she has a chance at winning a stripper's dance contest. And then, finally, she gets her breasts done. I get her phone call straight off, "Come see me tonight. I got some new tits to show you."

I drive over to the house where she's staying with her mother over in St. Louis. She gets a couple beers from the fridge and we sit down together on a swing set.

"What do you think of them? Feel my tits," she orders me as she takes off her tee shirt."

So, I feel her breasts, which are larger than they've ever been before. But they are also as solid as a board.

"I like them better when they melt in my mouth and get bigger as you become aroused," I tell her.

Well, Zoey might have thought getting those new silicone breasts would keep a man distracted from having to look at her eyes. but it sure didn't work with me.

*****

Two weeks later, Zoey's on the phone with me again.

"Goddam it, my tits are all fucked up now!"

"Why? What happened to them?"

"I just had a car accident. This bitch ran right into me, and I got jostled around and now my right breast got twisted around. It's crooked. Now I got to get them redone. I'm going to sue that fucking bitch."

This could only happen to Zoey. Which is what I was telling Skie as we played around with my desktop computer.

“Hey, I got a great idea, Skie. Suppose you show me your breasts. I'll take some pictures of them. Then I got some old pictures of Zoey's breasts on my computer, and also a few of Renee. You have natural breasts. Zoey used to have them, and Renee is natural also. Then I am sure I have a few more pictures of girls who are natural, and I've got hundreds of pictures of Feature Entertainers with their huge silicone breasts. Then I can put a form up on my website and have men vote on whether they like natural breasts or silicone breasts better.”

“That sounds hilarious, Jack. Let's do it. And here's my breasts,” Skie replied as she took off her blouse.

Skie had bigger breasts than I thought. That were far more attractive than any tit job I'd ever seen. As she sat next to me in front of my computer monitor I called Renee up on the phone.

“Sure, you can use that picture of my breasts, Jack. This is a great idea you have. And tell Skie hello for me. I wish I could be there with both of you.”

Skie stayed with me the entire afternoon helping me sift through a few hundred pictures I had taken of entertainers. Then I cropped each image until all I had left was a pair of disembodied breasts. By the time we had finished I had six sets of natural breasts and six sets of breasts that had been enhanced with silicone. As Skie continued to watch, I created a web page and put the six natural breasts on the top line. Then a few lines below the row of natural breasts I pasted the pictures of the Feature Entertainers' enhanced breasts.

That night I created a feedback form offering two choices: 1. I prefer natural breasts, or 2. I prefer silicone breasts. And pasted it on the web page showing the twelve pictures of women's breasts. I called the web page, “Tits.”

I've always wondered what most men prefer. Whether they really like huge breasts that much, or if they prefer natural breasts. I thought about taking a poll in strip clubs I'm visiting, and then Skie and I came up with that idea of putting that web page together. But even that didn't work. I got over 4000 hits on that Tits web page and only two guys bothered about voting on that sign up form. What a bunch of gutless wimps most men are today. Men don't have balls anymore. They are even scared to vote yes or no on a simple sign up form.

Getting Kicked Out Of Hustler

While doing my photoshoots for Pure Talent I was oftentimes joined by four other photographers: Mike Dunn, Bob Ferguson, Kloey, and Trace Grundstrom.

Of the four the best known was Bob Ferguson, who worked for Cheri Magazine, a magazine that was similar to Playboy, but far raunchier. Which would straight off give you a bad impression of Bob. But Bob also did a lot of promo for Feature Entertainers and House Dancers aspiring to be Features. Later, I would wind up shooting promo for a dancer from Council Bluffs, Iowa, who paid me $250.00 for shooting nude pictures of her. But I spent many more hours touching up her pictures thanI spent shooting her pictures. The dancer would later send the promo I had done of her to Pure Talent and other agencies. But she never became a Feature, due to her getting married to a friend of mine.

I don't know if Bob had someone help him touch up his promo pictures or not. Because being an employee of Cheri, he was stuck using his Nikon film camera while the rest of us had moved to digital. But whenever I asked Bob why he didn't get a Nikon D-1x like mine, he would tell me that Cheri wouldn't buy one for him. I also found out from Bob that Cheri did all his post processing for him, and that the magazine had its own film processing department, which is why it was so slow to move onto digital.

I did nearly all my own touch up work using Paintshop Pro and similar software. And that entailed a lot of hard work considering I oftentimes shot 1000 pictures a night when I was covering big events such as a Pure Talent Feature Showcase; not that I'd individually process each picture; because I'd focus only on the best pictures I took.

Kloey was a woman in her late twenties or early thirties. I always thought of her as Bob's accomplice. Like Bob she was shooting for Cheri.

Mike Dunn was a quiet spoken free lance photographer, who oftentimes took his models to Central, or South America. He might have once been affiliated with an adult magazine, but when I was shooting next to him I always thought of him as a freelancer, and he would not have been shooting in the same room with me had Anne Marie and Jim not thought highly of him.

I first started encountering Trace Grundstrom at Nudes-A Poppin, or at several of the Las Vegas Exotic Dancer Expos. Trace looked like a hippie being short and long haired, but he looked odd for being a hippie. For one thing, he moved fast, and walked fast, and usually had a big smile on his face. I had found most hippies didn't smile so much, due to their constantly being worried about the latest earthshaking social issue.

But I didn't get to know Trace very well until we were shooting together at the three day Miss Nude Great Plains pageant at Club Cabaret in Kansas. Whereas, Mike Dunn was usually quiet, he'd still make occasional flippant remarks about one of the Feature Entertainers, or Club Owners he knew. But Trace would often times make sarcastic comments about one entertainer or another, the club we were shooting at, a club manager, or doorman. So, obviously Trace had spent years in the adult entertainment industry. I already knew that he had been recognized as Exotic Dancer's Photographer of the Year. But it was at Club Cabaret that Trace first told me he was shooting a lot for Hustler and Deja Vu.

Bob Ferguson had an excellent reputation for shooting dancer promo; which was partially due to his having such a good way about him; I found him to be very helpful while being the epitome of a true gentleman.

Either Trace got hold of me, or I got hold of him first, but Trace would be in the Saint Louis Metro East for a very special event. The event was the transformation of the Washington Park Deja Vu strip club into a Hustler Club. This was starting to happen across the country as Hustler was now rapidly expanding its adult night club franchise. I had always thought of Hustler as a smutty, adult magazine and never encountered a Hustler strip club. But I learned later when I first watched “People vs. Larry Flynt” that Larry Flynt was managing strip clubs before he founded Hustler Magazine.

A few minutes after joining Trace at the Hustler Club, we got word that Larry Flynt had just arrived at the club. So, Trace and I rushed outside the club where we saw Larry being helped out of a limousine into a wheel chair. Years earlier Larry had been shot by a white supremacist and paralyzed from the waist down.

Which soon led to his becoming addicted to pain killers and having a stroke. So, the Larry Flynt Trace and I encountered was only a shadow of his former self.

Although Deja Vu was now a Hustler Club, it still retained its two Managers, Mike Parker and Ted, while Larry Trost still owned the club. Had we been shooting our pictures in Larry's Springfield Deja Vu strip club, Trace and I wouldn't have been having nearly as much fun as we had that afternoon at Hustler. Where we drank a lot of alcohol together and I shot two or three hundred pictures of naked women.

The Washington Park Hustler club, as one might expect of a Hustler franchise, was a first rate place to visit. It also had a great location being right off Interstate 64 on Highway 111. It would have taken me almost another five minutes to get to the other Washington Park clubs such as Dollies, C-Mowes, and Chameleon. Although Miss Kittys was just across Route 111 from Hustler.

By this time I was rarely paying a cover charge at any club in the Saint Louis area, with Hustler being no exception. And it certainly helped that I featured its manager, Mike Parker, in at least two magazine articles I wrote, such as "Last Bastion for Bad Boys." So I'd oftentimes stop in at Hustler, either by myself, or with one or two of my lady friends. That would include Sahara and Selena where Selena often wound up buying drinks for our entire table.

One night a handsome guy who had been standing near the bar approached me at my table where I was sitting alone and asked me if he could join me.

The man remembered me from the last Exotic Dancer Expo at Las Vegas where I had an exhibitor's booth. So, he already knew a lot about me.

"I am wondering if you can do me a favor," the young man asked me. "Do you think you can interview my wife for one of the magazines you are writing for?"

"Who's your wife?" I asked.

"She's right over there standing at the bar. It's the blonde. She's the Feature Entertainer who's performing here tonight."

"I didn't even know that Hustler was having a Feature Entertainer here tonight," I replied. I live only ten minutes from here so I just stopped in for a drink or two."

The man's wife was absolutely stunning. As in gorgeous. I had rarely encountered a stripper or a Feature Entertainer who could compare to the woman standing at the bar.

"What's her name?" I asked the man.

"Gina Lynn. I am her husband. Gina's a Porn Star."

“You have a very beautiful wife. Let me give you my card. I'd love to do an article about her, but I must first get permission from “Xtreme Magazine.”

****

When Jeremy got my email about how I had just met Gina Lynn, he replied within minutes.

“Gina's really hot. Yes. I will put her on the cover of "Xtreme". “Get over to Hustler tomorrow if you can, interview her and try to score as many pictures as possible.”

I arrived at Hustler early the following afternoon. Where I found out that both managers, Mike Parker and Ted were out of town. Since it was imperative that I get management approval for getting pictures of Gina I wanted to square things away with management first.

Normally, in situations such as this it is up to the Feature Entertainer whether pictures should be shot of her, or not. I could have taken pictures of Adara Michaels at PT's Diamond Cabaret, but her boyfriend, Hitler (oh, I'm sorry I mean Eddie), would not allow it. This is because Eddie felt that my digital camera was inferior to film cameras and also because he never let anyone take pictures of Adara, no matter how qualified the photographer was.[1] Whereas, at PT's Sports I could take all the pictures I wanted of Nikki Lynn, which was due entirely on Nikki's say so. And as for Platinum Club, I would later shoot pictures of both Leslie Wells and Devon Lee.

But here I was having to deal with John, a DJ working for Hustler, who would be the club's manager, due to the absence of Mike and Ted. I had already printed out a copy of Jeremy's email to me with his instructions on how to handle my upcoming article of Gina Lynn, which I now gave to John. Who promised me he'd call Mike about my shooting pictures of Gina.

I arrived at Hustler early that night. But when I told the doorman that I

---

[1]Ironically "Hitler would change his tune about digital cameras. About a year later while I was at Nudes-A-Poppin I heard a friendly voice calling out to me. It was Hitler smiling at me. When I saw he had a Nikon D-1 X camera around his neck, I said, "Eddie, I thought you didn't like digital cameras." Hitler continued to smile at me and said. "I've changed my mind, Jack."

was a special guest of the Feature Entertainer and that I had management approval to go into the club and not pay a cover charge, the man made a quick phone call. And then told me, “Gina and her husband don't want you to be in the club tonight.”

I just couldn't believe what I had just heard. Because the previous night I had not even noticed that Hustler even had a Feature Entertainer. And I hadn't ever remembered seeing either Gina, or her husband at the Exotic Dancer Expo. It was Gina and her husband, hat in hand, practically begging me to do an article of Gina for “Xtreme Magazine” and here they were having me barred out of the club? Unbelievable!

The next morning I got an email from Gina's husband that said, “Where were you last light? Gina and I kept waiting for you to show up to do that interview of her.”

To which I replied.... "I showed up, but the club told me that you and Gina didn't want me in the club at all. The doorman refused to allow me entry."

“Xtreme” eventually wound up doing the interview of Gina, but I wasn't to be the one to handle the interview even though Jeremy put my name on the article. Because by the time the dust had settled Gina and her husband had long vacated the Saint Louis area.

*****

A few weeks after this entire sorry episode happened, I had scheduled a photoshoot with Vic Meyer and his wife Tammy. Although I had already taken several of my models to the Meyer residence I would be taking a very special girl with me this time.

Arianna a Del and her girlfriend arrived in Collinsville by 5 or 6 pm after driving 320 miles from Louisville, Kentucky. They would spend the night at my apartment and then the three of us would drive out to the Meyer residence where I would do a photoshoot of Arianna for “Xtreme Magazine” featuring the M-16 rifle.

Before taking the girls out for dinner, I decided to take them to Hustler. I should have known better because I was already having problems with Ted. I had never had any problems with Ted before, but about right after that night Hustler had refused me entry to do an interview of Gina Lynn, Ted had started accusing me of making all kinds of derogatory comments about him.

But since I always enjoyed joking around with Ted, I could not understand how he could accuse me of badmouthing him.

Fully confident that I wouldn't be having any conflicts with Ted, or anyone else working that night at Hustler, due to my bringing Arianna into the club with me, I never made it past the doorman. Who immediately informed me that I was barred from the club and would never be welcomed there again.

When I asked the doorman to talk to Mike Parker, the doorman told me, "It's Mike who's barred you. Both Mike and Ted." And when I asked the doorman why Mike had barred me, he replied:

"Some of the dancers here have complained about your taking pictures of them outside the bar."

Which didn't make any sense to me at all. For one thing I couldn't recall shooting any of the Hustler dancers except for that afternoon Trace and I had been shooting them on opening day. And for another thing, what difference would it have made anyway? Because I had already done photoshoots of four or five PT's dancers at my apartment and at the Belleville gun range. And even if Hustler felt it was the top dog club of the Saint Louis Metro East, PT's Diamond Cabaret was generally regarded as the best of the best. I knew most of the PT's Managers, starting with Mike Oscello who was General Manager of all 14 PT's clubs, and never had problems with any of them.

And I just couldn't see Mike Parker barring me for shooting pictures of a couple of girls. Because once again, I had done several articles about Mike in two adult magazines, which made Mike look very professional.

I still can't say for sure what went wrong over that entire Gina Lynn episode, but if I were a betting man, I would say that John, the DJ was the sole cause of all my problems with Hustler.

Someone had been telling Ted that I was badmouthing him. And I really couldn't see it as being one of the dancers, and John had the personality of a wet mop. And here I was a favorite of many girls, having brought several into the club such as Selena and Sahara, and Angel. And here's this guy writing and doing photography for these adult magazines? And a beautiful Feature Entertainer and her husband seeking him out?

So, here I am at the front door of Hustler Club with Arianna a Del looking sensational. And her girlfriend, although not as riveting as

Arianna, but still more attractive than your average Hustler dancer. The three of us walked back to my Dodge Dakota four wheel drive, laughing our asses off.

******

I took the two girls to Vic and Tammy's country home the next day. Vic was a computer programmer and if I recall his wife was working with computers also. Tammy was no stripper, representing a normal American woman if there is such a thing. I always found her to be a very well mannered, helpful, intelligent woman. Who surprisingly, totally enjoyed the company of all the strippers I was bringing to the Meyer farm for photoshoots.

The Meyers had several horses, a couple cows, and a few deer which they kept penned up in an area that they had enclosed with a high fence. Oddly enough they also had a few llamas, and a couple of ostriches. The house was spacious and kept up to perfection thanks to Tammy. Vic had a sizable gun collection that included several automatic weapons, and most important of all, an M-16 rifle that Arianna would be posing with for my upcoming article "M-16, How Many More Soldiers Will Our Own Battle Rifle Kill."

I have failed to mention that out of all the nineteen Feature Entertainers I shot at the Feature Showcase at Big Al's that Arianna's pictures would have easily been called the sleaziest pictures of them all. At least that's what some people would have called them. Whereas, I would have called them the most sensual out of all the pictures I had taken.

But the real Arianna doesn't come off this way at all. She's vibrant, talkative, very beautiful, and very pleasant to be around. She was one of my absolute favorites out of all the girls I had met and would be meeting.

Surprisingly, it was Tammy who would instigate the most suggestive pictures I took of Arianna with the M-16 rifle. It was for example neither Arianna's idea, or mine, for me to take closeups of her buttocks with the rifle's barrel lying right up alongside the cheeks of her backside. Which suggests rear entry sex like no other pictures I had ever taken, or would take in the future.

Although in so many ways Tammy would seem like the girl next door, I truly believe that had her life gone in a different direction that she could have become very successful as an adult night club owner, or even an Anne Marie Hyatt running her own talent agency representing Feature

Entertainers.

I now ponder while writing this latest book of mine in my Thailand condo, 'why did I love strippers so much?' And 'why did I keep going to strip clubs in the United States and now in Thailand for the last 27 years?' There's a huge difference between the bar girls here in Thailand and all the strippers and Feature Entertainers I went with in the United States. But here's Tammy, this very intelligent normal middle class American woman, who keeps hitting it off with every entertainer I bring into her house. The reason is, which I will always contend is the absolute truth, the kind of strippers and Feature Entertainers I hung around with were more honest, a lot more fun, and much more intelligent than the average American woman outside the American Adult Entertainment World.

Getting Hired by Big Daddy and Vic Robinson for Maximus

Tornado agreed to room with me for the upcoming Las Vegas Exotic Expo, but he'd meet me later in the day at the Luxor Resort where we had booked a suite. Although most of the conventioneers would be staying next door at Mandalay Bay, which was where the Expo was being held, Tornado and I preferred the Luxor. Aside from the Luxor being cheaper than its sister resort next door, there was a certain ambience both of us found captivating.

The Luxor was shaped like a pyramid; while inside the overall theme was ancient Egyptian; with one section being devoted to showcasing ancient Egyptian artifacts; while the Nefertiti Bar had a mysterious ambience conjuring up images of ancient tombs and mummies.

The two sister resorts were both owned my MGM. While Mandalay Bay was the more expensive of the two, even the thought of ancient Egypt made the Luxor a far more exotic choice, and as for being next door to each other; next door meant one large city block; because the larger hotel-casino complexes were huge.

Upon my arrival at the Las Vegas airport's baggage claim, I noticed a man picking up his bags a few feet away from me. The man had adult professional written all over him, which you would only understand if you had been nearly totally absorbed in strip clubs as long as I had been. When I approached the man he looked up at me, and asked, "Are you going to the convention?"

"You mean the titty bar owner convention?"

The man replied. "Yes. The Exotic Dancer Expo."

"My name is Jack Corbett. I have an exhibitor's booth there. But I'm just a photographer."

"Glad to meet you, Jack. My name is Vic Robinson. I'm the General Manager of Club Maximus in Wichita Falls, Texas. What kind of photography do you do?"

"Vic. Are you familiar with Pure Talent Agency?" "

Yes. I know Anne Marie and Jim Hyatt, pretty well."

“I shoot a lot of their Feature Showcases. I also do a lot of writing and photography for “Xtreme Magazine.” It's a great adult magazine located on the East Coast, and now they even have me doing pictures of Feature Entertainers I put into my gun articles?”

“Did I hear you correct? You are writing gun articles for a titty bar magazine?”

“Yes. Every month I can choose any woman I want provided “Xtreme” thinks she's sexy enough. Then I can also choose any gun I want to write about. I get the gun and the girl together, shoot a lot of pictures, and then I write the article.”

“Well Jack, if you are doing all that I want to hire you three months from now. Club Maximus is having its annual M.S. Texas Pageant. It takes three nights and on the third night we have our Judges determine which entertainer has done the best performances for those three nights.”

“Sounds like a Pure Talent Feature Showcase.”

“Yep. Our M.S. Texas contests are run a lot like Anne Marie and Jim run their Feature Showcases. That's why you will be very good at shooting our next M.S. Texas Pageant. Here's my card Jack. I will see to it that Club Maximus pays your hotel room for three nights and $250.00 a night that you are shooting all the contestants.”

The next afternoon, after Tornado and I finished setting up our booth, Big Daddy stopped by.

"Jack, I remember how good a job you did shooting that Pure Talent Feature Showcase at Regina's. Currently I'm only the General Manager of the thirteen Regina's clubs, but three months from now I'm starting my very own club that I'm going to call, Big Daddy's Cabaret."

“And where will your new club be?” I asked.

“Dixon, Missouri. It's a little town you have probably never heard of, but it's just three miles from Fort Leonard Wood. I'm sure you have heard of Fort Leonard Wood."

“Never been there but I've heard a lot about it. It's a military base where they train American soldiers.”

“And not just that, but the Marines, US Navy guys, and the Air Force.

Anyway, we will be having our Grand Opening in three months and I would like for you to shoot my club and my girls for two days. What would you charge me for that?"

"Well, believe it or not, Club Maximus just offered me $250 a night plus my room and other expenses to cover the M.S. Texas Pageant, and I don't even know the guy who says he's their General Manager."

"I'll match it, Jack."

Leah Layne Does A Photo Shoot For Me

During the first day of the trade show when Leah Layne came up to our exhibitor's booth, I asked her if she wanted to do a photoshoot over at our Luxor suite.

“Why I haven't ever been to the Luxor before,” Leah replied. “What do you want to take a photoshoot of me for?"

“I'm not really sure Leah. Because you are really good looking. Because you have a great body. Because we already know each other. Anyway, Tornado and I want to get a real Feature Entertainer to do a photoshoot and not just one of these House Dancers. You have a pretty big name already, so there's a very good chance that I can get your pictures in “Xtreme Magazine,” and I can do a good writeup on you.”

“That sounds great, Jack. When do you and Tornado want to do the shoot?”

“How about tonight at 8:00 p.m?”

“Where shall we meet then?”

“Just meet us at the main bar over at the Luxor. It's called the Nefertiti Bar. It should remind you of an old Egyptian tomb.”

“I wouldn't know what an Egyptian tomb is like since I have never have been in one before,” Leah replied.

“When you see it you will be thinking of Egypt. We will see you at the bar tonight.”

True to her word, Leah arrived right on time. We started out shooting our pictures right in the bar. With Tornado, then me putting our heads in Leah's lap close to her ample bosom. Then we took her up to our suite.

We started out doing more of the head in the lap kind of pictures although this time Leah was exposing her naked breasts to my Nikon D-1x. Then Tornado and I got Leah into the hot tub where Leah went all the way down to the bone. I must have taken over 200 pictures of her. The last ones were of her in the shower.

Now Leah's got a great body and she knows it. She's trim and firm, and yet she's muscular. So once we got her into the shower, Leah started strutting her stuff by showing us her acrobatic moves. With one foot planted firmly on the floor she'd raise the other leg over her head. And then after I clicked off a few shots, I saw a dark filmy trail coming out from between her legs.

“Oh my God, Mike, Leah's actually pissing in front of my camera.”

Some time ago I had stopped calling Mike Tornado and started using his real name, Mike. We would end up doing many adult entertainment events together and ultimately Mike's visiting me in Thailand, which ended up with him marrying his Thai girlfriend, and his bringing her back with her eight year old daughter to the United States.

Shooting M.S. Texas

I don't think it's possible to find a more outgoing, friendly, and helpful group of people anywhere in the U.S. than you are going to find in Texas.

Wichita Falls, Texas, is almost 1000 miles from Collinsville. But the roads were good most of the way, and I was covering the last 200 miles by going 90 miles an hour in my Miata, top down with the wind in my face. Although at 143 horsepower it was far down from the 180 I with my supercharged 1993 Miata. I had a 6 speed gearshift, which helped the car feel letter perfect at 90, but I could get her up to 125 or so, if I really tried.

I didn't know what to expect. Here I had met Vic and spoken to him for just ten minutes and on the spot he hires me to shoot his club. And just recently he had emailed me the name and address of the motel he had promised to pay for. But did he? Or, would I have to pay my hotel expense in advance and hopefully get paid back by Maximus later on?

My hotel was more than I expected it to be. And you can imagine my relief when as soon as I checked in the front desk clerk told me, "Maximus has covered your bill."

An hour after I checked into the hotel I drove to the club, which I had no trouble finding thanks to Vic's clear directions. But when I walked into the club carrying my laptop and Nikon D1x; it was almost like having a welcome committee waiting for my entrance; I was immediately approached by several men, one introducing himself as the Assistant Manager.

While I was being escorted to a small booth, I told the Assistant Manager that it was imperative that I have an electrical connection near me to keep my laptop charged.

Who replied, "No problem. Here let me plug your laptop in," as I took a seat at the booth.

The booth had a good view of the women's dressing room ten feet away, while offering a 45 degree view of the main stage that was about 25 feet to my left. Which meant I'd have to walk over to the stage and stand directly in front of it to get any decent pictures.

A pretty waitress soon took my drink order. After bringing me a beer, she went around the room to take drink orders from other customers.

And after ten minutes, sat right next to me. Where she would remain for the next few hours when she was not waiting on customers.

I already knew Raven Raines, a Feature Entertainer who I became acquainted with at the Springfield, Missouri, Pure Talent Showcase I had shot at Regina's. And had more recently become well acquainted with Montana Steele at the 2002 Big Al's Pure Talent Showcase where I first met Arianna a Del. And at an after hours party in L.A. La Mann's (another well known Feature Entertainer) hotel room, Montana told me she would be competing for M.S. Texas and how Montana and I both teased Arianna that we would be having a blast together in Texas while poor Arianna had to stay home in Louisville, Kentucky.

When she was not actually performing her shows, Montana spent most of her time sitting with me and our waitress. Where all three of us got a good view of the contestants coming in and out of the dressing room.

Megan was just twenty, and although she was a waitress and not one of the club's strippers, she would often ask me to do special photo sessions of her performing on the stage. Aside from her being a non-stripper, she wasn't a Texan like the House Dancers competing for the M.S. Texas title. She was from Oklahoma, from a town not far from Wichita Falls. I found her to have an entirely different attitude from the Texas House Dancers. Not that I found anything wrong with the attitudes of the Texas dancers. I just found Megan to be more helpful and a lot more impressed with me, which was most likely due to her thinking I had to be pretty competent to be hired all the way out of St. Louis when there were so many other photographers who didn't live 1000 miles away.

A lot of the customers were a younger audience than I was finding in most American strip clubs. Primarily because it was next to a large military base near the club. Before each night's shows were over, I found Maximus to have a good crowd, with a lot of the men rising to their feet cheering their favorite dancers on. This often made it difficult for me to get an unobstructed view of the contestants through my Nikon's viewfinder.

Victoria Daniels, an out of state House Dancer, turned out to be an excellent pole dancer who put on some pretty exciting shows. But from the first night on, the front runner was Paige, one of the two Maximus House Dancers competing for the title.

By the end of the first night's performances, Vicki asked me to give her and her boyfriend a ride back to our hotel where all the non-local talent was staying. Which put all three of us cramped together in my Miata sports car.

Out of the Feature Entertainers, Montana Steele, had done the best shows, and that held true through the second night, but Montana ended up still far behind Paige who had a sizable following from Wichita Falls cheering her on.

By this time I had done quite a few photoshoots of Feature Entertainers thanks to Pure Talent. I had traveled to Philadelphia, Pennsylvania, Providence, Rhode Island, and Mobile, Alabama, where I stayed in the same hotels with the Pure Talent Feature Entertainers and a second time at Big Al's. As well as in Las Vegas where Pure Talent had a Feature Showcase at the Trade Show, which is where I first saw Montana Steele perform.

Montana and I spent that second night together, but it wasn't at all what you might think. I knew and liked her husband for one thing. So, we started off having a late night dinner together. Which was after Maximus closed at one in the morning. After dinner, Montana confided in me her concern that she would not win the M.S. Texas Pageant and that she wanted to go over her choreography with me.

Like nearly all Feature Entertainers, Montana had brought at least half a dozen outfits with her. While I had brought three lever action Winchester rifles with me: a 30-30, a .22 Magnum and a short barrel Winchester 94 Trapper chambered for .45 Colt. I had brought them with me for the upcoming article I would be doing for “Xtreme Magazine,” which I would entitle “America's Gun, the Lever Action Winchester.”

“Montana, the first night you performed your show in a cowboy outfit. I think you should wear it again tonight. I have three Winchester rifles in my hotel room. I'll bring all three of them to the club tonight. You have seen some of my “Guns and Babes” articles I've been doing for "Xtreme." I think if we do this together that you will knock the ball out of the park. When you go on the stage with those rifles all these Texans are going to go crazy. Because in their hearts most Texans like to think of themselves as cowboys.

Even though she had gone an entire night without sleep, Montana performed brilliantly. But first she made sure that Maximus would schedule her to do the last show. It was the 3rd and last night, and Maximus had drawn a big crowd with everyone trying to anticipate who would be crowned M.S. Texas. Once again my favorite waitress sat next to me, but she sure wasn't rooting for Paige. I keep saying it: the good

Feature Entertainers are a class act. So, by the time Montana got on the stage for the last time, Megan was one hundred percent in Montana's camp.

But Montana didn't waste a lot of time hanging around with Megan and me. Instead, she mingled with the crowd, and even signed autographs for some of the customers. She was wearing tight fitting black pants that accentuated her slender body and a matching shirt with chrome ornaments that contrasted sharply against her cowgirl garb. Meanwhile, several of the club's employees put up a prop that Montana had put together in her hotel room. The prop was a lightweight stand with a cardboard back. Montana had glued wallpaper on the cardboard of a wagon similar to what American pioneers used during the 1850's. To complete her set, Montana brought an axe, a lariat, a saddle, and several large wooden buckets.

Due to her gracious handling of the crowd and her painstaking attention to detail creating her props, Montana had already won the M.S. Texas title before she even started her show. Once again, Paige did very well–for a House Dancer. But other than hanging around several of her friends who had come in to watch her perform, she stuck pretty much to herself, which hardly endeared her to the spectators who had come into Maximus expecting big things from M.S. Texas.

Although she hadn't slept, Montana was still able to put on a sizzling dancing exhibition. By the time she started sighting down the barrel of my Winchester 30-30, she had nearly everyone in the house cheering. Finally, the judges announced their verdict–a come from behind unanimous vote for Montana Steele as the new M.S. Texas.

Montana would stay behind an hour after the club closed posing with my three rifles for my upcoming gun article for “Xtreme.” I hardly had to do a thing other than to shoot the pictures for Montana had already provided the perfect background that is presently the front cover of my book: Extreme Guns and Babes for an Adult World.

Nude Wrestling at Big Daddy's Cabaret

I found the drive to Big Daddy's Cabaret to be a fabulous outlet for my new Miata's sports car's abilities. Although the traffic can get heavy going through Saint Louis and its Western suburbs, the terrain gets progressively hillier as one drives toward Fort Leonard Wood. I mention Fort Leonard Wood instead of Dixon because Dixon's just a little hole in the wall town several miles off Interstate I-44. If you didn't know it you would hardly guess that this is Jesse James territory. Within ten miles of the club there's an enormous cave one can visit. And the beautiful Gasconade River where I'd later do a photoshoot of three of Big Daddy's dancers for my 1903 Springfield Rifle gun article for "Xtreme Magazine."

Upon my arrival at the club, one of Big Daddy's employees had me follow him to my hotel where I found out Big Daddy had gotten a room for a star entertainer he had booked for the evening. The new guest is a professional wrestler who wrestles as the "Honkey Tonk Man."

Most of the customers at Big Daddy's are young guys in their early twenties who are members of the U.S. Army, Air Force, Navy, or Marines. Who are perfect for Big Daddy's weekly wrestling shows that pit two of his strippers against one member of the U.S. Armed forces. The performance is held in a large vat that had been filled with cooking oil. Big Daddy asks the young crowd for a volunteer. A young Marine stands up, who Big Daddy introduces to the audience. Cocky and full of himself the Marine takes off his shirt and flexes his muscles. Then he joins two half naked strippers in the vat and stands in several inches of oil. At first the Marine does well. But the skin of the girls is too slippery for him to get a hold on either one. While the girls, who have often practiced wrestling in oil finally manage to bring the Marine down on his back.

"And now," Big Daddy announces into the microphone, "we are going to have these two girls compete totally nude, and gentlemen there's nothing like a couple of naked babes in a tank of hot oil."

After a few minutes chasing each other around the ring on their hands and knees one of the girls gets a good grip on her opponent and wrestles her onto her back. The Honky Tonk man towering massively over the two strippers counts up to ten, but he's counting far to quickly. Out of the crowd comes a very irate man who starts screaming at the Honkey Tonk Man. Who has had enough of the angry man's bullshit. There's a guitar standing on its bottom, which the Honkey Tonk man grabs and sends crashing down on the customer's head.

It's all an act of course, but the young servicemen in the audience give the Honkey Tonk man and the now prostate man a huge applause.

I spend the next night taking hundreds of pictures of Big Daddy's strippers. When the club finally closes a group of us join Big Daddy for a very late dinner. I have Big Daddy's brother Terry sitting next to me, who after drinking a couple beers tells me, “You know Jack, you will find me to be a pretty straight up kind of guy, but my brother, Paul, now he's a different story.”

Pure Talent at the Lumberyard

I really couldn't see reviewing a .44 Magnum for "Xtreme," because I had already reviewed the .454 Casull. And while Clint Eastwood brought the big .44 to world wide attention as the most powerful handgun on earth, there's one double action revolver that towers over all the rest. And that's the Colt Python, which is chambered for .357 Magnum. Although many fine shooters might prefer a Smith and Wesson, an out of the box Python is more accurate, twice the cost, and to most eyes more beautiful with its svelte lines and ventilated rib running along the barrel. As soon as I got mine I sent it back to Colt for an even smoother trigger and Colt's ultimate stainless steel finish. When I got it back I could even see my face as clearly as I would looking in a mirror.
Now that I had the ultimate revolver, the genesis for a new gun review started to form in my mind. If Smith and Wesson's .44 Magnum had Eastwood's Dirty Harry for its champion I'd find a stripper whose attitude would make Eastwood look like a cream puff.

I found the Heather I had met at "Nudes-A-Poppin" to be up for just about anything. And since she had bragged so often about her fighting prowess, I asked her if she wanted to be in my next gun article for "Xtreme Magazine," but when she drove 400 miles down to my Collinsville apartment she came with a friend, who she introduced to me as Ted.

I took Ted and Heather to Shaw's Botanical Garden on the Missouri side of the river where I had taken both Angie and Sahara a few weeks earlier. Here I found that Ted was the kind of guy who'd be up for just about anything, so it was no surprise that Ted was a strip club DJ we would soon start calling Krazy Ted.

We were all in a great mood when we came up to a statue of a sheep. Which reminded me of the sheep blow up doll I had brought into Dollies and how much the strippers enjoyed playing with it. So I asked Heather, "Would you go over and hump that sheep while I take your pictures?" Heather didn't hesitate five seconds before she mounted the backside of that concrete sheep statue. Nor did Ted who wanted to show that he could outdo Heather as he screwed up his face in mock pain as he pretended to have sex with the statue.

By the time we got around to doing the photoshoot later in the afternoon Heather was in a kick ass mood as she contemplated how she could outdo Clint Eastwood.

After we had dinner that night I took Heather and Ted once again to

Saint Louis. It was time to celebrate, so I took them to the Clayton Inn, an English style hotel where my sister had long ago had her wedding reception. Inside the Clayton Inn there's a suit of armor and various medieval weapons in a hallway that leads to Foxes and Hounds.

Foxes and Hounds is, as you might expect, an exquisite English styled pub emitting a special atmosphere that will make you believe you are in London. But the main attraction for many was Mark Pulliam, Foxes and Hound's bartender, who had gained quite a following, due to his actually writing books about bartending and a four page article the Saint Louis Post Dispatch had written about him.

As one might expect Foxes and Hounds had Guiness Stout and several English and Irish beers and Ales to choose from. But I had Mark prepare a Mark Pulliam special beer concoction composed of fruit and beer for my two friends. After having two or three Mark Pulliam specials, Krazy Ted suddenly became very excited.

“I got it, Jack. In this article you are doing for “Xtreme,” how about calling Heather, Dirty Heather?”

I about split a gut as I contemplated the article's title as “Dirty Heather and the Colt Python,” while the smile on Heather's face indicated total approval. But Mark, on the other side of the bar, spoke up: “I don't know if that's a good idea. But it's up to Heather.”

“I like it. 'Dirty Heather,' you can call me that in your gun article,” said Heather.

I didn't know it at the time, but Ted had started something that would grow into an event that was far bigger than any of us could imagine.

******

Since Pure Talent was having another Feature Showcase at the Lumberyard in Des Moines, Iowa, and I'd be shooting it, I asked Heather if she wanted to join me.

I had never been to Des Moines before and never expected very much out of it, due to it's being in a farm area. I had already driven 400 miles when I picked Heather up along the way. When we arrived at our hotel in Des Moines I found Des Moines to appear a lot larger and busier than I expected.

But, I was even more impressed with the Lumberyard. The club had both an upstairs and a downstairs. Heather and I sat upstairs where I introduced her to several Pure Talent Feature Entertainers. Since I expected to be shooting over 1000 pictures of the Pure Talent girls doing their shows, I started out drinking Red Bulls to help keep me alert.

By the time the Feature Entertainers started doing their shows, I got very busy, snapping off pictures of the girls on stage and returning to download my pictures from my memory cards to my laptop.

The Feature Entertainers enjoyed seeing their pictures on my laptop, which encouraged me to continue working non-stop. Thankfully, I soon found a friend in Victoria Daniel's boyfriend, Danny, who had accompanied her to the Pure Talent Feature Showcase. By this time Vicki had reinvented herself as Lollytops, which she named after her large silicone breasts. Danny proved to be a Godsend by keeping me well supplied with cans of Red Bull that he kept getting for me from the Lumberyard's refreshment stand. While I was keeping busy shooting pictures and setting my laptop up so the Features could soon see their pictures, and Heather was becoming increasingly helpful to me by showing them their images.

I never met the Lumberyard's owners who I learned kept themselves pretty much in the background, who were Doctors who preferred keeping their involvement in a strip club quiet. This was not the case with the club's General Manager they had hired. Who was a tall, young guy with baby cheeks wearing a baseball hat.

The General Manager called himself Big Mike. I found Big Mike to be a huge bundle of energy who had a lot of progressive ideas in his head about where he wanted to take the Lumberyard. Big Mike was good enough on computers to devise a system that would track which dancers were working that night that he would then put on the Lumberyard's website. This and other Big Mike innovations were responsible for the Lumberyard being able to generate a lot of new fans.

A few weeks later, I ran into Big Mike again, at the Exotic Dancer Expo in Las Vegas. By this time I had probably already visited Big Daddy's club a good half dozen times. Paul had paid me to do a photoshoot of his club a second time. But I enjoyed Paul's company so much that I started coming down to Big Daddy's Cabaret every two or three weeks. But now I was shooting for free while staying at Paul's house instead of a hotel. It was inevitable that Big Daddy and Big Mike would soon meet at the Exotic Dancer Expo. But once they started talking about Big Daddy's strippers wrestling in hot oil; I came up with the idea of pitting Dirty

Heather; the Iowa Female Wrestling Champion; against one of Big Daddy's strippers to determine who's the United States Champion. But, I didn't expect Big Mike and Big Daddy to run with my idea.

By this time the Lumberyard was getting to be a pretty large sized operation. And Big Mike had already met Dirty Heather and had seen the gun article I had done of her in "Xtreme Magazine." In Las Vegas, I also introduced Big Mike and Big Daddy to Pleasure and Pain, a mother and daughter stripper duo I had met at "Nudes-A-Poppin," who I was able to convince to join me in Las Vegas. Leah Layne was there as well, who became the last piece of what would soon become "Death Match 1, The Battle For Supremacy Between Iowa and Missouri."

The whole thing came together with Big Daddy's hiring Leah Layne to be his club's Feature Entertainer for the weekend. Krazy Ted brought Dirty Heather down from Iowa and Megan, a girlfriend of Heather's. They met me at my apartment and followed me to Big Daddy's the next day. Pleasure and Pain drove over from Columbus, Ohio. While Leah Layne drove down from Michigan to Rolla, Missouri, where Big Daddy was paying for her hotel. Big Mike brought his head of security with him.

The Missouri wrestler who was to take Dirty Heather on was Killer Kloey, who actually was the best female wrestler in Big Daddy's stable. We had quite the party that night with a good mix of very outgoing, fun loving people that was represented by the top bosses of two strip clubs; the extremely outgoing Feature Entertainer, Leah Layne; Pain and her beautiful daughter, Pleasure; the two Iowa girls and all the Missouri girls; not to mention, last but not least, Krazy Ted.

One should keep in mind that Big Daddy just didn't simply come out of an egg as, "You are born to be a strip club owner." While neither, Leah Layne, nor, Killer Kloey, were created to become strippers. Both Kloey and Leah Layne had done their time in the U.S. Military. While Big Daddy was acting out his fantasies being a professional wrestler who would be on television three times as one of the two "Assassins." Then he injured his back and became a professional DJ for night clubs, so that he could earn enough money to put himself through college.

Paul might never have become Big Daddy, who members of the American Mothers for a More Boring Nation might be calling a "seedy strip club owner" had it not been for his voice crapping out. Paul thought he had throat cancer. It wasn't, but whatever it was he had lost his voice for a few months. So not being able to play DJ anymore, Paul found himself becoming a strip club manager and eventually a club owner.

Paul had "Death Match 1" carefully planned. As an ex-professional TV wrestling star he knew how to get the crowd going. Which a lot of nudity certainly helped, and Killer Kloey and Dirty Heather would go completely nude in their final round. And with the curvaceous Leah Layne as the referee what could go wrong?

Out of Big Daddy's fertile mind, this is what happens in "Death Match 1."

Somewhere along the line of his brief career as a professional wrestler Big Daddy acquired a heavy and showy wrestling champion's belt. Dirty Heather enters the ring carrying the championship belt because she is after all "Iowa's Female Champion Wrestler." Then Killer Kloey struts proudly into the ring. The two female wrestlers are soon joined by Big Daddy, Leah Layne, and Krazy Ted.

Big Daddy's on the microphone introducing the two wrestlers. Then he hands the microphone to Killer Kloey who is facing Heather. Killer Kloey tells Dirty Heather, "You might be the champion of Iowa while I'm Missouri's champion, but you only wrestle against women while I have to wrestle men."

Heather pretends to be totally mystified and not able to understand Killer Kloey's insults. Big Daddy now takes the microphone away from Kloey and tells Heather: "What Kloey's telling you Heather, is that you are a completely worthless piece of shit."

Now it's game on! An angry Dirty Heather loses her temper and swings the heavy weight belt at Big Daddy. Who loses his footing in the oil filled ring. But as Big Daddy falls he knocks Krazy Ted down. But before Ted goes down the heavy weight belt appears to catch him in the face. When the two men finally get up Krazy Ted's forehead is bleeding profusely. The two naked strippers now go at it, crawling around the ring each girl seeking her opening. Then they start to grasp at each other. This goes on for a few minutes until a huge disturbance takes place. Pain, rushes into the ring screaming at the referee, Leah Layne. Then several men start to carry her out of the club. Pain, a striking blonde is lying in a horizontal position as the men carry her out of the bar over their heads.

Finally, Killer Kloey is able to pin Dirty Heather. With Killer Kloey's being the new champion Big Daddy goes to give the wrestling belt to her, but as soon as he announces that Killer Kloey is the new champion, Macy, who is another entertainer who believes she deserved the shot at the Championship Belt, comes out of nowhere and knocks Kloey down. Leah Layne rushes over to Kloey who's now pinned down by Macy and quickly counts her out. Macy who Leah Layne has now crowned as the new Champion proudly holds onto the new Championship Belt.

It turns out that Heather never hit Krazy Ted in the face with the weight belt. This is because Big Daddy's got a razor blade hidden between his knuckles, so when the two men go down in a pile Big Daddy slices Krazy Ted's forehead, which causes Ted to bleed like a pig in front of an ecstatic audience.

With Pure Talent in Baltimore

What's great about doing Feature Showcases with Pure Talent is every place is different, and although I found myself shooting a lot of the same entertainers, I'd always be meeting new ones.

This club in particular had excellent shooting possibilities. The lighting is perfect and there's a balcony above the club's main stage that allows the photographer to get right down on top of the naked entertainers performing below.

There were three new Feature Entertainers who I would be getting better acquainted with here. Although I had done a very special photoshoot of Lauren Kaine at "Nudes-A-Poppin," and also taken pictures of her doing her robot show on the "Nudes-A-Poppin" outdoor stage, I had never watched her put on a sustained performance. I had run into Lauren several times at the Las Vegas Exotic Dancer Expo, but I hardly ever saw her with a group of Feature Entertainers, so I was getting the impression that Lauren was pretty much a loner. But now for the first time, she had joined up with Pure Talent.

There was a new woman here who I met for the first time using Amber Rose for her stage name. She seemed older than most of the other women, but you wouldn't know it by watching her perform on stage. I don't think she had ever tried featuring before, and if I recall she had even stopped dancing for awhile.

I was also starting to become much better acquainted with Lori Alexander, a black dancer, who had outstanding acrobatic abilities that enabled her to do spectacular back flips. Lori had brought her pet snake along, that someone said was a Boa Constrictor.

Lori would get up on the stage holding onto the big snake, which she would make an integral part of her show. And that would prove later on to be a fatal mistake for Lori's career as a Feature Entertainer.

There were some really outstanding features here in Baltimore such as, Serenna Starr, who would soon be crowned "Miss Nude World." But personally, I liked Lauren Kaine's style. I had always felt there was something very special about Lauren that made her stand out from the rest of the pack. The first night I watched her performing totally nude on the Baltimore club's stage I thought of her as a real superstar. But as I have said, Lauren appeared to be pretty much a loner, so it's possible that she didn't get the backing she could have gotten that could have made her one of the most famous Feature Entertainers in the United

States.

I had always found Lori Alexander to be super friendly and very approachable. And since it was a warm early November day in Baltimore, I invited Amber Rose and Lori Alexander to have lunch with me. We had heard there was a Thai restaurant not far from the club. So, I had both women join me in my Miata sports car, which turned out not to be as crowded as one might think although it had seating for only two. So, here I'm driving about 30 miles an hour top down with two beautiful women and suddenly we spot a police car.

It's against the law to have three people in a two-seater sports car, but as luck would have it, both girls were hardly more than five feet tall. So I said to them, “One of you get down on the floor.” Both women were very agile, so it wouldn't have made much difference which one of the girls would cramp her body onto the floor. Both of them could easily manage it, but Lori Alexander got there first. And luckily the policeman only saw two us in the car.

It wasn't long after we got to the Thai restaurant that we spotted Lauren Kaine walking down the street. So, one of us invited Lauren to join us. At this point in her career Lori Alexander was one of the hottest features on the circuit. So Lauren asked the younger woman, “What do you like best about being a Feature Entertainer?”

“I got a new four wheel drive pickup truck and a big trailer I can pull behind it to put all my clothes in. I'm buying my own house now, and later on I want to buy one for my mother. And I get a lot of attention from men telling me how sexy I am.”

Lauren listened attentively to Lori and then she asked a question I will never forget. “But Lori, all this that you are telling us about is totally superficial. I know all about that. I really want to know about you.”

Which was vintage Lauren; because I had never felt there was anything superficial about Lauren Kaine; who I never saw to be a part of the crowd. I don't know exactly what Lauren had, but she was a very special woman you hardly ever find.

With Skie in Providence Rhode Island

Club Fantasies is in "Xtreme Magazine" territory. Due to Providence Rhode Island being on the East Coast, close to New York City and where my editor, Jeremy McTeague, had bought a house in Pennsylvania.

When I first started writing for "Xtreme Magazine" I had gone to New Britain, CT, where Xtreme's main office was and I booked a hotel room there. Then I had gone out at night with Jeremy who was in Connecticut at the time to keep him company distributing magazines. Jeremy had a Dodge Dakota two wheel drive back then in which he could store a few thousand magazines, which he would distribute to various adult outlets throughout the area such as strip clubs, tattoo and massage parlors, and adult book stores. One of the clubs Jeremy took me to was Club Fantasies in Providence, Rhode Island. While another one was in New York City, which Jeremy and I visited because the club owner still owed "Xtreme" one-thousand dollars for a one page full color ad.

By then, "Xtreme" had four franchises. There was the New York franchise, the New England franchise, the New Jersey /Pennsylvania franchise, and a new franchise just starting up in Maryland and Virginia they called the Mid-Atlantic edition. But Jeremy would not be my Editor much longer due to Andy's (the main owner of Xtreme) having bigger plans for him running the New Jersey/ Pennsylvania & the Mid-Atlantic franchises, which would include a lot of sales work.

I had shot Club Fantasies for Pure Talent once before. But this time I would bring Skie along as my accomplice who proved to be a great asset to me. For starters she would be helping me with the driving. It took us all night and most of the next day driving my Dodge Dakota four wheel drive over 1000 miles from Collinsville to Providence. And once we got to Providence it was great having Skie with me as a second pair of eyes, due to all the narrow, badly lit streets between our hotel and the club.

Once we got to the club, we were able to set my laptop up on the bar where I had Skie running my laptop. She had become very good at it due to all that time she had been spending with me at my apartment. Since I would be shooting more than a dozen of the Pure Talent Feature Entertainers, which could amount to doing over a thousand pictures a night, I expected to be overwhelmed.

Keep in mind that most of the other adult photographers were still using film cameras back then. So my shooting digital and having a laptop computer with me in a club gave me enormous advantages over the competition. For one thing I could crank out three or four times the number of pictures as the man shooting film standing next to me.

And with Skie on board, I could stick a memory card into my digital camera that was good for over 500 pictures. So, I'd shoot several hundred pictures of two Feature Entertainers doing their shows at Fantasies. Then I'd run back to Skie, hand her a filled up memory card out of my camera, and then she'd give me an empty card from which she had just transferred several hundred pictures to my laptop. And Skie was quick, because she'd often empty one of my memory cards while I was still shooting one of the Feature Entertainers, and then she'd run up to the stage and give me a fresh card.

You can imagine also what a lot of the Feature Entertainers were thinking as most of them hung around the bar when they were not doing their shows. And here's Skie showing off my most recent pictures to them on my laptop. There's nothing like instant gratification. People want to see their pictures now. Not three days later, or perhaps not at all.

And in Skie I think I had the prettiest, as well as one of the brightest and most personable girls in the entire bar. Who soon proved she could dance with the best of them. Because when she wasn't busy helping me, she would oftentimes practice her pole dancing tricks on one of the club's stages.

The Feature Entertainers loved her. Skie could have become an excellent Feature Entertainer. Anne Marie and Jim would have taken her on in a heartbeat, and talked to both Skie and me about it. Instead, unknown to me at the time she was already pregnant with her young boyfriend's child.

We wrapped up our trip by finally getting up to see Jeremy at his new house in Pennsylvania. Which was in an idyllic, rural Pennsylvania setting with deer coming up to the house each evening.

Southern Hospitality at the Candy Store in Mobile Alabama

Once again Pure Talent would be paying for my hotel room, which ultimately would come out of the club owner's pocket. But this did not apply to Tornado who would be meeting me at the Candy Store's Pure Talent Showcase being held in Mobile, Alabama. I had done a Pure Talent Feature Showcase in Mobile a year earlier in February when it was still cold in St. Louis. Where I found the weather in Mobile to be close to being ideal. So, I was in a good mood after driving my Dodge Dakota four wheel drive eight hundred miles to my hotel.

But when I went to the front desk to get my key, the desk clerk told me I had a roommate. When I asked the desk clerk, who am I staying with?" she told me, "Arianna a Del." I was happy with the choice. Whoever made it, but was it Arianna who told Anne Marie and Jim she wanted to room with me? Or did Anne Marie and Jim decide that since Arianna and I seemed to get along so well, that they'd simply put us in the room together?

Everything went well again. But this time the Candy Store provided us with even more Southern hospitality than it had a year earlier. This came in the form of the club owner's inviting us all to an open house he was having at his home. By this time Arianna had moved into Carrie Bare's room just down the hall while Tornado became my roommate. I don't recall why, but for some reason neither Arianna, nor Carrie showed up for the party at the club owner's house.

Tornado and I took two other Feature Entertainers with us to Darrel's house. One of them being Tori Blake who by this time had gotten to know me pretty well, due to both of us attending most of the Pure Talent Feature Showcases over the past year. The food was both ample and excellent. Darrel had also provided us with drinks on the house. So, not only did Tornado and I get to spend a pleasant few hours at the club owner's home, we were also able to do a photoshoot together for my upcoming gun article for "Xtreme Magazine."

I had brought my accurized Ruger Mini-14 along. But this time, Tornado and I could choose from close to a dozen of the Pure Talent Feature Entertainers to work with for this shoot. Still at the club owner's home, we got Brittany Love, to be my female model. As always I shot the pictures, but once again, I had a partner in Tornado to help me with the shoot, which Tornado had done once before at "Nudes-A-Poppin" where he posed with Darien Ross with my 1861 Springfield Civil War rifle.

That photoshoot had turned out exceptionally well. Darien was staying at the same hotel with Tornado and I where we found a grassy area close to the hotel. I had Tornado lie down on his back in the grass with my rifle across his chest as if he had been killed in a Civil War Battle. While a tearful, fully nude Darien Ross hovered over him. Darien was with all of us in Mobile, but since I had already featured her in two of my Xtreme Weapons gun articles, we ended up picking Brittany Love for my Ruger Mini-14 Xtreme article. Who did the photo shoot with Tornado at the Candy Store owner's home.

In Vicksburg with Damien

Tornado and I had visitors on our last night at the Candy Store. I had met Damien while shooting the Miss Nude Great Plains Pageant in Kansas City. But I really didn't remember her because she wasn't one of the Feature Entertainers. Similar to Maximus's M.S. Texas Pageant, House Dancers could compete for the titles the judges were handing out to the winners. While the woman who would be crowned Miss Nude Great Plains, would get a free trip to Hawaii and a thousand dollars cash. So, I just figured that Damien was another Club Cabaret House Dancer.

Several weeks later, I received an email from Damien who wanted copies of the pictures I had taken of her. Little did I know how often I'd later be dealing with the uknown House Dancer from Vicksburg. Mississippi.

I can't remember if I advised Damien to travel to Indiana to compete at "Nudes-A-Poppin," or if she came up with the idea on her own, but Damien and I knew we were both going. And later, when I found out I'd be shooting another Club Maximus M.S. Texas event I was able to convince Damien to drive to Texas to compete for M.S. Texas.

This was the third time Maximus hired me to shoot their pageants. With the first one being won by Montana Steele. And then Vic hired me a second time to cover the Maximus M.S. Texas West pageant in Abilene, TX, where my little waitress friend who hung out with me in Wichita Falls wound up winning the title of M.S. Texas West against a group of far more experienced Feature Entertainers. Competing now as Mirage, the ex-waitress put on a dazzling pole dancing exhibition as the Feature Entertainers stood up to cheer her on. Mirage would later become the centerfold model for the Xtreme Weapons 2004 calendar featuring the AK-47 rifle.

On my third outing with Maximus, Vic Robinson, had a group of us spending the pageant's last night at his home. Damien was one of the women staying at Vic's that night. I had brought several of my guns to Texas once again. So, we had a photoshoot at Vic's the next day with Damien posing with my M-1 rifle. I had by then already featured Skie in my M-1 rifle gun article for "Xtreme," but by this time Jeremy and I had concocted our latest scheme, which would turn out to be the creation of the 2004 Xtreme Weapons calendar. Since Damien was becoming increasingly interested in becoming a Feature Entertainer and aggressively promoting her career, she would be featured on the calendar instead of Skie.

Miss Nude World

Inevitably I would be called upon to cover, Miss Nude World, which was one of the most prestigious pageant events in the adult entertainment industry. For the first time, Miss Nude World, would be held in Iowa, a state which is much more renowned for its corn fields than top ranked adult entertainment. I would have thought Las Vegas, New York, or San Francisco to be much more suitable for the event than Des Moines, Iowa. But times were changing fast.

Pure Talent was now having the Lumberyard host its Feature Showcases on a regular basis. While the Lumberyard was giving a huge account of itself at "Nudes-A-Poppin." Because "Nudes-A-Poppin" was now crediting those night clubs that were providing the most contestants to the two day pageant. The winner–for being the most recognized provider of contestants soon became the Lumberyard, thanks to Big Mike and the club's owners who gave Big Mike a blank check for promoting their night club from Midwest ho-hum mediocrity to national prominence. To say the Lumberyard was starting to make a prominent appearance at "Nudes-A-Poppin" was a gross understatement. Thanks to Big Mike's practice of bringing an entire bus load of Lumberyard strippers to the pageant, and not just once, but several years in a row.

By now I was becoming great friends with Big Daddy who I was visiting on a twice a month basis. Meanwhile Death Match 1, that had pitted Dirty Heather against Killer Kloey had expanded into S.P.E.W.–which stood for Sexy Professional Exotic Wrestling. One month five Iowa strippers would head 400 miles to Missouri to wrestle five of Big Daddy's strippers. The next month five Missouri girls would ride up to the Lumberyard in Big Daddy's van. While I'd serve as S.P.E.W.s photographer.

Eventually, Big Daddy and Big Mike agreed to host most of S.P.E.W.'s events in Iowa, due to the Lumberyard being far less isolated than Big Daddy's Cabaret. Des Moines for example has 215,000 residents.

The S.P.E.W. events were exceptionally well done. With Big Daddy and Big Mike requiring the Missouri and Iowa strippers to meet at the Lumberyard during the day to rehearse their evenings soap operas. And I do mean soap operas. For example, Big Daddy would announce an upcoming match as a grudge show no mercy battle between two sisters. That had been initiated by one sister's having sex with the other sister's boyfriend. While on another occasion, Big Daddy had called me into the girls' dressing room to take pictures of blood pouring down the face of one of the contestant's that Big Mike had sliced with a razor blade.

I don't know if the audience was naive enough to believe all the hype or not, but S.P.E.W. was hugely successful drawing men and women alike to the riotous wrestling matches. If any strip club had ever hosted nude oil wrestling matches before, they couldn't compare to what S.P.E.W. was doing. Before long, Big Mike and Big Daddy would start offering S.P.E.W. to other night clubs. One of them being the Iowa Playhouse in Council Bluffs, Iowa. It started off with the Missouri strippers traveling to Council Bluffs where they would meet up with the Lumberyard strippers. But later on, some of the Iowa Playhouse girls would get in on all the fun.

Eventually, the owner of the Iowa Playhouse offered Big Daddy the General Manager's position, which Paul accepted, and sold his share in Big Daddy's Cabaret to his partner, Ishmael, and moved up to Iowa.

By the time the owners of the Miss Nude World Pageant decided to host their event at the Lumberyard I was spending a good amount of time in Iowa shooting a lot of pictures for S.P.E.W. and Pure Talent.

I wound up shooting fantastic pictures of the Miss Nude World event. For one thing, I already knew more than half the contestants. I also was well familiar with the Lumberyard knowing the lighting conditions and all the best spots where I could get the best angles of the contestants. The trouble was, I couldn't do anything with all the great pictures I would end up taking. The reason being the owners of Miss Nude World required all photographers to give exclusive rights to themselves. So, I could not even offer my pictures to "Xtreme Magazine."

Women did in fact compete from all over the world for the Miss Nude World title. For example, one of the contestants was Arianna Star, Miss Nude Australia. While another was Denise Molder from Holland who would share the Miss Nude World title with Serenna Star, the following year. Aspen Reign who had won the title the year before turned in a dazzling performance although as the previous year's winner she was not allowed to compete in 2003.

There were eighteen contestants in 2003 that included the likes of: K.C. Cannons, Kloey Love, Leslie Wells, Tristan Blue, Regan Anthony, and Lolly Tops. I had met Lolly Tops in Wichita Falls when she was dancing as Victoria Daniels.

To give everyone an idea of the immensity of the event, the first winner would get $25,000. While some of the props the contestants used were surprisingly extravagant and expensive. For example, XXXena who was Miss Nude Universe 2002, arrived on the stage in a cage like contraption that was suspended by a steel cable 20 feet in the air from the club's ceiling. While K.C. Cannons performed one of her shows in a robot suit that was rumored to cost $3,000.00. Keep in mind that's just for one show. As Feature Entertainers of K.C.'s caliber are expected to be able to perform a dozen unique shows and have enough outfits for each one. And Aspen Reign, who did not compete, put on a special guest performance in front of a stage setting that must have been at least 20 feet high.

One of the front runners was expected to be Lori Alexander. Lori had brought her large snake with her, which she was keeping in her hotel room. So, I soon visited Lori and her snake in her hotel room, due to my fascination with big snakes and wanting to wish Lori luck in the upcoming events.

I think Lori could have won the title. Although winning meant a lot more than just putting on a great dancing performance such as great choreography, the beauty of the entertainer, and the originality of her show. Although there were a lot of excellent performers here, with Denise Molder perhaps being the best pole dancer to name just one example, Lori was by far the best acrobat in the entire group. It takes a certain amount of originality and guts to dance while being wrapped in the grips of a large snake.

When I heard that Lori had been disqualified by the powers that be of Miss Nude World I joined her in her room where I found her in tears. Later I'd talk to Big Mike about it and found out that one of Lori's rival contestants badmouthed her for cruelty to animals, while another contestant told me in confidence that Lori had been robbed by being deprived of the opportunity of competing for the prestigious Miss Nude World title which she had an excellent chance of winning. Eventually, Big Mike agreed with the verdict of the owners of the pageant. But now that I look back on the whole thing, I believe that Big Mike, even though I respected him a lot, was relatively young back then and possibly too impressionable when being pitted face to face against those who had many more years of experience in the adult entertainment industry. When I reflect on it, I'm not saying she would have won, but I do think she was robbed of the opportunity of competing.

K.C. Cannons wound up winning the 2003 title, which I'd say she deserved to win. But on the other hand, there were several others who deserved the title just as much.

Selling the S.P.E.W. DVD

S.P.E.W. was proving to be enormously popular due to the monumental efforts the girls were putting in traveling from state to state, the golden voice of Big Daddy, and the raw energy of Big Mike with his willingness to try just about anything that offered a decent chance of success. So, when Big Daddy and Big Mike informed me that they were going to start producing S.P.E.W. DVDs that the girls could sell to their customers and on the Internet, I started to get excited about just how big S.P.E.W. could get. And not just for the girls, and Big Mike and Big Daddy, but for myself as well.

After Death Match 1, Leah Layne had come back to my apartment where I did two interviews of her discussing how the match had gone between Dirty Heather and Killer Kloey and who would likely win a rematch. Leah was funnier than hell with her answers and a real cut up; which vindicates a lot of what I keep saying about adult entertainers; there are a lot of reasons such women wind up stripping in a topless club; and a couple of really important ones for many is that they are very talented and creative. I believe that a lot of them want to go to Hollywood to become famous movie starlets, but unfortunately their chances of becoming movie starlets are very remote.

Most times after they have gone into the adult profession, no movie studio is going to touch them. Take Marilyn Chambers for an example, as I had mentioned earlier in the book. After performing in "Behind the Green Door" at Mitchell Brothers she became labeled as a "Porn Star." Marilyn was, however, a very beautiful, intelligent woman who it so turns out could actually act. But in the eyes of the mainstream film industry Marilyn had already sullied herself by doing Porn.

I think a lot of women who enter the adult profession want to do something creative with their lives but they know their chances of making it in the mainstream movies are virtually non-existent. And this is why so many House Dancers want to become Feature Entertainers who have to act out a variety of roles while wearing clothing that fits the parts they are playing.

Most of the women wrestling with S.P.E.W. were putting out a lot of effort for little gain. Take Pleasure and Pain, the mother daughter duo from Columbus, Ohio. Pleasure was only 20 or 21 when I first met her at "Nudes-A-Poppin." While Pain, her mother was about 39. If Pleasure was not the most beautiful girl at "Nude's-A-Poppin," she was pretty close. While Pain being 39 knew her career as an entertainer was about to end. So, Pain went balls out to advance the career of her daughter who had every chance of being a superstar. So, when I told Pleasure and Pain about the Exotic Dancer Expo in Las Vegas, they met me there at considerable expense to themselves. And later when I told them about the Maximus M.S. Texas pageant they drove over 1000 miles all the way from Columbus, Ohio, to Texas to compete in the pageant.

I'm sure Pain must have felt that S.P.E.W. would help put her daughter on the fast track to success in the adult entertainment business. I believe Pain wanted her daughter to hang around with me as much as possible. And when they came out twice to visit me in Collinsville, so I could do photoshoots of them for my "Xtreme Magazine" gun articles; I think there was even more to it than being featured in the magazine; because I started noticing that momma kept trying to get me one on one with her daughter; while momma would go into the other room; or at various events, leave the two of us alone together. In retrospect, I believe Pain wanted Pleasure and I to establish a comfort zone that might eventually lead to our forming at least a close, professional relationship together.

I am aware that several of my friends felt that Pain's clock was ticking, and that she had been hoping to be able to cash in on her beautiful daughter's success provided that she made it in the big leagues. But, I truly believe that Pain was looking forward to the end of their mother daughter stripper acts, and that her daughter would have to face stardom alone, and for this Pleasure needed good friends in the adult entertainment world she could trust.

I never visited Pleasure and Pain at their home club in Columbus. But I'm sure that the pair did pretty well financially on their home turf. But when they traveled to Big Daddy's Cabaret in Missouri, or the Lumberyard in Des Moines they were no longer able to make nearly as much money as they could have had they stayed in Columbus. They were too busy wrestling for one thing, and when they were not wrestling they were sitting with some of the other wrestlers at a long S.P.E.W table where they were expected to hand out S.P.E.W. promotional materials and socialize with customers coming up to their table. So, here they are traveling all the way from Columbus, OH, while making very little money for their efforts.

Now this is where Big Mike and Big Daddy made their fatal mistake. Big Daddy in particular enjoyed having good music being played in his bar. So, the pair of them decided that the S.P.E.W. DVD had to include music. But the problem then just as it is today, "Copyright Infringement." So, both men knew that if they put popular music on the S.P.E.W. DVD, that all of us would be sued for copyright infringement.

To avoid the problem of copyright infringement Big Daddy and Big Mike went into business with a local Iowa Rock Band, which created the master DVD for S.P.E.W. By going into a partnership with the band Big Mike and Big Daddy could avoid being sued for music copyright infringement. This is because the band was creating its own music for the S.P.E.W. DVD. The first problem with this arrangement with the Iowa rock band is the music turned out to be total crap.

But even worse–because the band had contracted to produce the DVD for Big Mike and Big Daddy, it had total control of the entire production process.

Being your typical egocentric rock band, the rock band members made certain that the S.P.E.W. DVD focused entirely on their band. There was nothing about either Big Daddy, or Big Mike on the DVD, and here they were the founders of S.P.E.W. And other than putting on some video footage of the S.P.E.W. wrestlers, there was nothing said about the girls starring in the video. The band members made sure that they were the only heroes on that DVD. I cannot begin to describe the anger I was feeling as I learned more and more about how much the talent and the efforts of Dirty Heather, Killer Kloey, Macy, Suzanne, Pleasure and Pain, Paradise, and so many other hard working women were being marginalized not to mention the pioneering talent and intrepidness of Big Daddy and Big Mike.

Had I done it, I would have made up a lot about Leah Layne the referee being this ultra, sexy Miss Nude Illinois bombshell. I would have made up all kinds of yarns about Killer Kloey putting over ten girls in the hospital and Dirty Heather having been rumored to have killed a man who had tried to rob her. I would have glorified or vilified each S.P.E.W. wrestler to no end. While making a big deal out of Big Daddy's once having been a professional TV wrestler.

As it turned out, I don't think anyone of the girls who had spent so many hours with S.P.E.W. gave a tinkers damn about selling any DVD's for Big Daddy and Big Mike. If we were to do the entire S.P.E.W. saga over again today, with the computer software and video editing programs I have now, and my ability to get copyright free music I could produce DVD's that the women would want to sell. There would be no self serving band.

Ironically, this is exactly what I have done with my Thai boxing videos I've put on You tube. And just as ironical that Big Daddy took me to the matches here in Pattaya, Thailand, where we sat next to each other in the front row.

The Xtreme Weapons Calendar

It was Jeremy McTeague's idea to produce the 2004 Xtreme Weapons Calendar. Which was immediately seconded by Vic Meyer who was by this time becoming a huge component to the success of my "Xtreme Guns and Babes" articles. I had taken Dirty Heather, Arianna a Del, Darien Ross, and Carmen to Vic and Tammy's house to do photo shoots for Xtreme. With Carmen being a twenty year old House Dancer working for Big Daddy's at the time.

I had done my second gun shoot of Dirty Heather at Vic and Tammy's with Dirty Heather and Krazy Ted posing with a .30 Caliber Browning machine gun. While a gun owner friend of Vic's brought his even larger .50 Caliber Browning machine gun out to Vic's where I did a photoshoot of Carmen pretending to fire it. I had done a photoshoot of Jada Deville at Big Louie's at Fort Leonard Wood posing with an AK-47 I had borrowed from Vic. And borrowed a Tec- 9 Automatic Machine Pistol from Vic and an AKS Russian assault rifle, so that I could take pictures of Leah Layne and Lollytops in Collinsville. While I was shooting my third Pure Talent Feature Showcase at Big Al's, Vic had joined me in Peoria, IL, where we did a photoshoot of Carrie Bare, Serenna Star, and Kelly Taylor at Tommy Gun's farm ten miles outside Peoria.

All three of the models we shot at Peoria were Feature Entertainers. While Serenna Star would become the best publicized out of the three after she went on to share the Miss Nude World 2004 title with Denise Molder. There were a lot of people who came to watch Vic and I do that photoshoot. Mike Dunn, being the freelancer photographer who often shot Feature Showcases while standing next to me was following our entourage, so that he could get in on the action. Jim Hyatt was there because he had wanted to shoot some of my guns, especially my .454 Casull after I told him how powerful it was.

Gary, a makeup artist and hair dresser who was very popular with the Pure Talent Feature Entertainers came with us that day to work on each model before she took her place posing with a gun after the model who had preceded her.

I had brought my new Springfield M1A with me, which Kelly Taylor wanted to shoot in the worse way. While Vic had brought along a couple FAL Battle Rifles and a Russian Dragunov Sniper's Rifle. Serenna Star drew the FAL Battle Rifle as her weapon she would pose with while we had Carrie Bare pose with the new M-16 I had just bought. Although I had done over a hundred terrific shots of Arianna a Del posing with an M-16, she had suddenly lost all interest in being a Feature Entertainer.

Who would prove useless when it would come time to be selling the new 2004 Xtreme Weapons calendars.

In many ways, Kelly Taylor was a lot like Marriah. Kelly had told me she had already shot a number of weapons and that she liked shooting guns. So, the Springfield M1A with its 20 round clips of high powered .308 shells intrigued her. Since we were at a farm far from Peoria's city limits we had an ideal spot to try out some of the weapons. Kelly did quite well firing the Springfield M1A, but when I told her that she had to model with the Dragunov Sniper's Rifle she suddenly turned obstinate.

"I don't want anything to do with that rifle," Kelly told me

"Why not Kelly? It's a great looking gun. You will hardly ever see anyone of those around, and it is a highly accurate rifle that's designed for killing men at long range."

"It's Russian Jack. They are a bunch of Communists and I hate all Communists."

About this time Vic interceded. Who was finally able to help me convince Kelly to allow me to shoot her pictures posing with the Dragunov.

As for Jim Hyatt, I had already hatched my evil plot I'd play on him. My Ruger Redhawk .454 Casull at close to 55 ounces was quite heavy for a handgun. I also had a Colt .45 Peacemaker Single Action Army that produced a fair amount of recoil while shooting the .45 Long Colt. I mean a fair amount, although not punishing, or earthshaking by any means. With my .454 Casull l could also shoot .45 Colt loads as well as the .454 Casull's, which had a lot longer casings. Shooting .45 Colt cowboy velocity factory loads in my .454 Casull was a real pussy cat to shoot due to its 54 ounce weight compared to my Colt Single Action Army's 43 ounces. But I had also been reloading my own ammo. I often times reloaded my .45 Colt shells with a lot more powder to bring the velocity of the Cowboy loads of 850 feet per second to around 1100, or so. This brought the power of my .45 Colt reloads to about the same level as a medium .44 Magnum load, which would have been ideal for shooting deer and wild boars, but a bit light for tackling grizzly, or brown bear. My reloads had a significant kick, but my Ruger Redhawk still shot very nicely with them, but I had something else in mind for Jim Hyatt.

In Peoria I was able to find a large gun store, that had a variety of .454 factory ammunition to choose from. So, I bought a box of 260 grain hollow points that would do over 1800 feet per second out of my

Redhawk. Keep in mind that this is over 700 feet per second more than my hand loads that I already considered enough for a lot of big game.

A .454 Casull shooting maximum loads is considered to be powerful enough for Kodiak bears, Elephants, and Rhinoceros. I don't know if Jim was expecting to shoot an Elephant load or not, but when I loaded six shells into my gun's chamber and handed it to him, Jim got off just five rounds before handing it to me, telling me while trying to hide his discomfort, “Ok Jack. I've had enough. You get to take the last shot.”

Which I did, but I was just a little too flippant and arrogant shooting that last round. I wasn't deliberate and careful enough. So, as the big revolver recoiled the cylinder release thumb latch cut open my thumb. When I saw blood starting to squirt out onto my shirt, I proceeded to suck on my thumb to keep the blood from getting all over me. But when I heard Gary scream out, “Oh, how awful.” I started to laugh as I thought about how squeamish some people can get over just a little blood.

I have totally forgotten how many calendars Xtreme finally printed up, or how Jeremy, Vic, and I broke down its financing. But I recall that both Vic and I might have paid Xtreme $1,500 to $2,000 each to print several thousand of those calendars, while Jeremy paid Xtreme something like $500 or $1,000.00. To make up for the cost differences Jeremy told us that Xtreme would advertise the calendar in full color and not charge Vic and I a thing for the advertising. Since Vic was traveling all over both Missouri and Illinois to set up his booth at gun shows, Vic was figuring that he should be able to sell a lot of calendars at his exhibitor's booth.

Xtreme had done a tremendous job on the calendars. There was of course a single page in the calendar for each month and on each page there was a large picture of one of my models posing with the gun of the month. Taking up the entire front cover of the calendar, was a picture I had taken at Fort Leonard Wood of an M-60 Heavy Tank with three of Big Daddy's strippers posing in front of the tank. While the back cover of the calendar had small pictures of the twelve entertainers with the guns they were posing with. Xtreme had placed a lot of text on the back cover displaying for example, “This calendar is dedicated to the members of our Armed Forces.” I was credited with all photos on the calendars back cover along with my email and website addresses, while Xtreme listed its corporate address in New Britain, CT, and its phone number.

The calendar turned out sensationally, since it had been designed and printed by Xtreme. I was every bit as good as if it had been done by Playboy. But it did not sell well. Although Xtreme advertised it in its magazine, hardly anyone bought any from Xtreme. While Vic had grossly overestimated how many he could sell at the gun shows. I think Vic must have felt that most American women were just as open minded as Tammy. But as it turned out time and time again, one man after another came up to his booth to tell him how much he liked the Xtreme Weapons calendar, but he could not hang one up in his house, garage, or machine shed because he was afraid his wife would object to its erotic pictures.

I don't remember if I just had Darien Ross staying overnight with me at my Collinsville apartment or Leah Layne, but one of the women was there when Serenna Star stopped by to get her share of the calendars I promised to give her. She didn't manage to sell many even though she'd soon become Miss Nude World 2004. But it was a true work of art that revealed the fine figures of the most exceptional models I could find. Altogether, I would do over 26 gun articles, which became the genesis for my book: Extreme Guns and Babes for an Adult World.

Club 64

When PT's bought the Platinum Club from Jim Lichty the owners must have felt that Platinum would keep making the same money it had been when Frank Marcella was running it. Which would have been a good bet that could have paid off in spades. After all, Frank had been managing Platinum for years and was the best strip club manager I had ever known. A total professional through and through, Frank could still pull off the unexpected.

For example, Frank had employed the largest bouncer I ever saw. The man was about six foot seven and he weighed 375 pounds. Have you ever faced a man that big in the boxing ring? Well I have. Thanks to Frank.

Leo was Yugoslavian. Frank had told me once that he had been the body guard of one the Yugoslavian government higher ups. I am not sure if this was true or not, but one night Frank told me he wanted Leo to get into professional wrestling. Then Frank asked me to shoot pictures and video of Leo training. This meant my driving over to St. Louis where I was to meet Leo at his father's house.

The house was just a normal sized brick home that was typical of so many South St. Louis old neighborhoods, but it had a very untypical garage. Which was filled with barbells, a bench press bar, and all sorts of punching bags, that included a platform bag that had been mounted to the ceiling as well as a speed bag, a heavy bag, and another bag that I had never tried before. This was a round bag mounted on a flexible steel rod, that would gyrate around as it was being hit. I watched Leo bench pressing over 400 pounds, which was about double what I could do, and then I watched him work out on the bags.

I used to be damn good with the speed bag, and could hit the heavy bag hard enough to become a pretty hard puncher for a middleweight. But I remember one time when I had a night job with the Coca Cola bottling company when I put the gloves on with a solidly built black guy. It was all in fun of course. We were about equally fast, but I learned real quick that he had the build of a light heavyweight. So, there was no doubt in my mind that if we were in a real boxing match that I'd end up the loser.

I weighed about 165 then while the guy I had just been boxing was probably about 175 to 180, which would have put him in the light heavyweight division had he been a professional boxer. Normally, true heavyweights go anywhere from about 190 pounds and up. And historically, about every time a light heavyweight fought the heavyweight champion, the heavyweight champion would knock the light heavyweight challenger out. Now I'm not saying this always happens, I'm only saying it if the heavyweight champion is a quality fighter and he's in good physical condition.

A really huge heavyweight boxing champion might be as heavy as 250, and here we have Leo, who's training every day, and although he is not a Professional Boxer he's using the same basic training techniques with the speed and heavy bags that a boxer would. Leo ends up convincing me to put the gloves on with him. I've not been doing any form of boxing training at all and I've been smoking a pack of cigarettes a day.

I get the first two punches in. Right into Leo's face. But they are only light jabs, which probably was just enough to piss Leo off. Because he just waded right in on me, and backed me right up against the garage door. Now, I don't care if I would have gotten in the luckiest punch in the world, there was just no stopping that 375 pound giant. He would not even have had to punch me. He would have just gone through me and I would have been mashed potatoes on the floor. I would take pity on any troublemaker who would have had to face Leo.

By the time PT's had taken over the Platinum Club it already owned 14 clubs in Illinois, Missouri, Kentucky, Colorado, and Texas. What PT's did not count on was Frank's complete refusal to work with them. Instead, Frank bought a little hole in the wall country western bar that was just off the main highway to Saint Louis.

In his past life Frank had been a Plumber, so he had a lot of contacts from the plumbing and carpentry professions. And he was pretty good at doing carpentry if he had to do a project with his own hands. A lot of his carpenter and plumber buddies used to visit him when he was the General Manager at Platinum, and now that he was remodeling an old country western bar, he started calling on all his old pals.

A few months later, Frank and his buddies had totally transformed the old bar into a strip club that was completely different from the Platinum Club, or Visions. The place was not glittery at all and there were no bright flashing lights. The bar had two large rooms on the ground level with several smaller rooms upstairs. One had a hot tub in it while the other two were bedrooms where his strippers could do their thing. What their thing was, I am not going to say because I never was a customer of any of Frank's girls. But the main entrance opened up into a typical neighborhood bar that was selling beer for only two dollars a bottle. At the end of the bar was a single small stage with a dancing pole.

The second room had a larger stage in the center of the room. On one side of the room there was a rustic loft that led to the upstairs rooms. And there were comfortable chairs, couches, and small tables throughout the place. But Frank's real masterstroke was the truck trailer he had bought second hand that he had transformed into a VIP Room. I think the trailer only cost him a thousand or two thousand dollars. But it gave him a very narrow room that was around twenty-three feet long. And all he had to do was to cut a hole in the side of the trailer, push the trailer up against the West side of his building, and cut a matching hole in his wall. Another hour or two spent fitting a door between the trailer and his bar, and suddenly he's got a very charming VIP Room. Add several dim lights, a couch or two, a 1500 watt space heater to warm the place in the winter, and he's got a very private narrow lounge for maybe four thousand dollars tops.

I'm sure that the top brass from PT's was not very happy. Frank called his new establishment--Club 64, and it was situated at a choke point on the road leading from Interstate 64 to Brooklyn. This is where the old stockyards used to be. Now it was a crime ridden neighborhood where I'd often see crack whores venturing into Club 64's parking lot. Club 64 is in East Saint Louis, which for many people spells CRIME in huge letters. Yet, it's only half a mile from where you can see the bright lights of Saint Louis and the Saint Louis Arch across the river. So, driving to Club 64 isn't scary at all, but in order to get to Brooklyn to visit the Platinum Club or Roxy's, which is right next door to Platinum, you have to drive another two miles down a dark two lane road to the seedy little town of Brooklyn with its dilapidated houses and crack whores.

On most nights Platinum and Roxys would be selling bottled beer for $5.50. Although on Tuesday nights Roxys had its $2.00 specials where you could buy nearly any type of drink for only two bucks. In general the PT's clubs were known for having a lot of pretty decent looking girls. While Dollies, C-Mowes, Miss Kitty's, Chameleon, and a few other titty joints didn't have on average the best looking strippers. So, you'd be paying around $4.00 a beer at these lower echelon clubs. But being a PT's club, Roxy's was able to attract more than its fair share of good lookers. But the atmosphere inside was not even close to being as spectacular as Platinum's.

I don't know if it was because Roxy's might have had better management, or because people had been going there for years and still expected a better looking group of girls, but after Frank left Platinum, it never seemed to get even half the number of customers it used to get during its glory days.

But what really must have angered some of the PT's people was when Frank hung six 48 by 30 inch pictures of his best looking girls on one of the outside walls of his club. He put the pictures in glass fronted frames and backlit them so that passing motorists could see them from half a mile away. Of course I was equally responsible with Frank for all those pictures. Because every week I'd shoot a couple hundred pictures of one of his girls with my Nikon D-1x.

I keep mentioning how terrific a manager Frank was. But Frank had his wife, Sherry, who had been the daytime manager at Platinum. Sherry had three things going for her: She was beautiful, smart, and she knew how to work. So, I got to work with Sherry doing all those photoshoots. Sherry would pick a girl out to be my model, and then she'd spend up to two hours having the girl's hair and makeup done, and then she would personally supervise all my photoshoots.

Although I had brought in several flashes, Sherry would help me locate a few special lights which we would position around our model. And then she would help the model get into various positions and angles that would show her off to the greatest advantage. I can't say enough about Sherry who had a keen eye for the correct lighting and which pictures had turned out the best.

Meanwhile, Leah Layne had visited me a couple of times, and had asked me if I could get her jobs in the Saint Louis Metro East clubs for a few days. So I asked Craig, who was the General Manager of Roxy's, if he would hire Leah. Now normally a PT's club would have no interest in having a girl work for only a few days and then run off to work somewhere else. But Leah was a well known Superstar Feature Entertainer. So Craig made an exception for us.

Leah got along great at Roxy's. The House Dancers viewed her as a mentor, and a dancer none of them could even hope to match. When Leah would get up on that stage they'd all just watch her with awe. So, I'd end up picking Leah up each night her shift ended, and then we'd often head to Club 64 on the way back to my apartment.

One night I started to walk into Roxy's when Leo strode across Platinum's parking lot to intercept me.

“You cannot go into Roxy's,” Leo told me in a voice showing how pleased he was with himself. And then he added, "You cannot come into Platinum either. From now on, you are barred from PT's."

And then Craig came out to talk with me.

“I'm sorry Jack. There's nothing I can do about it. I don't understand what's happened except I've got my orders from above.”

I didn't know what to think. Craig and I had always gotten along exceptionally well. And I knew a lot of the top brass from PT's. They had seen me several years in a row at the Exotic Dancer Expos in Las Vegas. They had seen me doing a couple photoshoots at the Pure Talent Feature Showcases. I just couldn't see any of the top PT’s executives barring me from any of their clubs.

But at least I could have a few beers over at Club 64. As soon as I went inside the door I encountered Frank, and told him, “I just got barred from PT's. Can you believe it?”

“Don't feel badly Jack. They've barred me too.” Frank replied.

The next morning I called Mike Oscello, who has been for years the General Manager over all the PT's clubs. I still don't know who barred me from PT’s, but Mike told me straight off that I was not barred and that he'd take care of the situation straight away.

Angel and Delilah

Although I had been kicked out of Dollies, I was still good friends with a few of the girls. Who would move around a lot among the Washington Park clubs. One week Angel would be working at Dollies, the next week she might be back at Chameleon. Or Alex who I first met at C-Mowes, would work at Chameleon for a few days, and then she'd be back at Dollies. By this time I was also getting to know several of the Visions girls quite well such as Angie, Sahara, and Selena. While up in Indiana I was still traveling there to see Doc and Sam, and each time I'd go Renee would wind up coming down to Stimmelators to see me and my friends.

But no matter what club the girls had come from, and with several of them no longer being strippers, such as Brandy and Renee, we were all connected through the Internet with the Lost Angels chat being our hub.

Angel even managed to get her own desktop computer that Allan Nilman and I helped her hook up at her house in Granite City. By now I was seeing a lot of Angel. And so did a lot of my friends such as Allan and PlONe when he was visiting us from California.

And we had another Lost Angels Annual Awards party a few months after I got kicked out of Dollies. I can't remember everyone who came to my apartment because by then we were all having so many parties. But Alex and her husband were there, and both Selena and Sahara had joined us after driving through a snowstorm from New Athens.

At first, Sahara told me that she couldn't come due to the hazardous driving conditions. And then Selena told me she'd rather get killed than to miss my party. So Selena must have pointed a gun at Sahara's head because they both came to my party.

Once again, we gave out trophies that I had bought at the Collinsville sporting goods store that specialized in altering trophies to fit the needs of its customers, but whereas we had all voted Alex as our “Dancer of the Year” the previous year that night at Dollies, this year we made Renee the Lost Angels “Dancer of the Year.”

Renee once went with me for two days to “Nudes-A-Poppin” as my photographer's assistant. A year later Renee and her husband Lee, joined me in Las Vegas where they helped me run my Alphapro booth at the Exotic Dancer Expo. The three of us shared a room together, and we shared the Alphapro booth with“Nudes-A-Poppin.” So there we were, Lee, Renee, and myself having Scarlett, (the owner of “Nudes-A-

Poppin,") her production manager and her head of security all at the booth together, with "Nudes-A-Poppin" and Alpha Productions sign boards identifying the booth as a joint effort. So, we all became even better acquainted. "Xtreme Magazine" had its booth there, so Renee and Lee got better acquainted with Jeremy and a couple of the new salesmen for Xtreme. And at night we all had a great time!

After returning home from Las Vegas I hit Renee up on my latest idea. Back then I was using Microsoft Front Page for my website development program. And Front Page had a feature I could use to build discussion groups. The concept I now shared with Renee was to start an advisory forum that I'd call, "Dear Delirious Delilah." Renee had not been dancing for several years, and Renee was never her real name having only been her stage name. So,once she quit dancing, I'd start calling her Delilah while keeping her real name a secret.

For a couple months, Renee kept "Delirious Delilah" cooking. Guys would go into the forum asking Renee some pretty strange questions such as: "My dick is only five inches long. What can I do to make it longer?" To which Delirious Delilah might reply, "Soak it in boiling water to soften it for 90 seconds and then tie a rope around it and fasten the other end to a door knob. Pull on the door twenty times, until you can't stand the pain any longer. Do this each night for ten nights and you will soon see some results."

Unfortunately, Renee could not come to our awards party, due to her living over four hundred miles from the rest of us. But we got into the Lost Angels chat with her where we put up pictures of her "Dancer of the Year" trophy.

Angel and I soon came up to visit her, but Angel had a drinking problem.

I had once taken her to the Platinum Club where we had a few drinks. And then Angel wanted to go to a small bar that was just up the street from Platinum. She wouldn't stay long, she assured me. So, I let her go by herself. But when she didn't return back to the Platinum, I went into the bar, and when I saw that she wasn't there, someone told me that she had walked off up the street drunk on her ass. Since she didn't remember how she got home, Angel decided it was time to stop drinking.

I had another trip planned to go up to Stimmelators and Angel decided to come along with me. And then we'd contact Lee and Renee in Michigan and see if they wanted to join us. But first we went to South

Bend where we spent the night at Tornado's apartment.

Lee and Renee met us at Stimmelators the next evening. I don't remember what Tornado did exactly. He probably just wandered off somewhere with Lee and his deer hunting buddies, which left me alone with Renee and Angel. Angel was still on the wagon. So, she had to sit there watching Renee and I having the time of our lives swigging one beer after the other. Eventually, Renee and I came up with the idea of our selling lap dances to all the Stimmelators strippers.

Renee and I had done this once about a year earlier at one of our Stimmelators parties where we were joined by Crazy Czech, Keith Miller, Tornado, and Philip21. One of the guys shot the video while I was lap dancing Renee by sliding my pelvis up and down her body and then turning around so that I could rub my backside up and down her legs. Then Renee lap danced me, while she kept crying out, "Oh Jack. I know you want me. I want you too!"

We were staying at Sam's house that night, but whoever was in charge of management came close to kicking Renee and me out of the club, due to some kind of rule that we were breaking that one customer could not be allowed to perform sexual acts on another customer.

Several of the Stimmelators dancers fell for our bait, so I ended up lap dancing them while Renee kept laughing at us. Angel looked miserable, not being able to drink and having to watch Renee and I having so much fun.

Eventually, we all wound up at Renee and Lee's house in Buchanon, Michigan. Where Renee and Lee took all of us to a couple of their favorite local taverns. Renee's sister joined us, and then someone came up with the bright idea of doing Dollies Trendy Toilet Sex here in Michigan.

Tornado got very involved and so did Renee and her sister. All of us doing weird things in the toilet. The girls would pretend to be defecating on the toilets--pulling down their jeans and playing with toilet paper. Although our senses of humor might have been sick; none of us were into porn; and some of the locals got into all of our antics with us. I got it all on my YouTube channel, which just shows that what we were doing in the toilet over at Dollies wasn't just a lot of degenerate, depraved acts that can only be dreamed up by a bunch of immoral strippers and strip club managers. No. It's the kind of degenerate, depraved acts that people like to do just about everywhere on Earth. Because most of the people drinking with us in those Michigan taverns probably never spent much time in a strip club.

After spending the night at Lee and Renee's I finally had to drive Angel all the way home. I don't remember what time I got her back to her house in Granite City. But a couple hours after getting back to my Collinsville apartment Angel called me, and she was very drunk. A neighbor of hers had come over and offered her a drink, as a joke, knowing that she had not touched a drop for nearly three weeks.

Picture Collage III

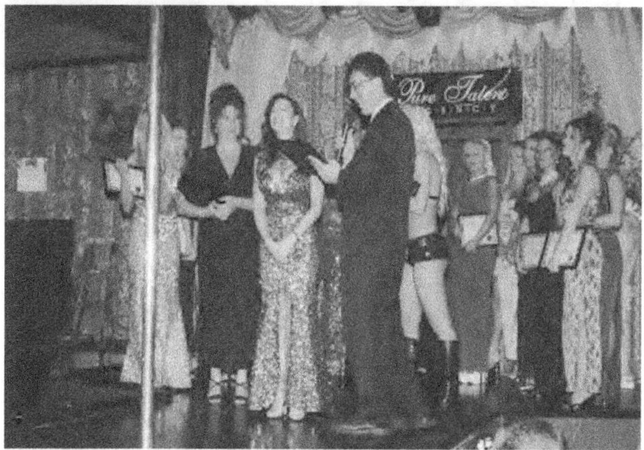

K.C. Cannons and Anne Marie and Jim Hyatt of Pure Talent Agency.

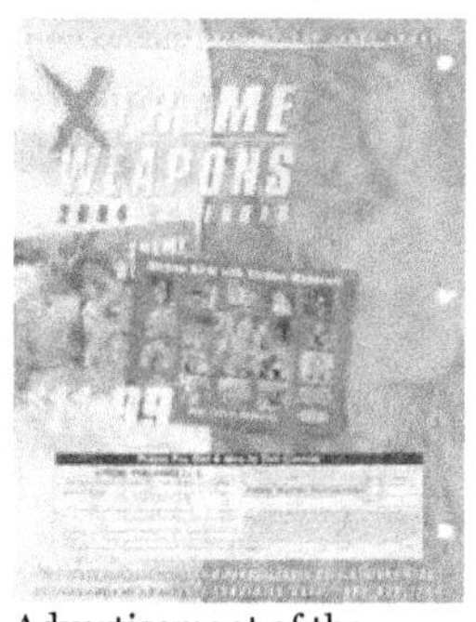

Advertisement of the Xtreme Weapons calendar in Xtreme Magazine. The calendar was published in 2004. The author has just published two new Xtreme Weapons calendars for 2021 and 2022.

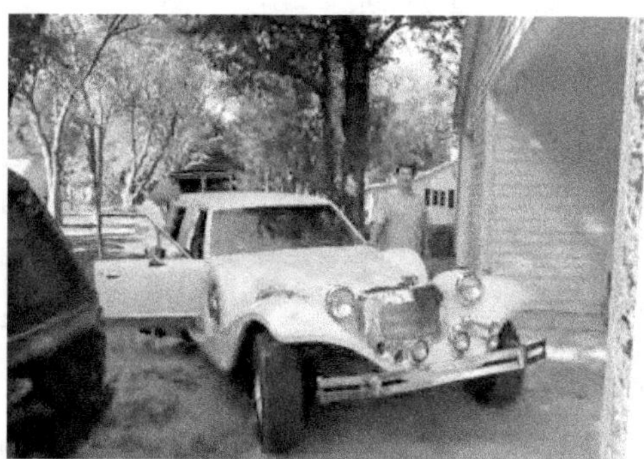

Doctor Doom and his wife Donna with his Lincoln Excaliber stretch limousine he acquired from Sam Stimmel.

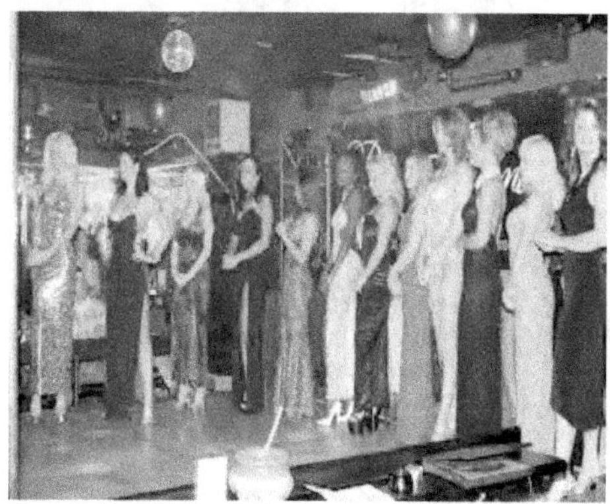

Pure Talent Feature Entertainers at a Pure Talent Feature Showcase in Mobile, Alabama.

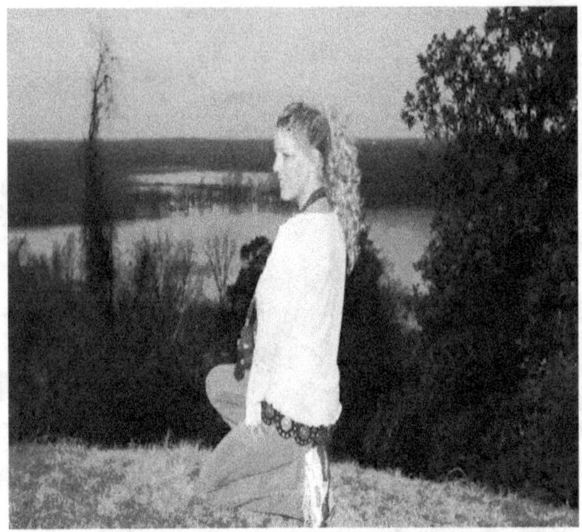

Damien and the author would travel together up to fifty miles touring the Vicksburg Civil War battlefields together.

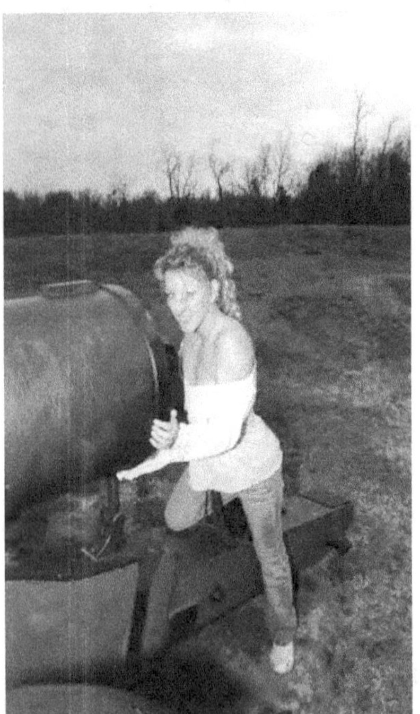

The author met Damien at Nudes-A-Poppin. He would later attend her wedding at 6:00 a.m. in Las Vegas.

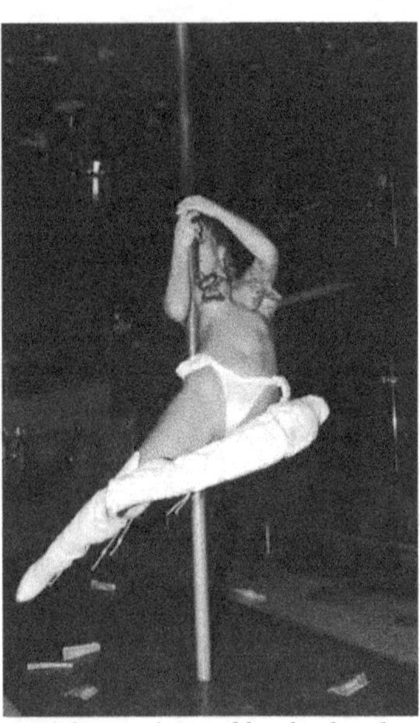

At night Damien and her husband would take the author to the Vicksburg strip clubs. (Damien pole dancing)

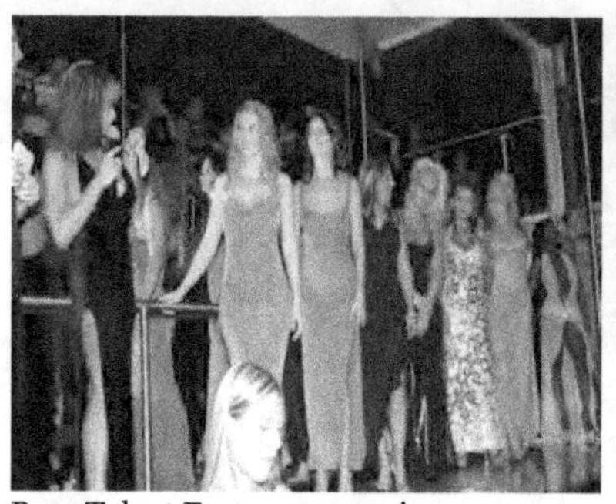

Pure Talent Feature entertainers at a feature showcase at Ritz Cabaret in Baltimore, Maryland.

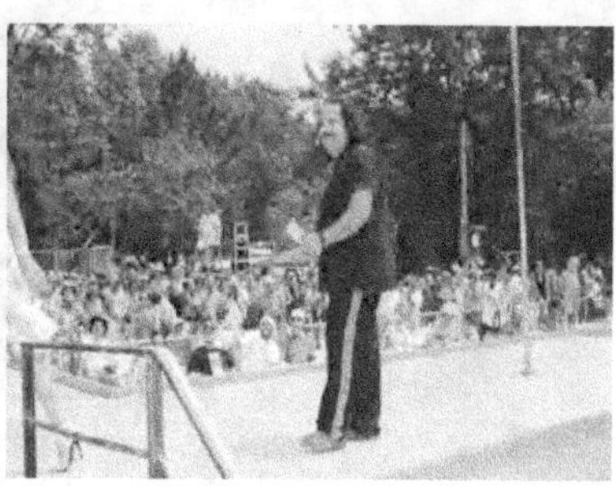

World famous xxx star, Ron Jeremy, the MC at Nudes-a-Poppin entertaining thousands of spectators.

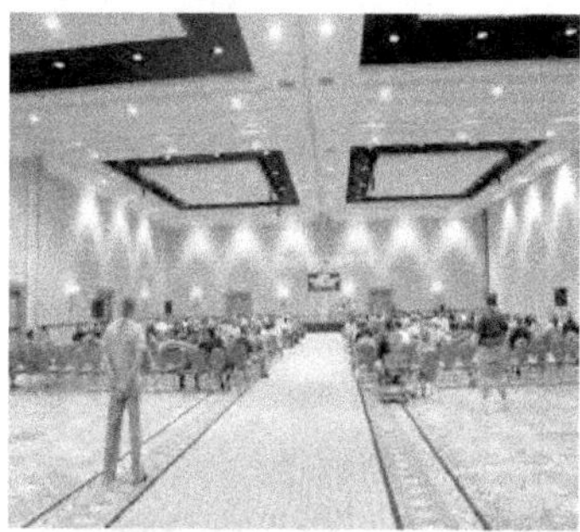

Striving for perfection. An Exotic Dancer seminar attended by club owners and other adult entertainment professionals striving how to improve their club's image in the community, marketing techniques, security methods, how to retain a quality staff, etc.

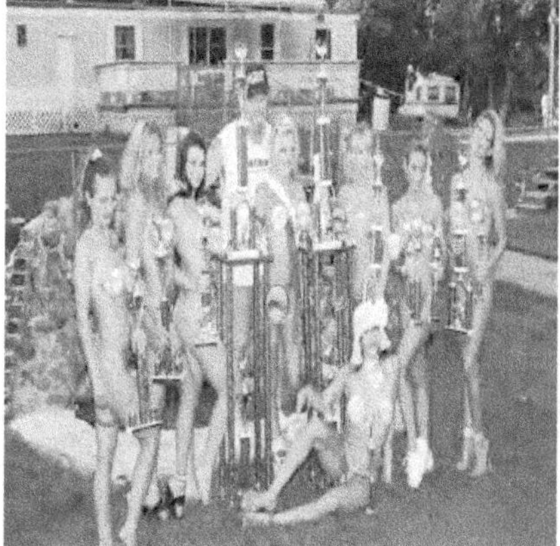

Nudes-A-Poppin contestants with their awards. Darien Ross on the left, Leah Layne to Darien's right. On the far right Lauren Kaine. Continental Agency's Ken Shinkel in the back row. Nudes-A-Poppin is one of the most prestigious adult events n the U.S.. This is because getting an award from NAP represents a significant credit in an Adult Entertainer's career.

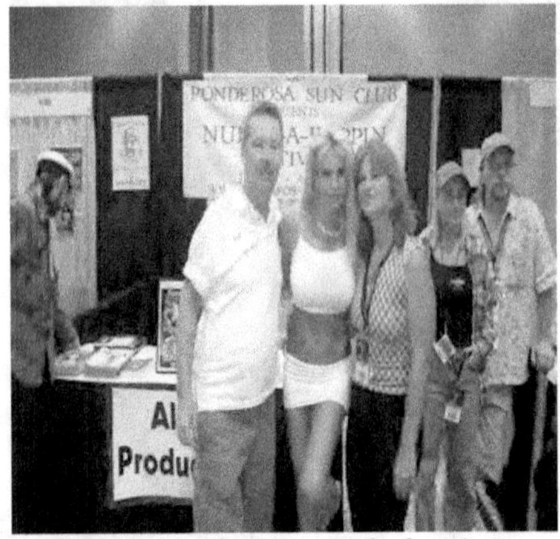

Booth at the Mandalay Bay trade show in Las Vegas. This was a shared booth between the author's alphapro.com web site and Nudes-A-Poppin From the far right Lee (Renee's husband), Renee, Scarlett, xxx star Teri Weigel, Rich Miller, Nudes-A-Poppins Head of Production.

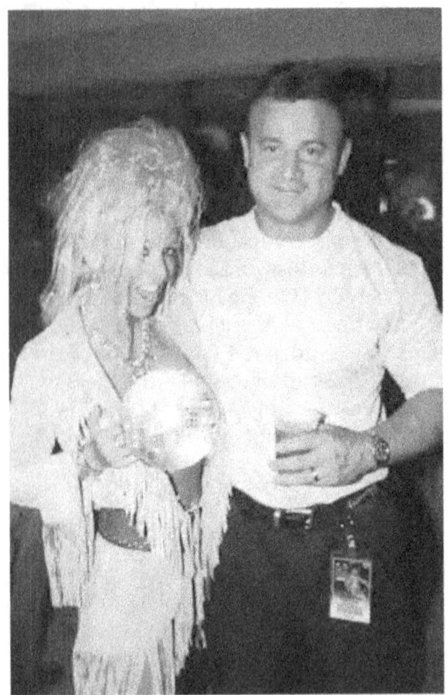

Andy Wielblad, the owner of "Xtreme Magazine" with L.A. Lamann, one of the best Feature Entertainers in the business and an excellent M.C. who Mced many Pure Talent Feature showcases and such major events as Nudes-A-Poppin.

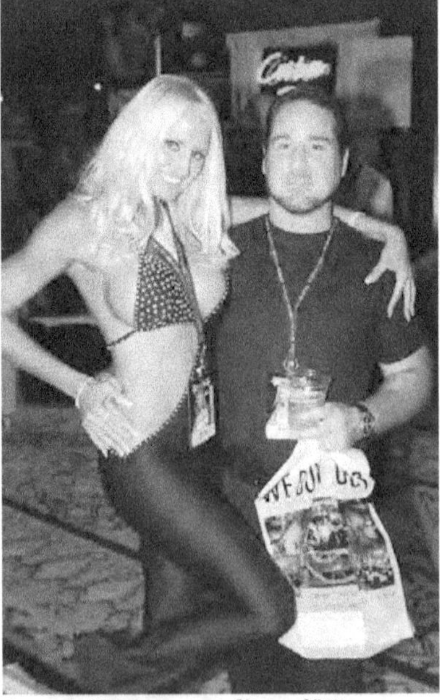

Jeremy McTeagues, editor of "Xtreme Magazine". A gifted writer, Jeremy was called upon by Andy to fulfill a variety of roles from sales, collections, franchise owner, and all around pinch hitter.

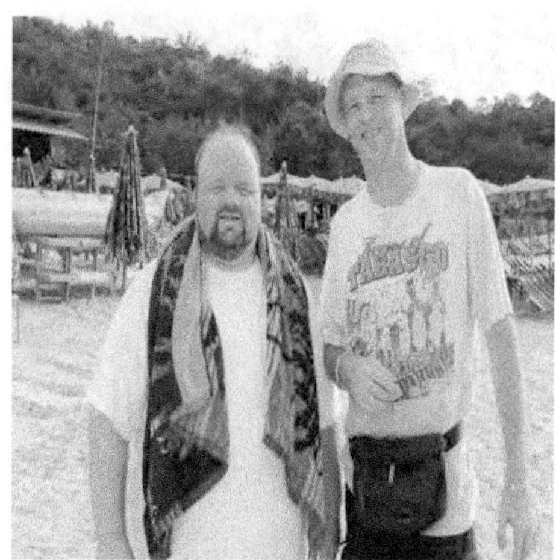

Big Daddy and Hawkeye in Thailand. Hawkeye wound up leaving the adult profession to get his Master's Degree and become a school teacher. Big Daddy has now become an actor.

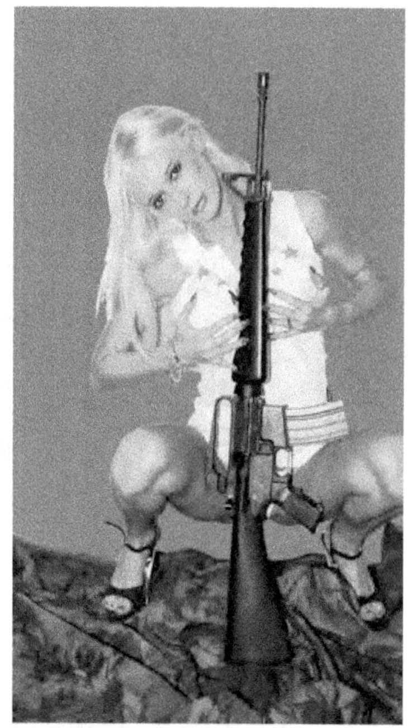

Modeling for Jack's upcoming M16 rifle article for Xtreme, Death on the Wild Side cover girl Arianna a del.

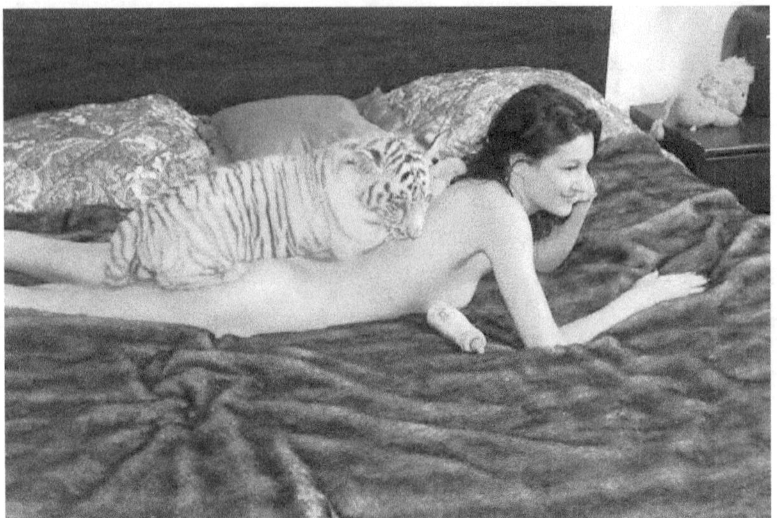

Meet Smokey, a 40 pound white tiger cub. The author was able to "borrow Smokey" for 24 hours, and when the ladies found out what we had in that hotel room, they came a knocking. We also got Smokey up on the stage in Club 64 in East Saint Louis, and the entertainers went wild.

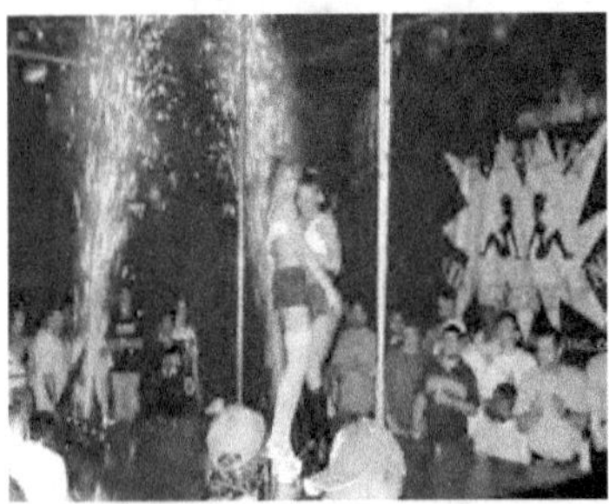

S.P.E.W. (Sexy Professional Exotic Wrestling at the Iowa Playhouse in Council Bluff, Iowa. We went all out to produce the S.P.E.W. wrestling events, including fireworks to introduce the contestants.

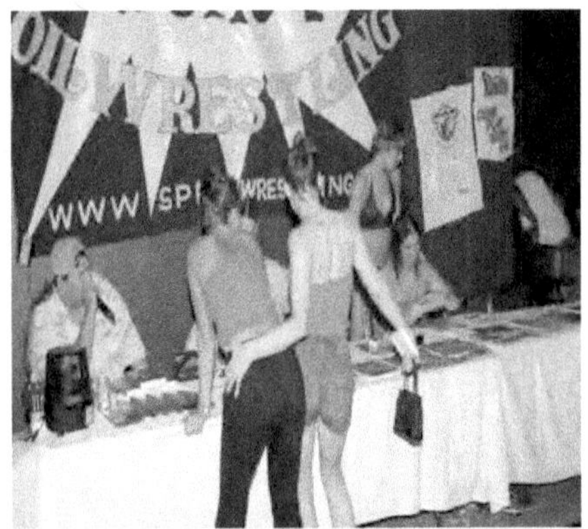

S.P.E.W. promo booth at the Iowa Playhouse. Lumber Yard's General Manager Big Mike on the left. Notice the S.P.E.W. DVD's for sale and copies of the my first book, Death on the Wild Side. I doubt if there will ever be the likes of S.P.E.W. again. Under Big Mike's leadership the Lumberyard became one of the most widely known and respected clubs in the U.S.

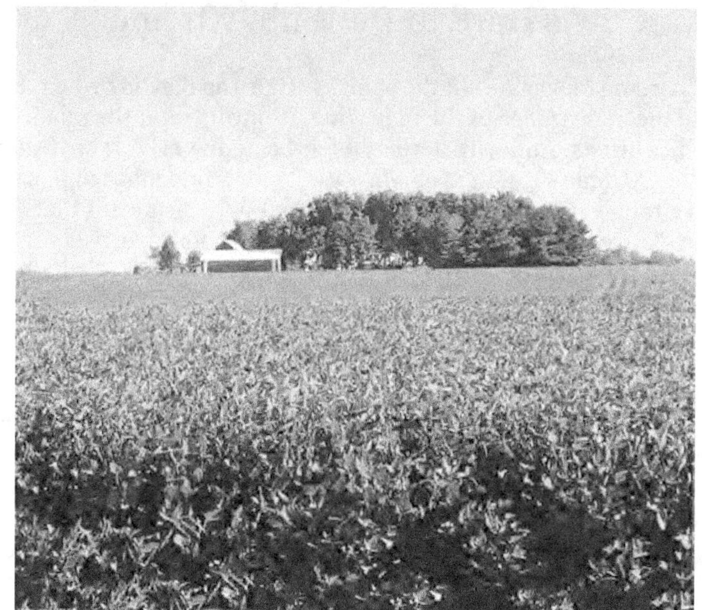

The author's farm near Springfield, IL

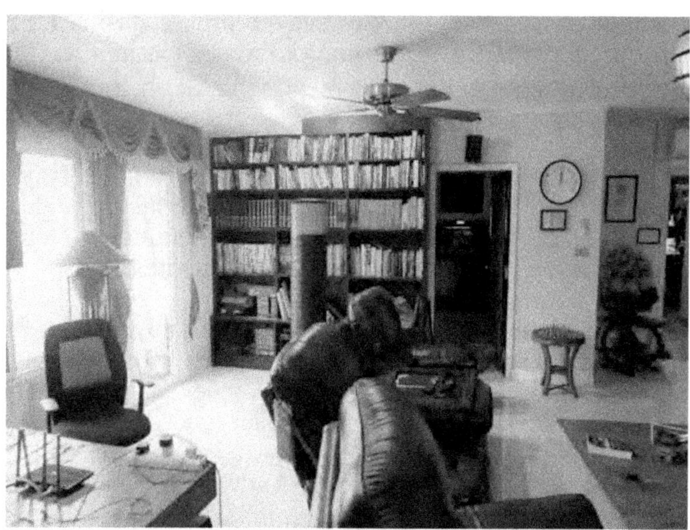

The author's condo in Pattaya, Thailand. Note the floor mounted punching bag in front of his book shelves.

Breaking up is Hard to Do With "Xtreme"

I'd put "Xtreme Magazine" in the same category as Playboy when it comes to the appearance of the magazine, its layout, and the quality of its graphics artists. And with Jeremy I felt I couldn't ask for anything more. But "Xtreme's" main problem was: it was a free magazine, which put it in a totally different category than Playboy. This meant that "Xtreme's" revenues were totally dependent upon its advertisers. While Jeremy had been Editor "Xtreme's" content was excellent. We had some of the top Porn Stars, and Feature Entertainers on the cover every month with full 4 - 6 page color layouts and interviews. Jeremy was continuing to do his horrorscopes, which I felt were totally warped. But have about the same sense of twisted humor as Jeremy, so I found his horrorscopes to be outrageously funny. At the same time I was getting my Dick Fitswell short stories into "Xtreme," and getting these awesome Gun's & Babes articles in each month. So, we had a magazine that had a satiric outlook, but also focused on some really good feature interviews and eclectic stories based on both fiction and nonfiction. But after almost three years Andy (the main owner of Xtreme) put a muzzle on Jeremy and me, which ended the monthly horrorcopes; Jeremy's Adventures of the Backdoor Man series; and my totally demented Dick Fitswell short stories.

But when "Xtreme" had hired two unproductive salesmen in a row, Andy decided to utilize Jeremy's other talents by having Jeremy take on the New Jersey / Pennsylvania "Xtreme" franchise, along with the Mid Atlantic edition franchise. This now made Jeremy responsible for both sales and collections along with his many other responsibilities. About this time "Xtreme" went full color glossy. Giving Xtreme the ability to now command a much higher price from its advertisers.

At the time I was writing my gun articles for "Xtreme," a lot of my articles were three or four pages long. But eventually Jeremy unloaded the bombshell on me: "Andy has decided to stop running your gun articles. But Jack, we've had a very good, long run with them."

I am not for one minute about to take pot shots at Andy. Putting this in perspective, can you see "Hustler," "Penthouse," or "Playboy" running gun articles for almost three years straight? I believe to this day that both Andy and Jeremy were way ahead of their time. And it didn't help that when Jeremy got promoted to take over two franchises, that his editing job went lock, stock, and barrel to Andy's wife, which became a huge wall for Jeremy to even try to penetrate, so he settled on becomig an Associate Publisher and focused more and more on the sales end of the business.

It wasn't long before “Xtreme” started cutting down the size of all its articles with an article normally being four pages long to now being just two pages long, due to its total dependence on advertisers and much higher printing cost because “Xtreme” had gone full color glossy;

“Xtreme” was increasingly becoming less content orientated and almost 80% advertising based; while I was stuck with the problem I had always had:

“Xtreme” was an East Coast outfit whose advertisers were from New York, Pennsylvania, Connecticut, Massachusetts, Rhode Island, Maryland, Virginia, Maine, New Hampshire and Vermont etc....overall covering thirteen states with four regional magazines. While I was a Midwesterner living 1000 miles from the East Coast. But somehow I was able to convince both Jeremy and Andy to allow me to do a lot of Midwest content. For example, “Nudes-A-Poppin,” the Pure Talent Feature Showcases at Big Al's, and Nude Oil Wrestling at Big Daddy's Cabaret. Or, my interviews with leading non East Coast top Managers and owners such as PT's Mike Oscello, or Hustler's Mike Parker. And interviews with top Feature Entertainers such as Nikki Lynn and Adara Michaels who I interviewed in the Saint Louis Metro East PT's clubs.

So, I was able to produce a lot of Midwest content through the backdoor. But I'm sure that a lot of East Coast clubs that were spending a thousand dollars a month or even more with “Xtreme” were not well pleased with seeing so much content coming out of the Midwest.

So, when Jeremy told me that my articles would from now on be limited to just a couple pages, and that I wouldn't be writing for “Xtreme” as often as I had been, I decided that I finally had to make a decision. It was no secret that both Jeremy and Andy were interested in starting up a Midwest “Xtreme Magazine” franchise. While I had developed some excellent contacts in Big Al, Big Daddy, and Big Mike who would almost certainly advertise in a Midwest “Xtreme” franchise. And I would be picking up a lot of new business due to my photoshoots with Pure Talent, “Nudes-A-Poppin,” and being S.P.E.W.'s photographer traveling across several states with Big Mike and Big Daddy.

But I figured I was getting too old. And I couldn't see investing a lot of my own money on start up costs for a Midwestern adult magazine.

If I felt it was too much to be starting up a Midwestern “Xtreme

Magazine" franchise, I thought my best option would be to team up with Jim Lilly who already had his own magazine, the "Wild Times," which was nowhere close to being of "Xtreme's" caliber. It was not even glossy, it was in newspaper print, while a typical "Wild Times" issue only ran to about 30 pages compared to "Xtreme's" 116 plus pages. But Jim Lilly was a smart guy, who I had always found to be a live wire of energy. Unfortunately, as I was starting to do more and more events in Iowa or at Big Al's, Jim for some reason, or another just didn't seem to be very interested.

Shooting Tigers

I still was doing a lot of traveling shooting S.P.E.W. events for Big Mike and Big Daddy. And it was likely that Club Maximus would still want me down in Texas to cover future M.S. Texas Pageants. While after sharing an exhibitor's booth with "NudesA-Poppin" at the Exotic Dancer Expo in Las Vegas, I was in a terrific position to keep meeting some of the best adult entertainers across the U.S.

One of my last gun articles for "Xtreme" featured the Mauser 98K German Military Rifle and one of Big Mike's House Dancers. At one of Big Daddy's S.P.E.W. wrestling events a Missouri man calling himself, Tiger Wayne, had brought a 40 pound Bengal Tiger Cub into Big Daddy's. Which many of the entertainers paid, Tiger Wayne, to take their pictures cavorting around with the playful Tiger.

A few weeks later, Tiger Wayne brought another Tiger Cub up to the Lumberyard. He called the new cub, Smokey, due to the cub being completely white.

So, I ended up making Tiger Wayne a deal by offering him at least one St. Louis Metro East night club where he could try to make enough money from the girls to justify his taking Smokey all the way up from the Lake of the Ozarks to Collinsville. I offered to pay for Tiger Wayne's hotel room, which he would share with Smokey and a young guy who was helping him take care of the white Tiger Cub.

Bringing a Tiger into a strip club isn't as easy as it sounds. Even a forty pound Tiger Cub poses huge liability risks for any night club that allows its guests to come anywhere near a big, potentially dangerous feline. So, I didn't even ask Mike Oscello if we could bring a white Tiger Cub into one of his PT's clubs, due to my being fully aware that a corporate structure such as PT's would never take on such a risk.

But Frank and Sherry Marcella and Club 64 was a different story. Because Frank and Sherry owned the place and didn't have any risk adverse partners. It didn't take very much for me to convince, Kiara, one of the Lumberyard's House Dancers to come down to Collinsville to do the shoot. Kiara brought her husband with her and she had also told several of the other Lumberyard girls what we were all up to. I had gotten, Tiger Wayne, a hotel room at the Best Western that was high up on a bluff less than a mile from my Woodhenge apartment. An hour after Tiger Wayne, and his young sidekick arrived I decided to look in on them to discuss our plans for the evening. After knocking on the hotel room's door someone told me to let myself in. But when I did, I felt an animal tugging at my pant's leg. Thinking it was a dog and how much I hated having dogs mouthing my pants legs I almost kicked back at the animal before realizing it was Smokey.

Club 64 was having a very special party that night, because it was Christmas Eve and two Feature Entertainers, Kloey Love and Leah Layne, were going to be there; not to do their shows; but as guests who had once been House Dancers for Frank. And even though both Kloey and Leah were two of the best features on the circuit the real star was to be Smokey. It seems that practically everyone in the bar took turns feeding Smokey milk from a baby bottle. We even had Smokey on the club's back stage and I still have pictures of Sherry Marcella playing with Smokey as if she were a little girl again.

We did the "Xtreme Weapons" photoshoot on Christmas the next day. Where we were joined by two entertainers who were working for the Heart Throbs Agency. Heart Throbs was not at all like Pure Talent or Continental Agencies, being much smaller it specialized performing for small parties. Amy, from Heart Throbs, had joined us the night before at Club 64 where I took pictures of her totally naked while she cavorted around with Kiara. I had also done a photoshoot a few months earlier of her with a Kentucky rifle for one of my "Xtreme Magazine" gun articles. On Christmas day Amy, brought a second girl with her who I had met at "Nudes-A-Poppin" when she was with the Big Mike entourage.

Smokey proved to be an unforgettable hit with the three entertainers.

Lolly Tops Gets Me An Advertiser

"Jack, I got you an advertiser for your new Midwest Magazine." The voice belonged to Lolly Tops who was calling me from Davenport, Iowa.

"What do you mean, Vicki?"

"I mean this man's the Club Manager. I'm here at his club working temporarily as a House Dancer. I'd like you to come up here and take pictures of me. Tell me if you can come and I will get you a hotel room next to mine."

It is understood, of course, that I will have to pay for my hotel room. But by now having an entertainer book my room for me is not an unusual event. Selena, (from Big Daddy's) used to book hotel rooms for me when I was coming to Big Daddy's. As would Leah Layne several weeks from now.

I soon found out that the name Lolly Tops didn't mean squat with the Iowa Club's customers. For one thing, Vicki hadn't really established herself as a Feature Entertainer—and never would. When she and Danny had visited me in Collinsville when I did a photoshoot of her for my SKS "Xtreme" gun article I had taken her and Danny to Roxy's. Roxy's was having its totally nude shower shows that featured two dancers going down on each other. When Vicki saw that, she said, "I can't believe they are doing all that here!"

And now, I'm talking to two customers who are telling me, "The girls here aren't that bad, except that one," one of the guys told me while pointing at Vicki. "She won't even let me touch her."

Which is probably the single most important reason Vicki would never make it as a Feature Entertainer. She hated to have men she didn't know touching her, and when they did she would get very angry with them. I can't blame Vicki at all for having a lot of respect for her own body.

Eventually the two guys tried to manhandle Vicki again, and this time she got the Manager to kick them out of the bar.

Vicki had it all set up for my having lunch the next day with her Manager. Who told me he wanted to advertise in my new magazine. The Manager remembered my doing a Pure Talent Feature Showcase at the

Oasis Gentlemen's Club in Philadelphia where he had been an Assistant Manager.

Vicki had put the whole thing together, after figuring out that the Manager must have been impressed with my shooting pictures of the Pure Talent Feature Entertainers and how I had come all the way over to the East Coast to cover his club.

By then I had already started up my online magazine, "The Looking Glass."

Leah Layne and Kasey Karrington

Voodoo was one of the youngest guys in the Lost Angels although his real name was Chuck. We were hanging around together in Collinsville when Leah Layne asked me to join her at a small club in Ottawa, Illinois. The Lampliter was up in northern Illinois close to Chicago, and as far as Chuck and I were concerned in the middle of nowhere. But this was Leah Layne calling us, and Leah definitely wanted me and my Nikon D-1x to be with her. And since Leah offered to book us a hotel room right next to hers, how could we refuse?

Leah was in between bookings which meant she'd have to work as a House Dancer for the time being. When Chuck and I got to the club, the game was on. I could shoot as many pictures of Leah and any other girl I wanted provided the girl agreed. But after a few minutes of our arrival one of the most attractive entertainers approached me.

“Do you remember me?” the woman asked.

“I think so,” I replied. “You look familiar.”

"I am Kasey Karrington. I've changed my hairstyle so I might not look the same anymore."

"My God, Kasey, what in the hell are you doing way up here?"

"I had to get away from Vic, Jack."

"I remember. Vic was on all of us to help him find you."

"I had to hide from him. Do you remember all those awful emails I sent to you about your being a terrible photographer and writer?"

"Yes. But I couldn't believe it was really you, writing them."

"It wasn't. It was Vic. He used to use my email address all the time to send emails out in my name. He was so controlling, Jack."

"It all makes sense to me now, Kasey."

"Promise me you will never tell anyone that you have found me here, Jack."

"Don't worry Kasey, I don't even talk to Vic anymore, and there's no need to tell anyone that I've found you here."

Chuck and I had a good time partying with all the girls that weekend. Because even after the club closed Leah's motel room was party central. But the whole event was remarkable in one fact alone; Kasey had just cleared up a mystery that had baffled me for over a year; thinking of it now, I have a better understanding of why I despise so many men; and why Lenny who I'd become friends with in Thailand many years later kept telling me: "95 % of all my customers coming into the Doll House Go-Go bar aren't worth a shit." I don't know if it's men in general, or the kind of men who go to strip clubs, or even here in Thailand, where they have bar girls for girlfriends, but most men I keep meeting are complete control freaks. They are morons, and can be disgusting representatives of humanity. Just the other night I saw one of my favorite Thai bar girls, who told me she wasn't about to shave her pubic hair because one of her customers had given her $300.00 if she didn't shave it off. Most Pattaya bar girls shave downstairs for a lot of good reasons I won't get into here. While another man is about to get a boob job for still another one of his Thai girlfriends. Then there's Scott the guy who pays his girlfriends to have his name tattooed on their bodies. I see this kind of behavior everyday and when I think of all these men I think of them as totally inconsequential idiots who I want to stay far away from.

The Kidnaping of Big Howard

Although I was no longer writing for "Xtreme," I was still able to cover a lot of events through the new Looking Glass Magazine I had recently put on my Alphapro website. Over at "Nudes-A-Poppin," Mike Dunn[2], was no longer being allowed to operate as a photographer, due to Scarlett's feeling that Mike had not been doing enough to publicize the event and was using her pageant as only a means of meeting new prospect models for his other projects. While Ken Shinkle, from Continental Agency, was barred for reasons I won't get into here. But when I promised Scarlett that I would do my best to publicize "Nudes-A-Poppin" through my new Looking Glass Online magazine, I was once again welcomed into the sign up shed where I had the entertainers sign my Looking Glass Magazine releases.

I even had Five Star Graphics create Looking Glass Magazine T-shirts for me, which I wore during the 2005 "Nudes-A-Poppin" Pageant. While I was even able to get a few writers contributing articles for me, and Scarlett was 100 percent correct by trusting me to do my utmost to publicize "Nudes-A-Poppin." For one thing I believe it was largely due to my influence that Scarlett and Big Daddy were able to get together on featuring a S.P.E.W. wrestling exhibition on the long stage next to the "Nudes-A-Poppin" swimming pool. But of even greater importance is that getting a huge pageant such as "Nudes-A-Poppin" in any adult magazine is just a one shot deal. The magazine comes out with say its September monthly issue covering the August 2005 "Nudes-A-Poppin" Pageant. Come October, the September issue of the magazine is now out of print. So, it's History. This was not the case for what I was able to achieve for "Nudes-A-Poppin" in the Looking Glass.

So far as I write this book, my Looking Glass 2002 article for "Nudes-A-Poppin" has had 71,767 views; while my 2003 article has generated 80,317 views; with a whopping 137,707 views for the Looking Glass 2004 article; and for 2005 it generated 56,282 views; and now almost twenty years later all four of my articles are still getting read every month. There is no adult magazine that I can think of that could ever have generated this kind of continued interest in "Nudes-A-Poppin."

As for writers, I was even able to convince Jeremy, my editor at "Xtreme" to contribute a few articles for the Looking Glass. Along with

---

[2]I believe Mike was reinstated the following year

Krazy Ted who would write a strip club DJ column, and perhaps the best writer of us all was - Morgan Hawke, who specializes in writing Erotic Fiction. There would be many other writers as well, while even after I moved to Thailand in 2005, the Looking Glass soldiered on for another eight years. Meanwhile, things started to heat up over in New Athens, Illinois. I was starting to spend even more time with my favorite bartender, Lori, who I had met at Visions. But I had become great friends with her husband, Ron, as well. So, I would oftentimes stay over in New Athens at their house where I wound up writing several of my new Dick Fitswell articles. But this time I was writing them for the Looking Glass. Both Lori and Ron loved my Dick Fitswell articles, and Lori even started calling me Dick Fitswell. I was seeing a lot of Sahara also, who I would often invite to stay with me in my Collinsville apartment. From there we would often go to strip clubs together. And of course I was still seeing a lot of Selena who was sharing an apartment with Sahara.

I even got Howard, my manager friend from Dollies, to go with me several times to New Athens where we would all hang out at the Marina. I also got a girl named Frankie to go to the New Athens Marina with me. Where we got smashed out of our minds with several of the New Athens women.

I had met Frankie when I first started going to C-Mowes. Those were in the days when I was going out with Nipples and when I met Alex for the first time. But after a couple years passed, I lost track of Frankie until she suddenly started working at C Mowes again. And since Frankie wanted me to do a photoshoot of her in the worse way, I ended up taking several hundred pictures of her and put one of them up on my Alphapro front page as my "Stripper of the Month."

And Frankie, like most of my other stripper friends, had become a huge fan of my Dick Fitswell character, which got Frankie and I planning a competition for the best original picture of Fitswell.

We put the competition up on my alphapro.com website, but we ended up having just two artists entering paintings that represented their concepts of what Dick Fitswell should look like.

One of the artists was my old pal, Greyghost. The other artist was a friend of Frankie's. Frankie's friend, who I never actually met, wound up winning the competition and the $100.00 reward I had promised to the winner.

Meanwhile, we had the same Canada versus U.S. rivalry going on. Even though I had managed to get myself barred out of Dollies. And even though Chid and Beater had lost a lot of the credibility they might have had if they had only given Tori plane fare back to the United States. One night when I managed to get Howard to come down to the New Athens Marina with me I was able to gather around us a pretty good sized group to do a Canada versus U.S. video. And not only that, I also have Lori and Sahara involved and have Lori's husband Ron totally into my latest scheme. Which also gets Rocker involved who's one of our latest Lost Angels members.

Our Video Went Like This:

With war brewing between the United States and Canada, we decide that only Howard can save the day. But I need to have a very smart and very sexy lady to help me convince Howard to go up to Canada to keep the Canadians from invading the United States. At first I try to get Sahara, who in the video is playing Secret Agent 008, to help me get Howard over to Canada. In the Marina I'm sitting at a table sweet talking Sahara to help me. Meanwhile, Lori's the bartender, not Sahara. When Lori sits at another table while taking a break from her bartending duties, I snuggle up next to her, trying to convince her that there's nothing between Sahara and me. And that it's Lori who is really my favorite bartender and my only true love. I promise Lori, “I will make you famous as the best bartender the world has ever seen. And together we will live forever.”

Then I go back to sit with Sahara who acts as if she's very upset with me. I tell Sahara, “Lori means nothing to me. I'm only trying to use her.” And then Sahara slaps the hell out of my face. We keep rehearsing Sahara's slapping my face, but Sahara keeps laughing every time she slaps me. Until after she slaps me about five times, Sahara starts acting serious enough to convince me that we now have a scene that I can actually put up on my website.

But, we still don't have Howard going to Canada, although I have been successful in convincing Lori to do what I'm asking her to do. So, the next scene is of Ron and Rocker planning out exactly how they are going to kidnap Howard and manage to transport him up to Canada. The third and final act is of Howard and me drinking tequila together with Lori as our bartender-waitress. I keep trying to convince Howard to agree to go to Canada and Howard keeps refusing to go. But Lori keeps coming up to Howard and me to bring us one tequila after the other until Howard passes out on the floor. At this point; Rocker, Ron, Lori, and two or three male customers at the Marina manage to pull Howard across the floor and out the door of the Marina bar. Where they are able to hoist his 300 pound body into the bed of my pickup truck. Someone slams the lid down onto my pickup bed, and as the lid latches a sign drops down in clear view of the camera lens. The sign reads, "Heading to Canada." Rocker soon became one of the new writers for the "Looking Glass," and over the next few years the "Looking Glass" would go through periods in which new writers would suddenly appear to replace writers who had preceded them.

I soon had several entertainers sending me their poetry, which I put into the "Writer's Nook" section of my alphapro.com website. The most prolific of them was Heaven followed by Alex, Sahara, and finally Selena who didn't send me a lot; especially when you compare her to Heaven; but I still keep rereading the following verse which would portend bad tidings for the future:

"Inside I Scream Out In Pain" Teresa Selena
Kay R
March 7, 1990

How can all this be?
I've lived through things I never, never
wanted to see.

I try to be good to all, but so many has hurt
me viciously.
I guess it's all life's lessons I never expected
I'd have to learn.

Outside, I try to appear cheerful and happy,
yet, inside, my emotions burn. Burning with
confusions of a realize sort,

so many times I've prayed for mercy, to let
my life abort.

I feel so disoriented, so emotionally drained.
Outwardly I smile but, Inside,
I scream out in pain.
Is there a chance
For my weak, weary soul?

Will I find salvation, or Will the torment win,
Taking it's final toll?
I feel the Evil all around.

It thrives from my fears
Like a never ending spinning sphere.
Still, I have no choice
But to patiently wait for blessings to come,
Wounds to heal and, to embrace the power
Of forgiveness that will come, freeing me.

Though for now it's still the same, On the
surface I'm happy but, Inside,
I scream out in pain.

Death of Selena

Lori and Ron used to live in the apartment complex Selena and Sahara were now living in where I used to visit them before they moved out to the house next door to Sexy Jessie and Bob's place.

I thought Lori, who I'd later call the World's Greatest Bartender, was the hottest woman in Visions. And she wasn't even a stripper. I got the idea for searching for the Goddess of New Athens right after Lori had given me her address and phone number.

PlONe was visiting me from California the day we started looking for the Goddess. I still had the Sebring supercharger on my Miata sports car then. While PlONe had his own Miata in Oakland, which didn't have a supercharger, air intake, sports exhaust and header, or even a roll bar. But he had made up for it with the four seater airplane he took to fly his dates around the San Francisco Bay area. Since it was a bright, sunny day both of us were up to going somewhere we had never been to before in my Miata. So, when I suggested that we look up the bartender friend from a strip club PlONe was all for it.

But where in the hell is New Athens, Illinois? We started out just outside my apartment at Woodhenge where we encountered two of my new neighbors, a young guy and his wife, going through their mailbox.

With PlONe standing next to me chuckling to himself, I asked the couple, "Can you tell me where New Athens is?"

"I'm not sure," the young man replied. "But it's South of us; I think if you head out past Belleville on Route 159 that you will eventually run into it."

"Thanks. My buddy here and I are just out for a nice afternoon drive with the top down. We are in no hurry. But I've got this address in my hand for the Goddess of New Athens."

"The Goddess of New Athens? Now that's one I never heard before. Who is she?"

"She's this beautiful woman I know who works in a strip club."

The funny thing is, both the young man and his wife should have found my behavior to be very unusual had they lived anywhere else. But the entire idea of someone searching for the Goddess of New Athens who worked for a strip club seemed perfectly normal to them, but that's Collinsville for you. The weather was perfect, being neither too hot, nor too cold as we rode together with my car's top down. Since PlONe had never driven a supercharged Miata before I let him do most of the driving. We could have taken a map with us, but that would have been too easy. We were, after all, out on a quest looking for a mythological Goddess. So, when we arrived in Belleville ten miles from my apartment I got out of the car and went into a Seven Eleven. Where I read off Lori's address to an attendant.

“Excuse me. But I am looking for the Goddess of New Athens," I told the attendant. It says here she lives in New Athens. Where do I go to find New Athens?”

Finally PlONe and I arrive in New Athens. It doesn't take long for us to find the two level apartment building. There's something like twelve units there. There's nothing unusual about the building that appears to have been built within the past ten years. So, it's not run down or falling apart, it's just a typical low rent kind of establishment, but it does have some nice trees surrounding its parking lot making it altogether a little bit charming.

It ends up being Sahara who answers the door. Her hair unkempt and wearing no makeup. While Lori's sitting at a table a few feet away looking totally nothing at all like a Goddess.

But I still address her, “My Goddess of New Athens. We have finally found you.”

I wind up taking Sahara in my Miata for a short drive. While Lori's putting on a little makeup and chatting with PlONe. But she's out of cigarettes, and I need to show off my souped up sports car to my Goddess.

That's the way we all were back then. I once made a twenty inch penis out of paper mache. Then I inserted a can of glade room deodorizer into that artificial dick and took it into Sahara's apartment. Where Sahara and I laughed it up shooting digital pictures of each other playing with Dick Fitswell's new penis. Had I been showing off the orgasmic qualities of my home aid, glade tipped penis at the local country club, I do not think its members would have been nearly as appreciative of my totally whacked out sense of humor as all my stripper friends were.

When Rocker had his hernia operation I tried to get him to join us at the

New Athens Marina. After all, when I had my last hernia operation I celebrated my surviving the operation by getting totally wasted at Dollies Playhouse. But when Rocker told us he was in a lot of pain I went out and got a few bottles of beer for him and a bottle of whiskey. Rocker had his apartment above Sahara's. This all happened twenty years ago, and I can't remember exactly who was living where and with whom back then, but I think Sahara was still rooming with Selena in Lori and Ron's old apartment. I was able to get Sahara to join Rocker and me in his apartment. Lori was bartending down at the Marina and Sexy Jessie was going to join me later at the bar for a few beers.

Rocker never made it out of his apartment and neither did Sahara, so eventually I joined them. When I did, I found that Sahara and Rocker were having their own party. After three or four much younger guys had joined them. I don't know where all of them came from, but they were all around seventeen to twenty years old. But one of them, who was nineteen and taller and more slender than the rest was living in an upstairs apartment with his father. So, I joined in on the fun and snapped off a few digital pictures, which I still have, and still look at every now and then, because the tall nineteen year old would soon end up murdering Selena.

I was still in close contact with Greg, Selena's husband. Greg wanted Selena back and had made no bones about it to either Selena, or me. And at least once had either driven from Marion to New Athens, or had planned to until Selena had called their reunion off. By this time, Rocker had started getting romantically involved with Selena, and as far as I remember about Selena, she was all over the place: Both mentally and physically. She'd be stripping at a club for a few days, and then she'd take a week or two off. She might have even stayed with Greg for several days.

As for Sahara, she sensed that something was about to go terribly wrong, and moved far away from New Athens. Although I continued to see a lot of her even though she had moved in with her mother in University City, Missouri.

University City used to have the finest public school system in the Saint Louis area. But that was when University City was 80% Jewish. There were a lot of huge mansions in University City then. Most of them still are, although the landscape has changed after a lot of blacks had moved in. When I was twenty-three I had done my student teaching at the University City High School. The class was about 50 % Jewish and 50 % black. A lot of the Jewish kids were the sons and daughters of Doctors,

Lawyers, and wealthy businessmen. I found most of them to be super achievers who would often stay after class to learn even more about whatever subject we had been discussing.

Although University City no longer had the number one public school system in the Saint Louis area, it still hadn't changed all that much. The big houses were still as impressive as they had always been. Washington University, is right next door although technically it's in Clayton, which had taken over the number one spot for having the best schools. While Delmar Boulevard had become a very picturesque center where one could find several used bookstores, an Indian, Lebanese and at least one Chinese restaurant and a good assortment of other eateries, that included the very well known Blueberry Hill.

I really didn't expect to find Sahara's mother to be living in such a nice area. But the more I'd see of Sahara's mother, the more I found her to be the least likely woman to have a stripper for a daughter. I found her to be a well educated, very ladylike, middle class woman who would probably never go near a strip club.

For that matter, Sahara was far more like the girl next door than the prototypical stripper. By this time, I was taking Sahara to a lot of restaurants and bars on the Saint Louis side of the river. We still frequented some of the Saint Louis Metro East night clubs such as the Platinum Club. But now I was picking Sahara up in a nice middle class neighborhood over in Missouri, and most of the time I'd chat with Sahara's mother. Half the time we went out, Sahara would tell her mother, “I will be staying all night at Jack's.” Which both ladies understood to mean, 'Where I will be safe and sound and we won't be driving back to Missouri late at night while all the drunks are out on the road.’

Around this same time, Selena had moved the nineteen year old boy who had been living upstairs with his father into the apartment she had shared with Sahara. Although I was seeing a fair amount of Sahara I was still spending a few nights with Lori and Ron at their house in New Athens. We'd often hit several small town bars around New Athens where I'd meet a lot of people through Lori and Ron while shooting digital pictures of whatever riotous, unforgettable moments we could create. And while staying with Lori and Ron I wrote several of my most satirical off the wall Dick Fitswell short stories I had ever written. By this time, Lori was calling me, Dick, more often than Jack.

Because I often stayed overnight with Lori and Ron, on several occasions Selena had me drive her to work at Visions, which was on the way back to Collinsville from New Athens. We usually took my Miata and often talked about Selena's marital problems with Greg.

I personally don't recall Selena's ever having bad manners. Unless one were to call her outspokenness bad manners. Like many strippers I found her to be energetic and boisterous. Sure, she often drank too much, and then she'd pass out. But Selena sure didn't think much of herself. She would tell me how inferior she often felt around Greg, his friends, or his family and how she felt Greg was eying her with disgust over her bad table manners while she was having dinner with such company.

I was with Selena the last day she was alive. After driving my Miata to the apartment complex, Selena asked me to drive her to Visions where she was working the day shift. I was standing just outside my car in the parking lot talking to Selena when Rocker came out of his apartment and told us, “I'm taking her to work, Jack.”

“No you're not, Rocker. I want to ride with Jack,” Selena replied.

On the way to Visions, Selena, confided in me that she was going to send her young boyfriend packing, and that she'd send him back to his daddy that evening. I had heard from several people that Selena and her new leech roommate had been doing a lot of drinking and drugs together in Lori and Ron's old apartment. While I had also gathered that Selena was only working a couple days a week at Visions, which was just enough to cover her bills whenever her money ran out. The leech boyfriend was, of course, unemployed and now entirely dependent upon Selena for his room, board, and beer money.

I had a dinner date with Sahara that night. I chose to take her to Busch's Grove in Ladue on Clayton Road only one mile from where I used to live with my parents while going to High School at the Saint Louis Priory. Although my Dad had taken me there several times he always told me he didn't like the restaurant. It was a great place. My Dad just didn't like it. And I think the reason was because a lot of wealthy West County St. Louisans considered it to be one of those spots you want to be seen in. So, my Dad felt that the restaurant had an air of pretentiousness that he just couldn't abide

.

I didn't have this problem. For one thing the restaurant had these small private cabanas that cost quite a bit more to dine in than one paid for normal seating inside the restaurant. And as far as being inside the restaurant itself, the food was excellent, and really not that much more expensive than you would find close-by. But this was in Ladue, and quite close to Clayton and University City where a lot of Saint Louis's West County elite lived. One expects to have first class food and service out here.

And if Selena felt that her own table manners were God awful, Sahara's were impeccable. Sahara might have been a stripper, but for me she had always been the quintessential lady. It is women like Sahara who truly appreciate all the little niceties such as private cabanas where you can eat an awesome crab dinner.

Since one or both of us had to get up early the next morning, I didn't bring Sahara back to my apartment over on the East side. Instead, I took her home to her mother's after we had a great dinner together. I think it was about 9:30 p.m. But when her mother answered the door, I noticed tremendous sadness in her face.

“Come inside Jack. I have something really terrible to tell both of you.”

“What is it, Mom?” Sahara asked.

“It's Selena. She was murdered just one hour ago.”

“How do you know, Mom. How did you find out?”

“Lori just called me from New Athens. That boy who has been staying with her just stabbed her to death. Lori came inside the apartment right after it happened, and Lori told me that the boy stabbed Selena at least thirty times.”

I took Sahara to Selena's funeral three days later. Greg was there, weeping, and either being unwilling, or unable to leave Selena's casket There were a few of us who had gone in a group to pay our last respects to Selena. There was Allan who had been with us at the Las Vegas Expo and accompanied me to Renee's wedding up in Michigan. And Morgana who had recently moved to New Athens who had worked now and then at Visions with Selena and Sahara and was now going out with Allan. Steve, who was one of Visions DJ's, who had posed with my supercharged Miata for the 1st edition of Death on the Wild Side came with us as well, and Rocker came too. Our little group found a bar afterwards, but Greg never joined us.

A year or two later I ran into Greg at the Platinum Club. He found me upstairs in the VIP Room where we sat down together for the next two hours talking about Selena. Contrary to Selena's phobias that Greg had found her table manners to be disgusting and that he felt far superior to her, Greg had actually found her manners to be refreshingly different from the manners of most other women. Once again, Greg confessed to me how much he had truly loved Selena. But I always knew that. And at the same time without his ever asking me, I knew that Greg always understood that I'd never ever try to have sex with his wife.

Scuba Diving with Big Daddy and Hawkeye

By mid 2004 S.P.E.W. amounted to a big triangle. Although its birthplace was Big Daddy's Cabaret near Fort Leonard Wood, Missouri, most of the S.P.E.W. action was now occurring in Des Moines, or Council Bluffs, Iowa. With Big Daddy spending more and more time at the Iowa Playhouse in Council Bluffs. In forlorn hopes of still being able to sell S.P.E.W. DVDs, I had started up a S.P.E.W. website. And at Big Daddy's request had even set up a mechanism with CCNow we could use to sell and collect credit card payments. Meanwhile, I had started becoming well acquainted with Big Daddy's new DJ.

Big Daddy and Hawkeye had known each other for years, but until now I had not heard anything about Hawkeye. Then out of the blue this energetic, young guy starts working for Big Daddy's Cabaret. He's a DJ, but I soon learn that Hawkeye is much more than your typical DJ. Whereas, Big Daddy never became very adept with computers and someone else usually had to put digital images of strippers up on the Internet for him, Hawkeye was able to take pictures of the girls and put them online about as well as I could

It didn't take long for Hawkeye to soon start joining Big Daddy and me in Iowa to attend S.P.E.W. wrestling events. But, I had no clue about how talented Hawkeye was until Big Daddy talked me into joining him and Hawkeye in a PADI Scuba Diving Certification Class.

Although it was hardly my life's ambition to take up scuba diving; I had tried it several times; first in Mexico when I was 18; and later on in Eilat, Israel, where I spent a total of half an hour in the Red Sea. So, when Big Daddy mentioned that he and Hawkeye would take scuba diving classes in St. Robert, Missouri, I agreed to join them.

We spent the first part of the course in a classroom where we had to learn a lot about the intricacies of air pressure we'd encounter under the water, how different depths affected the amount of time we could stay under water before coming up for air, and rescue techniques we'd need to use when, and if something would go wrong. Then at the end of each class we'd all have to take a written test.

Big Daddy and I had to struggle through the written tests until our instructor told us our time was up. While Hawkeye would just breeze through the tests in a few minutes and then he'd leave the classroom to smoke a cigarette outdoors.

The next part of our PADI training took place in a swimming pool where we learned how to put our air tanks on, how to adjust its valves, and how to deal with a variety of situations under water. This included taking our masks on and off under the water, switching mouth pieces to a buddy's tank, under water rescue and so on.

And then we had our final two class sessions in a rock quarry where we found the water to be cold and murky.

It wasn't very long after we had gotten our PADI certification that Big Daddy started talking up "The Man Tour."

As much time as I had been spending with Big Daddy, I really didn't miss him when he went to Thailand. When suddenly he's telling me he's going back to Thailand, and Cambodia. "You have got to come with us," Big Daddy tells me on the telephone. "I think I got Hawkeye talked into it."

"Thailand? Why would I ever want to go there?" I replied. "I'd just soon as go to Mexico if I'm going anywhere outside the United States."

"I'll send you a DVD," Big Daddy added. "When you play that DVD you will be booking your flight to Thailand with the rest of us."

"The rest of us?," meant a group of men from all over the United States who would fly into San Francisco where they would meet, Joe Grant, their fearless Tour Leader who would escort them all the way to Bangkok and beyond.

After watching the DVD I was sold. The Man Tour promised eleven days of total bliss where a man could live like a King while attracting more beautiful women than a Rock Star. My flight from Saint Louis to San Francisco ran about $400.00. And another $1,100.00, or so round trip to Bangkok and back. Which I had to pay directly to, Joe Grant, along with another $1,500.00 to cover my hotels and transportation costs once we reached Thailand. And after being able to convince PlONe to join us, we had concocted a vacation none of us would ever forget.
We stayed near Nana Plaza once we arrived in Bangkok, which was within walking distance of some of Bangkok's most infamous Go-Go Bars where a man could get a beautiful young Go-Go Dancer to spend the night with him for only $50.00.

After spending several days in Bangkok, Joe Grant, took us on a bus to Pattaya, which is on the Gulf of Thailand just two and a half hours from

Bangkok's airport. Here we spent another three or four days savoring Pattaya's boisterous night life, before returning to Bangkok where we would spend our last few days before flying back to the United States. But once we got back to Bangkok, Joe, gave us the option of flying to Cambodia for a couple days where we would stay in Phnom Penh for two nights along with a day trip to Angkor Wat, where we would visit the largest ancient temple complex in the world. Big Daddy, Hawkeye, and I, and a dozen of the other guys accompanied Joe to Cambodia while PlONe stayed in Bangkok.

Big Daddy and I soon learned that although Hawkeye shared with us an equal interest in enjoying Thailand's sinsational night life; he was even more interested in exploring the archeology of Angkor Wat's vast temple complex; which led him many years later into getting his Master's Degree in teaching and becoming a school teacher. Having his undergrad in Anthropology, he would have preferred getting an Anthropology Master's degree but chose the much more marketable teaching degree with an emphasis on Physics.

But staying in Thailand for just eleven days was not nearly enough for me. So, I started planning on a one month trip in order to find out if spending the rest of my life there was a viable option. I got Joe Grant to find me some one month prices for Pattaya hotels he was familiar with, until PlONe came up with an even better idea.

Being a high powered computer programmer having the best possible Internet service in Pattaya was critical to PlONe's being able to stay for an extended visit. PlONe's solution came in the form of the Skytop Guest House on Pattaya's Second Road just one block from Pattaya's infamous Soi Six. Skytop was owned by, Pete Long, an Australian, who soon became my best friend.

Skytop had only seven guest rooms Pete could rent out. While what would have been his hotel lobby was an Internet Café, which took up his entire first floor. I reserved one of Pete's largest rooms for $500.00 for the entire month, which would include unlimited Internet access. While PlONe was able to stay only two weeks, due to his having to get back to his computer software company business in Oakland. I soon became good friends with both Pete and an Englishman who owned a restaurant just two doors away from Skytop. But the month went by far too quickly, which made me think: 'If one month turned out to be terrific, two months ought to be twice as good.'

When I returned again to the United States, I started to look at a much more permanent arrangement. While staying at Skytop PlONe and I visited a condominium complex in Jomtien, which is a Pattaya suburb roughly six miles south of where we were staying at Skytop. We looked at several two bedroom units before the desk clerk showed us a much larger three bedroom unit.

Which got me thinking of all of us having this wonderful little family of PlONe, Big Daddy, and I buying the large 3 bedroom condo, and having all our wonderful parties drinking cocktails and beer together while watching the sun set over the Gulf of Thailand. Of course, the idea of all three of us purchasing a single condo together was only a pipe dream, which I realized as soon as I returned to the United States, but the two bedroom units were definitely a realistic alternative that I could finance by myself.

They were high priced though. At a starting price of around $100,000 for the smallest two bedroom unit. Back in the United States I started planning my next trip to Thailand, and I would soon be staying at Skytop for two months, and I already started planning what I should do with my life after that two months was over. Should I rent an apartment in Pattaya for six months, or a year? And if so, where? Or should I go all balls out and buy a condo where I would live happily for the rest of my life?

It's one thing to be staying somewhere for six months or a year, but an entire lifetime is a different matter. Living close to the ocean would be the only thing that would be right for me if I had to live somewhere in Thailand for the rest of my life. So, I did a lot of research into both renting and buying a condo. The condo building in Jomtien that was just one block from the Gulf of Thailand seemed just about perfect for me except for my having to shell out over a hundred thousand dollars for it.

Then I found it – a listing for what seemed to be exactly what I wanted. A group of Germans were building a condo complex in Naklua, which I assumed to be very close to Pattaya. On their website the Germans had put up pictures of what the complex would look like when it was completed. Wongamat Residence would be situated just two hundred yards from Wongamat Beach on the Gulf of Thailand. The Germans promised German quality in the building's construction. While the drawings and pictures of the actual units looked a lot like the condo units PlONe and I had looked at in Jomtien. Most of the units were larger, however; while being about 20 percent less expensive.

Arriving finally at Skytop I asked Pete, "Where is Naklua and where is this Wongamat Residence that's being built on Naklua Soi 16?"

Pete replied. "Naklua's up north in Little Germany where all the Germans live. And there's a lot of crime up there."

But regardless of what Pete had to say about it, I had to check the place out, so I started walking to Naklua the very next day. But I didn't find it due to my walking down Naklua Soi 16/1, instead of going further north to Naklua Soi 16.

I didn't make the same mistake the next day. Wongamat Residence had been planned as a seven story structure that would encompass sixty-two condo units. But the basic structure of just one floor had been built out of concrete blocks. I did find two showrooms on the first floor that had been outfitted with new drapes, full kitchens, and furniture. The two showrooms were next to each other, both were two bedroom, two bathroom units. The larger one, measuring 145 square meters (1566 square feet) seemed overly large for my needs while the smaller 118 square meter unit appeared to be just about ideal.

But that was in 2005, when the entire area was very quiet. It had only four or five condominium communities near it then. And just one Family Mart with no Seven Elevens. But right next door was the Long Beach Hotel with two beautiful swimming pools with a picturesque waterfall accentuating one of them. It was exactly what I was looking for. So from that moment on, I would walk, or run all the way from Skytop to Wongamat Residence where I'd buy a bottle of water, or Coca Cola from the Family Mart. And then I'd make mental notes on the progress of the building's construction. Then I'd walk, or run back to Skytop.

The Wongamat Residence sales office was just one block from the construction site. The first of the two Germans had put his picture up on the Wongamat Residence's website as the building's Architect. His name was, Achim Geiso, but he was not actually the Architect. Achim later admitted to me that he was not a licensed Architect although his father had been. A few days after meeting Achim, I met, Helmut, who I assumed to be his partner. Although I had found Achim to be competent, he was quite a bit older than Helmut and much more laid back. Whereas, Helmut seemed only too anxious to please and a fireball of energy.

After being at Skytop about a month, I decided that it made a lot of perfect sense to purchase a condo from Helmut. I had predicted that the Wongamat area would soon become a very high dollar place to live and that if I was going to buy a condo there I had better do it right away. Also, back in 2005, the American dollar was worth 40 to 41 baht. My feeling was that the American dollar would go down to around 30, and possibly quite a bit lower than that. When I told PlONe my thoughts about the American dollar plummeting to 30 he told me that I was nuts.

Helmut and Achim both represented a German Corporation calling itself Nova Sunset. Planning on buying a condo from them, I found a reputable Thai lawyer to handle my end of the sale. But I decided to take Pete, and then Greg, who owned the restaurant next to Skytop over to Wongamat Residence to get their thoughts on the honesty and reliability of the two Germans. After meeting Helmut and Achim, Pete and Greg both told me that they didn't even think I needed a lawyer, due to their feeling that both Germans were totally honest men.

The deal was: one had to first give Nova Sunset 50,000 baht[3] in order to reserve a condo at Wongamat Residence. This was about $1,250.00. And then after a month, pay Nova Sunset 20% of the purchase price. Which would amount to 700,000 baht for a three million five hundred thousand baht unit. At 41.5 baht to the American dollar I was expecting to pay $86,000 for the 118 square meter first floor unit. Helmut and Achim were expecting to complete the entire project by November of 2005, which meant that the 80 percent of the unpaid purchase price would be spread out over so many months.

With 50,000 baht in my hand, I walked into Helmut's office and told him that I wanted to buy the 118 square meter unit on the 1st floor. But Helmut replied that although he'd be happy to reserve the 118 square meter unit for me, that perhaps I'd prefer buying a corner unit on the 2nd floor and that he could show me the unit right now.

The shell of the 2nd floor had just been constructed, which meant that I could actually go inside the corner unit Helmut was describing to me. But whereas, the 118 square meter unit on the first floor was facing the ocean, the 126 square meter corner unit was facing Naklua Soi 16. This meant my having a street view instead of a sea view. However, due to the trees just west of the building one had to purchase a unit that was at least 4 floors up to be able to see the ocean above the trees. So, there

---

[3]Example of this foreign exchange rate. If I pay 100 baht for a hamburger in American dollars this is 100/41.5 baht or $2.41

wouldn't be a sea view from the 118 square meter unit either, although it was on a much more quiet side of the building.

As soon as I walked into the 126 square meter corner unit I fell in love with it. Every room, even the two bathrooms had a window in it, which promised a cheerful sunny atmosphere. The condo's living room was big enough to encompass a large bookshelf that I would certainly have once I moved in. And although the main balcony overlooked Soi 16, the entire East side of the condo faced the Wongamat swimming pool.

“I'll take the corner unit,” I told Helmut as soon as we went back to the Wongamat sales office. “But, what price will you give me if I give you the entire purchase price at once. Say one month from now after I'm back in the U.S. and can get the money from my bank?”

It took Helmut just thirty seconds to calculate the time value of money if Nova Sunset received the full purchase price by Mid May compared to having to wait until November for my final payment.

"I'll knock 200,000 baht off the purchase price of 3,650,000 baht," Helmut told me. So the price now is 3,450,000 baht.

Everything went about as smoothly as could be expected. Looking back at my paying the entire 3,450,000 baht purchase price in May 2005 amounted to my taking a huge risk. Because only the second floor of the seven story building had been completed, and this was only the basic concrete and brick shell. Because if the Germans wouldn't be able to sell most of the condo units, they'd probably never be able to finish the project.

Figuring on being able to move into my new condo in November, or in a worse case scenario in December I reserved a room at Skytop with Pete starting in August of 2005. This left me three months in the United States getting all my affairs in order. I had an apartment full of furniture and exercise equipment to dispose of, and thirty six firearms, and since I wasn't planning on ever living in the United States again, selling my special edition 2002 Mazda Miata roadster and my Dodge 1997 four wheel drive pickup truck.

I gave my nephew eight of my rifles and pistols. And sold twenty-eight guns to the Belleville shooting range.

By this time, Angel had fallen in love with and married Terry. Terry was an American who was 50 % Korean by blood. Who Angel met while

Terry was making deliveries for UPS to Chameleon. Angel had always told me that while she was working at Chameleon she could never fall in love with a man who was paying the girls for sex. Which Terry never did. He was just a six foot two strong and handsome guy whose visits to Chameleon consisted of only doing his job for UPS.

Terry had bought a nice house way out in Saint Louis's westernmost suburbs where Angel and her three children moved in.

I was able to sell Angel and Terry my exercise equipment and a fair amount of my furniture for something like two thousand dollars, which I set aside to buy furniture for my new condo in Thailand.

I shot my last adult entertainment event at "Nudes-A-Poppin" on July 18-19, 2005. Big Daddy was with me wearing a bright red tuxedo orchestrating S.P.E.W. wrestling matches on the long stage next to the swimming pool. Two weeks later I'd be on the airplane to spend the rest of my life in Thailand

Epilogue

Doctor Doom: I was able to visit Doctor Doom and his wife, Donna, again in their new house in Syracuse, Indiana. Sam Stimmel had found a large house on Lake Syracuse that had absorbed a lot of water damage. Sam bought the house at a fire sale price after making a deal with Doc that he'd lend Doc the money at zero interest if Doc and Donna could make the place look like new again. After working many months Doc and Donna got the property to drain correctly while restoring it to its original magnificence. A few months before moving to Thailand I sat with Doc on his porch as both of us sipped our gin and tonics. My former heroin addict friend now had his own Lincoln Excaliber stretch limo and a house befitting a millionaire. Upon his mother's death Doc was able to pay Sam off, but several years ago Donna called me up to inform me that Doc had passed away.

Sam Stimmel: Eventually Sam vindicated the article I wrote about him in two adult magazines. "The Devil Incarnate, They Want To Shut This Man Down." Years after the two customers got away with pepper spraying his club, Sam messaged me after I moved to Thailand about a new lawsuit his club had to fight. Several underage men came into Stimmelators with fake ID's showing they were 21. When the club employees realized the young men had become very intoxicated they stopped serving them alcohol. While giving them coffee to sober them up. When the young men finally left the club, they had a car accident. The car hit a tree and one of the young men was killed.

Stimmelators argued in court that it was not negligent, due to the young men producing fake ID's. While the parents of the deceased argued that the club's bartender had over served the driver.

Years later Sam lost his Indiana club when he made a mistake on his application to buy a new club in Texas. His mistake was claiming residency in Texas, which according to law he could not do, because he was already a resident of Indiana.

Four days before this book's publication, Renee messaged me that Sam had died of a heart attack.

Angel: After living a few years in a nice house out in Saint Louis, West County, with her husband and children, Angel died at the age of 36 from the lung disease she had inherited as a child.

Renee: Renee stripped for only several years after I met her.For the past twenty some years she has continued to live the typical life of a small Michigan town girl taking care of her children while working traditional jobs.

PlOne: With the huge headway Thailand's made at achieving very fast Internet, PlONe found out he could continue doing his work as a Computer Programmer and not have to live in the United States any longer, which resulted in his buying a condo here in Pattaya only three miles from mine.

Big Daddy: After selling his share of his Big Daddy's Cabaret to his partner, Ishmael, Big Daddy became General Manager of the Iowa Playhouse where he continued to do his S.P.E.W. Wrestling matches. Then he bought Teaser's Cabaret in Dixon, Missouri, with a new partner, Bruce Middleton. Twelve years ago, a young customer went off the deep end when he was evicted from the club for abusing one of the dancers. He went out to his car, grabbed a 9 mm semi automatic pistol, and shot to death Big Daddy's twenty year old son, the dancer, and a customer. Since then Big Daddy's changed careers, doing voice overs, and playing bit parts in the movies.

Bruce Middleton: Bruce had been making a good living in construction when he became Big Daddy's partner. He had no experience running bars whatsoever, until after the murders took place. Bruce would tell me later that the killer had mistaken the customer for him when he shot the customer down. Devastated by his son's murder, Big Daddy turned the management of the club over to Bruce. Although business had nearly disappeared after the murders, Bruce brought Teaser's back to a profitable business. Big Daddy and Bruce are in the process of selling the club while Bruce has been living for the past four years in Thailand in the same building I'm living in.

Big Daddy's Cabaret (Matt Wagner):
A few months ago, I found out about Big Daddy's Cabaret's final demise in Dixon, Missouri. I met a very boisterous Texan managing "Where Angels Play," a bar on Soi Six, in Pattaya, Thailand. The first night I met Matt, I could hardly believe the story he told me. And when I asked Big Daddy later on about Matt Wagner, I found out that everything he had told me was true.

In 2007 Matt bought Big Daddy's Cabaret from Ishmael Balazi, where he continued to run the nude oil wrestling matches that Big Daddy had started. When Matt told me he had been living in the same house Big Daddy's had next to the club, I could hardly believe the irony of my staying in the same house Matt had been living in those many times I had visited Big Daddy. So, I had probably been sleeping in the same bed Matt had slept in and here we were both meeting for the first time over 8000 miles away in a Pattaya Soi Six bar.

Matt and I bonded immediately and wound up having many drinks together over the next several weeks. After having a successful eight years as the club owner, Matt, lost the bar in 2014, due to his allowing some of his bar girls to dance topless, which is illegal under Missouri state law. Although Matt had continued Big Daddy's wrestling events for seven years and looked after the club's strippers like a doting father (feeding them when they were hungry and loaning them money) the state of Missouri would not tolerate a night club displaying a woman's breasts.

Big Louie's: Is no longer a strip club. With its insistence for not allowing strip clubs to serve alcohol; not allowing customers to come within five feet of dancer's on stage; and prohibiting nudity in even the mildest forms; I suppose Big Louie's had just had about enough and had decided to convert his club into another form of business.

Tornado: Visited PLONe and the author in Thailand twice where he met a beautiful Thai woman. Tornado married here. I joined him for his wedding up in Sisaket to be at his wedding.

The Pursuit of Excellence of Athens and the Downfall of American Exceptionalism

On January 6th, 2021 thousands of Americans attacked the United States Capital, breeching its walls and threatening the lives of the government officials inside and the policemen who were assigned to protect them. Make no mistake about it, this is treason. And everyone entering the walls of the Capital are traitors and need to be punished as such. While the ringleader of all those traitors has gone unpunished for urging his followers to attack what is most sacred to the entire U.S. experiment. Which is our system of democratic government, our elected leaders, the U.S. Constitution, and the Capital itself. If this isn't treason, then what is?

Our gutless Republican Senators with the exception of only ten, have failed to convict Donald Trump of fomenting insurrection. By showing the world that any treasonous act is permissible, these men have forever tarnished their reputations and the party they represent. They have betrayed their country, and if technically they might not be called traitors, they certainly have proved themselves to be scumbags who are unworthy of holding public office.

And yet, most of rural Missouri and Indiana supported Donald Trump's claims that this last election was fraudulent. While still supporting the actions of those thousands of traitors attacking our Capital. While these same people are claiming that strip clubs like Big Daddy's or Stimmelators are evil and that they corrupt the morals of our youth.

I claim the exact opposite to be true. And urge everyone to compare the values and morals of such people to the values and morals of Ancient Athens, which is considered to be the cradle of democracy. And then compare those same Athenian concepts and values to so many members of the adult profession I have worked with.

The Athens of over 2000 years ago stood for Democracy, Education, and physical accomplishment as a well balanced whole that Athenians should try to emulate. Athenian schools put a lot of emphasis on physical education for two reasons: The first reason was, Athenians believed it to be necessary to have a sound body and brain to be a healthy and well balanced citizen of the Athenians City State. The second reason was the necessity for providing capable soldiers and sailors for the defense of Athens in an era when prowess with swords, spears, and hand to hand combat meant the difference between life and death. The Athenian ideal of the well conditioned male or female found expression in totally nude Athenian sculptures. These statues presented sharply defined muscles, firm bellies, and strong backs serving as examples of physical perfection that all Athenians should aspire to.

Just as Athenian sculpture depicted what men and women should aspire to, the same holds true for the Entertainer displaying herself totally, or partially nude. And I will even go so far as to include boxers such as a Muhammad Ali exposing much of their bodies, which inspires other men to emulate them.

And whereas Athenians, used to revere the logic and superior intellect of a Socrates, Plato, or Archimedes; in the world of Donald Trump; scientists and all their teachings are despised. I find this anti-intellectualism to be especially prevalent in rural communities such as Missouri, Illinois, and Indiana.

Whereas, in the adult entertainment world that I've experienced I find the exact opposite to be true. We find a Renee, who revels in her ability to build computers, or a Heaven who has published (at least on my website) page after page of poetry. Or an Aspen Reign whose best performances are never good enough in her quest for perfection. And speaking of Aspen, I cannot possibly imagine her appearing on stage wearing a gunny sack. Aspen is as I called her in "Xtreme Magazine," a "Magician in Pursuit of Excellence." Who performs at lightning speed--a Naked Goddess, who is an inspiration to every other entertainer in the house.

And how about topless club owners such as Big Daddy and Matt Wagner, introducing nude, oil wrestling to thousands of U.S. Servicemen at Fort Leonard Wood on their way to our wars in Afghanistan and Iraq? These men should be our real heroes. Because they are the ones who entertained our troops who were on their way to getting their limbs being blasted away while serving their country.

Missouri is a beautiful State, especially in the Ozarks where it's hilly. The State has more types of trees than any other State, but it's a cultural wasteland. Gone is any clue of the Athenian ideal of what a beautiful woman should look like. The Mothers for a More Boring Nation have put over 120 billboards all over the state accusing strip night clubs of causing lobotomies and Leprosy in children who live within a mile of such a club. There's 25 churches advertised on Google serving Dixon, Missouri, that has a total population of 1260 souls hoping for salvation.

Which might help explain why this last presidential election and its aftermath clearly showed that rural Missouri has been a breeding ground for conspiracy theories, and Donald Trump cultists.

I am proud to have been a part of a much more select minority of Americans from the American Adult Entertainment Industry. Who are far more logical, rational, creative, and loyal to their country than all those Congressmen and Senators who gave Trump a pass when he so obviously incited rebellion against the country he swore an oath to protect. I do not know a single ex club owner who would give this traitor a pass.

As Sam Stimmel commented to me a few weeks ago on Messenger:

> "He is guilty of insurrection. Even Mitch McConnell admitted that. 57 to 43 said he was. Everyone is afraid to lose votes and he does have a lot of followers. I got my certification in Hypnotherapy. His followers will never leave him. Jim Jones has nothing on him. However Jim Jones started out good. He has been the most intimidating politician in my lifetime. He tried to completely control all branches of government and fire anyone who did not show absolute loyalty to him. Mike Pence somehow managed to make it until Jan 6th. Nikki Haley was the only person who made it out unscathed and she has now turned on him. I have spent many, many hours following his reality show and have listened to all sides.

The following words spoken at the legal seminar at the Las Vegas Exotic Dancer Expo in Nevada would prove to be so prophetically true as did my article for Xtreme Magazine. "The Devil Incarnate, They Want To Shut This Man Down", which I wrote about Sam Stimmel.

> "Gentlemen, you are on the front lines of a tremendous struggle between those who want to silence you and to take away your given rights to freedom of expression. Make no mistake. You are in a war between those who want to shut your clubs down and those who wish to continue providing all the entertainment you are providing."

And now over 20 years later I am still calling these control freaks the "Mothers for a More Boring Nation." And they have won. When I measure how exciting and vibrant my new home in Thailand is compared to the wasteland of what had been the American Adult Entertainment World, I feel saddened and exhilarated at the same time. The real Devils Incarnate are the people who eventually shut Sam Stimmel and Matt Wagner down. They are the ones who urged all those far right extremists to attack the United States Capital. And who still are members of the Trump Style cult, which requires total obedience and conformity. But every time I look at the pictures I took as an adult photographer, I feel an immeasurable amount of pride in taking my part in an adult entertainment world whose likes will probably never be seen again.

www.ingramcontent.com/pod-product-compliance
Lightning Source LLC
La Vergne TN
LVHW020658110826
845149LV00012B/2043
* 9 7 8 0 9 8 4 8 9 3 4 6 1 *